What readers are saying about *Design Accessible Web Sites*

Jeremy Sydik has comprehensively and yet succinctly addressed web accessibility in a manner that will assist any web developer in creating a truly welcoming and usable web site for all who visit it. The ten principles provide clear and understandable guidance.

► **Christy A. Horn, PhD**
 ADA/504 Compliance Officer, University of Nebraska

Always informative and often spunky, Jeremy sheds light on the menacing shadow of web accessibility, revealing that it isn't the scary law-and-guideline straitjacket we think it is. Jeremy shows how we can capture wider audiences and create more humane interfaces by embracing accessibility from the get-go.

► **Aza Raskin**
 President, Humanized, Inc.

Jeremy Sydik's book is a valuable tool for all web developers. Where other accessibility books tend to go standardista on you, *Design Accessible Web Sites* takes a pragmatic approach to making web interfaces accessible. The many markup examples make it possible to dive right in and start coding.

► **Peter Krantz**
 Developer, Standards-schmandards.com

Jeremy Sydik's *Design Accessible Web Sites* covers a wide spectrum of practical accessibility solutions to common problems. It addresses the concerns of managers, developers, designers, and content providers in a way that lets everyone on a project own accessibility and communicate a

► **J**
 K

If you are putting information on the Web, then you need to be sure that everyone and anyone can get it. In this book, Sydik teaches you how to ensure there are few barriers between your information and the person who is accessing it.

► **Mike Hostetler**
CTO, Heartland Stores, Inc.

Jeremy keeps it light and understandable. Yet, when there is a need to dig into the details, he does so effectively. Through this, he convinces me that usability and accessibility go hand in hand and then shows me how to do it.

► **Ian Scheitle**
Technical and marketing writer

Jeremy has a no-nonsense view of accessibility and a passion for the subject that shows throughout this book. He approaches the material in a straightforward, personalized manner that is informative as well as entertaining.

► **Warren Werner**
Developer, The Crucial Realm

Design Accessible Web Sites

Thirty-six Keys to Creating Content
for All Audiences and Platforms

Design Accessible Web Sites

Thirty-six Keys to Creating Content
for All Audiences and Platforms

Jeremy J. Sydik

The Pragmatic Bookshelf
Raleigh, North Carolina   Dallas, Texas

Pragmatic Bookshelf

Our Pragmatic courses, workshops, and other products can help you and your team create better software and have more fun. For more information, as well as the latest Pragmatic titles, please visit us at

http://www.pragmaticprogrammer.com

Contents

The journey is the reward.
► Zen Proverb

Acknowledgments

Every journey has a beginning, and in the case of this book, the journey truly began more than ten years ago at the University of Nebraska–Lincoln's Accommodation Resource Center. Dr. Christy Horn first showed me the importance of accessibility and has continued ever since to shape me as a professional and as a person. Thank you for your mentorship and your friendship. I also thank Christy, Roger Bruning, Barbara Robertson, and everyone else at the Center for Instructional Innovation for contributing to the supportive environment that makes working on a project like this possible.

The road to this book would have been impossible to navigate without help along the way. Mike Hostetler, Peter Krantz, Jason Kunesh, Florian Ockhuysen, Aza Raskin, Ian Scheitle, and Warren Werner read early versions of this content, reviewed chapter drafts, and called me to task when I oversimplified or underexplained. This book is much better for your help (but I'm still taking credit for all of the mistakes, so there!). Susannah Davidson Pfalzer had the (sometimes extremely) challenging task of being the development editor for this project. I know I'm not easy to negotiate with, so thank you for pushing when you knew this book could be better and for trusting my judgment when I was convinced we were on the right path.

I'd also like to thank Dave Thomas for listening to the original concept for this book at RailsConf 2006 and believing in the idea of a principles-based approach to web accessibility. Dave, along with Andy Hunt, also answered many of the questions that came up along the way about production, layout, copyright, and all of the other things that turn a bunch of words into a book. It has been an honor to write a Pragmatic Bookshelf title. Each of the Pragmatic Bookshelf titles is of outstanding quality, and this is in no small part due to the efforts of Steve Peter, Sara Eastler, Kim Wimpsett, and Janet Furlow. The value of their careful attention to the fine details of book production can't be overstated.

To get where you're going, you need to remember where you came from. My mom and dad are responsible for teaching me to believe in doing the right thing, helping people who need to be helped, and trying to be the best person I can be. (The rest is my own fault.)

I'd also like to thank Gerry, Susie, Steve, Jeannine, my grandparents, and the rest of my family for their faith and prayers for this project and their understanding when I sometimes nodded off on a couch at family gatherings. For every blessing I have received, for giving me strength along this path, and for *all* things, I thank God.

The difference between journeying and being lost is knowing where home is. I want to thank you, Kate. You've been my editor, reviewer, cover designer, and first audience for this project. More important, you are the mother of my son, my girlfriend, my best friend, and my wife. The things I do here and elsewhere are meaningless without that. Finally, I'd like to thank my son, Aidan. You're young enough that you won't remember much about your dad wandering around late at night muttering about chapters, edits, markup, and guidelines, but my favorite part about late-night writing was sitting with you long after your mom was asleep and sharing a snack after I was done for the evening. You remind me every morning *why* I want a better world and every evening that, with you in it, I'm already in a better world.

Jeremy J. Sydik
August 2007

Part I

Laying the Foundation

New information and communications technologies can improve the quality of life for people with disabilities, but only if such technologies are designed from the beginning so that everyone can use them. Given the explosive growth in the use of the World Wide Web for publishing, electronic commerce, lifelong learning, and the delivery of government services, it is vital that the Web be accessible to everyone.

▶ William Jefferson Clinton, **Statement of Support for the Web Accessibility Initiative**

Chapter 1

Introduction

It was a dark and stormy night...

Actually, it was a late summer afternoon a little more than ten years ago when I first began to *get* accessibility. Back then, I was working as a student web developer and sysadmin, and we needed a system for a blind user to work on a paper. Simple enough—we had some new systems. Just grab one, install it, add the specialized software, and we're done. I was fairly happy about the job—it was my first time through this kind of configuration and I finished with plenty of time, so I added (what I thought were) nicer speakers and a nicer keyboard.

Our user came in and started to use the system—or at least *tried* to use the system. Everything started to fall apart. The keyboard was one of the newer (at the time) ergonomic keyboards, which the user had never worked with. The speakers were an even bigger problem. They came out of the box set to a low volume, and I hadn't thought to set them to a higher volume so they could be controlled from software. The user began to panic when the interface to the system was completely disrupted. Two decisions that wouldn't have usually been a problem turned the afternoon into a disaster.

Of course, the *real* problem was human, not technological. My mistake was in my assumption about how people use computers, which, of course, was how *I* used a computer. I knew that blind users needed to use special software on their computers, but I didn't consider the real difference in user *experience*.

Later that evening, I got curious about my web sites—seeing how much difference something as simple as a different keyboard could make, how would my sites behave for users with screen readers instead of monitors and with keyboards but not mice?

It wasn't pretty. I knew I needed to design my sites differently, but what exactly did I need to do?

It turns out that accessibility isn't really that much about *what* you do—it's a matter of *how* you do it. What I really needed was information on what being accessible *means* and how to think from the perspectives of many kinds of users.

Accessibility for the Web is about designing content to be reachable by the largest number of users possible. There are a lot of ways to be accessible. Content can be accessible from a variety of hardware platforms or browsers. Accessibility can also be in terms of which technologies are assumed to be available to the user—less is more. Finally—and most important for us since it will be the primary focus of this book—content can be made accessible to *users with disabilities*. This kind of accessibility means tailoring our content to be useful for people with a wide range of physical, mental, and sensory abilities. As far as the other kinds of accessibility, we'll get the best of both worlds. Content that is made accessible for users with disabilities is usually well on the way to being ready for multiple platforms and browsers as well.

1.1　Getting to Know Each Other

This book is about learning to apply accessibility principles to your web development practices. In other words, if you have anything to do with building web sites, there's something here for you. You could be a project manager, a designer, a developer, an author, or an artist. (Refer to *Making a Team Effort*, on page 29, to see how different people fit into the accessibility process.) I've written information that will be useful for anyone who wants to produce accessible web sites. You might want to do this because you believe it's the right thing to do, because you know it'll make your sites more portable to different platforms, or because you are concerned about the consequences of accessibility laws. These are all valid reasons, and for each of them, you'll find plenty of useful principles and techniques here.

I'm also going to assume, however, that you understand the basics of web development. We'll be looking at accessibility as it relates to HTML, CSS, images, video, and sound. We'll also make brief excursions into accessibility for external document formats, JavaScript, Flash, and Java. We're not going to be looking at how to use these technologies beyond what we need for using them accessibly, but I'll do my best to point you toward plenty of good resources to check out if you feel you need help getting up to speed.

It's important to mention, however, that I'm not a member of any of the committees you'll read about in this book or the developer of any of the tools. When I give a recommendation, it's because I find the tool/book/web site/whatever useful when I write pages.

I *won't* be doing three things in this book, however. I won't be spending a lot of time explaining (over and over and over) that accessibility is a good thing. I'm assuming you're already partly convinced if you're reading this, so we'll take look a quick look at *why* accessibility is a good thing in Chapter 2, *Why Be Accessible?*, on page 9. After that, it's down to business. I also won't be ripping apart good visual design. Great visual design is an important element of the Web, and I welcome every designer who wants to add accessibility to their toolbox to come along—there's plenty of information here for you as well. Finally, I'm not going to focus primarily on accessibility guidelines. I don't think this is a useful route for understanding the principles that underlie web accessibility, so we're going to take a principles-first approach. We'll get to the guidelines after we have a better understanding of what they *mean*.

1.2 Finding Your Way Through This Book

Web content is often referred to in terms of *places* such as sites, home pages, stores, and so on. That works fine—if we're building places, we can look at our users as visitors or, better yet, as *guests*. With that in mind, we'll look at the concepts in this book in terms of building these places. I've laid out the concepts in this book in order from basic concepts to extra details:

- Part I, "Laying the Foundation": All good buildings start with a strong foundation. Here, we'll get you started with a basic look at accessibility, why it's important, and how to get started with accessible development.

- Part II, "Building a Solid Structure": Like the framing of a building, markup gives our site a defined form. In this part, we'll look at web semantics and at understanding how to use markup and styles in an accessible way.

- Part III, "Getting the Perfect View": When a building is well designed, the views from it are remarkable; when it isn't, the views are lacking. When we add accessibility features to our images, videos, and sounds, we provide the best view possible for our entire audience. In this part, we'll learn how to add alternative information for accessibility.

- Part IV, "Putting on Some Additions": We might want to put some extra features into our buildings. There are also extra things such as external documents, scripts, and plug-in technologies that we can use in our sites that are at the edges of the Web itself. In this part, we'll look at applying accessibility principles to these as well.

- Part V, "Understanding the Building Codes": Before a building is complete, it's inspected. Web sites should also be checked for correctness, and in this part, we'll wrap up by looking at the standards and how they connect to the techniques we've learned in the rest of the book.

It's not strictly necessary to follow the entire book in order. You should start with Chapter 2, *Why Be Accessible?*, on page 9, as well as Chapter 3, *A Brief Introduction to Disabilities*, on page 17, but after that, you should feel free to move in the order you find most useful. If you're managing site development, you should probably continue into Chapter 4, *An Environment for Access*, on page 27, but if you're a graphic designer, you might find it more useful to jump ahead to Chapter 9, *A Picture Is Worth...*, on page 147.

Chapters 3 through 12 are comprised of a series of thirty-six *tips*. These tips are meant to stand on their own—you should be able to spend a short time with each tip, get the information you need, and walk away to apply it to your own projects. The "Act on It!" sections are there to give you some ways to get started. Don't just read these—give them a try!

After you've been through the tips, read the discussion of guidelines and laws in Part V. They'll make a lot more sense once you've been through the rest of the book; however, if they're still confusing, my commentary will point you to the part of the book where the underlying principle is covered.

1.3 Principles Before Guidelines

This book is going to take a "principles-before-guidelines" approach to accessibility. Staying focused on compliance issues is a frequent approach to accessibility, so it may seem surprising that I'm going to push the guidelines out of the way for now. Guidelines are useful for sorting out details and testing for compliance, but they're not written as instructional documents. Our goal is helping as many of our users as possible get the information they want—not learning to be "rules lawyers." When we add video to our sites, we don't want to be thinking this:

> "Section 508, §1194.24(c) says: All training and informational video and multimedia productions which support the agency's mission, regardless of format, that contain speech or other audio information necessary for the comprehension of the content, shall be open or closed captioned."

This places our priority on compliance instead of on our users. We really want think about it like this:

> "OK, we're using video. Which of our users does this affect? Well, for users who can't see the video, we should add audio descriptions, and we'll add captions for people with hearing disabilities. Hmmm—some of our users might not have the video player we're asking for. We should also add a transcript of the video. Is there anyone else we might be missing?"

This approach is user focused, and at the end of the day, that's what accessibility is all about. We're going to follow ten rules when we design accessible sites.

Because these rules are so important, I'm going to put them on their own page.

Ten Principles for Web Accessibility

1. Avoid making assumptions about the physical, mental, and sensory abilities of your users whenever possible.

2. Your users' technologies are capable of sending and receiving text. That's about all you'll ever be able to assume.

3. Users' time and technology belong to them, not to us. You should never take control of either without a really good reason.

4. Provide good text alternatives for any nontext content.

5. Use widely available technologies to reach your audience.

6. Use clear language to communicate your message.

7. Make your sites usable, searchable, and navigable.

8. Design your content for semantic meaning, and maintain separation between content and presentation.

9. Progressively enhance your basic content by adding extra features. Allow it to degrade gracefully for users who can't or don't want to use them.

10. As you encounter new web technologies, apply these same principles when making them accessible.

These principles apply to just about everything you'll need to do to design accessible sites. Of course, you'll need to understand *how* to apply them. That's good, because we're just getting started.

Injustice anywhere is a threat to justice everywhere.
▶ Martin Luther King Jr.,
 Letter from Birmingham Jail; April 16, 1963

Chapter 2

Why Be Accessible?

We're going to spend a few hundred pages learning about web accessibility and how to apply the ten principles introduced in Chapter 1, *Introduction*, on page 3. In this chapter, we'll look at reasons *why* you should want to do this. There are plenty of good reasons to build accessible content. Some, such as legal requirements, aren't terribly pleasant to think about. Others, such as opening your sites to new markets and increasing your skill set, are more exciting to pursue. By the end of this chapter, you will be able to understand what *your* reasons for developing accessible web content are. With that in mind, let's look at some benefits of understanding accessible web development.

2.1 It's the Right Thing to Do

Although the Web was originally designed for scientific communication, it was rapidly adopted as a new form of publishing with the promise to be wide-reaching and open to everyone. As web developers, we haven't always lived up to this promise, however. As web technologies grew in complexity, many features appeared that threatened the openness of the Web. In some cases, certain browsers were restricted from accessing content; in other cases, multimedia was provided without alternative means of access. These changes have made the Web less accessible over time.

Shutting out users this way is entirely against the nature and intent of web communication. We should also keep in mind that accessibility to information and services is an issue of civil rights. The Universal

Declaration of Human Rights[1] states it best: "Everyone has the right freely to participate in the cultural life of the community, to enjoy the arts, and to share in scientific advancement and its benefits." When we create accessible content, we help to realize this promise for our users.

2.2 Accessibility Is Good Business

The biggest advantage of developing content for the Web is gaining access to an audience that was once beyond the wildest dreams of the largest publishers. If you create inaccessible content, you ignore part of this audience. Some developers write off this audience because they think the population in need of accessible web content is too small to consider. Just how small of a potential market are we talking about? Not so small at all, actually. Let's take a closer look.

The Market of Users with Severe Disabilities

In 2000, the United States census found that nearly one in eight people has a severe disability. Because accessible web content can be read with assistive technologies and is available from the home, people with disabilities can find information and make purchases with less hassle and inconvenience than by traveling to another location and seeking the assistance of others. This is really the same reason most of us use the Web, but for people with sensory or mobility disabilities that make it difficult to travel or communicate, it is even more appealing. The bottom line is that 10 million people with severe disabilities represent a $46 billion market that wants access to web-based services.

The Aging Population

The reality of an aging population is beginning to make a huge difference in the way we approach web development. Over the next two decades we will reach a point where one in five U.S. citizens will reach the age that vision, hearing, and mobility problems become more common. The Baby Boomer generation is used to having control over their consumer environment, and there is no reason to expect this to change as they reach retirement age. They will be expecting our sites to cater to their needs, and they represent a large enough market that it would be unwise to disappoint them.

---

1. Article 27.1 (http://www.un.org/Overview/rights.html)

The market for accessible web content and services is out there and growing. These are our potential readers and customers to the tune of $100 billion a year—why would we choose to ignore them?

2.3 Accessible Sites Are More Usable

When we look at usability, we typically pay attention to elements such as hardware devices, browsers, and operating system support of plug-in technologies. The capabilities of our users and the ways that they use the Web are even more variable.

Our sites need to have good usability characteristics. Usability expert Jakob Nielsen finds that increasing the overall usability of a web site can improve visitor traffic and productivity.[2] This is compelling: increased visitor traffic translates to higher purchase and click-through rates, and productivity is a solid selling point for web services. Unfortunately, that isn't the end of the story. Another study by Nielsen shows that users with visual impairments experience reduced usability in conventionally designed (inaccessible) web sites.[3]

People with visual impairments aren't the only ones who have problems with usability. When a site doesn't give multiple descriptions for its content or provide easy-to-use navigation, it also causes less obvious usability problems for users *without* disabilities. Accessible design serves the needs of people with disabilities, but it's more than that; it makes your sites more usable for *everyone*. The advantages of accessibility increase usability for all users, however. Think about curb cuts in sidewalks. Originally these ramps between the sidewalk and the street were meant to assist people with mobility impairments, but the concept was so useful that most people would object to their absence. Similarly, by providing full access to information and functionality for visitors with disabilities, we increase usability for *all* users.

2.4 It's the Law

Legal requirements are a major reason to be concerned about web accessibility. Unfortunately, when it comes to accessibility, the law seems to be all that anyone wants to discuss. This isn't to say that

---

2. http://www.useit.com/alertbox/20030107.html
3. http://www.useit.com/alertbox/20011111.html

> ### A Word About Universal Design
>
> Occasionally, you'll find developers who claim they don't need to worry about accessibility practices because they practice "universal design." Universal design is a general method of designing interfaces that are usable by everyone. The ideas behind universal design are good ones, but they don't necessarily do enough to make our sites accessible. Sometimes proponents of universal design overfocus on the parts of accessible design that benefit everyone and overlook that some disabilities require specific adjustments that aren't necessarily useful for every user. The result is that some developers are misled into believing that their "universal" sites are accessible when they're not. For this reason, I advocate caution regarding the idea of universal design unless it is mentioned alongside specific discussions of accessible design principles.

the laws are bad or unimportant, just that there are more inspiring reasons to create accessible content than fear that the "accessibility police" are going to come in and ruin our day. Still, we can't escape that we're required to comply with laws governing accessibility. In Part V, I'll guide you through specific guidelines and legal requirements, but here are a few starting points.

If your company or a client has a presence in the United States, your web site falls under the jurisdiction of the Americans with Disabilities Act (ADA). The ADA, signed into law in 1990, is a comprehensive piece of civil rights legislation for citizens with disabilities. It guarantees access to employment, public services, public accommodations, and telecommunications. Because the ADA was written in an open-ended manner, there is a lot of discussion and debate (and litigation) to determine how the ADA applies to the Web. The general rule at this point is that web sites are held to the same standards as physical locations.

Some will tell you that the ADA doesn't have much impact because many suits have been settled out of court. This is pure nonsense. Even assuming that a settlement could be reached, you need to ask yourself three questions about the *real* costs of settlement:

- Do I want to pay legal fees for the coming months or years to get to the point of settlement?

Equivalent Access

Many people misunderstand what is meant by *equivalent access*. When we make claims of equivalency, we are ensuring that the alternatives we create are providing the same *quality of experience* to the user, not simply the same information. This can be a really difficult task, particularly when alternatives use different communication mediums. For example, you might consider adding a toll-free phone and Telecommunications Device for the Deaf (TDD) service for a web store. You need to ensure that this service is available whenever your site is (likely twenty-four hours a day and seven days a week) and ensure that the quality of interaction available through the service is at the same standard as the site. In many cases, this approach is impractical or outright impossible. If your service relies on live interaction, as with an auction, you need to have enough people on hand to handle as much traffic as you would ever expect to have. Sometimes, providing personal assistance undermines the purpose of a site. If you promote to your visitors the ability to seek information or make purchases in an environment of privacy, a live operator is clearly an unacceptable solution. For these reasons, this kind of substitute equivalency is one I don't recommend.

- Can I afford the cost of settling the case privately? (Remember, closed settlements still have a price tag attached.)
- Is the potential public relations and branding damage from an accessibility lawsuit something I want for my business? See the sidebar on page 178 for an example of what can go wrong.

In general, unless you really enjoy fielding lawsuits and recovering your reputation, it is far better to build accessibly in the first place.

Work in the public sector has more specific legal constraints. If you contract with the federal government, compliance with Section 508 of the U.S. Rehabilitation Act is *mandated*. The laws in many states have also adopted the terms of Section 508, and the notion of "contracting" in this case has been interpreted very broadly. More about Section 508 is in Chapter 15, *Section 508*, on page 263.

Clearly, the legal issues of accessibility will be of concern to us as we move forward. As creative people, we don't like doing things because we *have* to do them.

Fortunately, we have other good reasons to develop accessible sites that feel much less like a hammer waiting to come down on us.

2.5 Building with Accessibility Can Make You More Capable

We spend a *lot* of our time as web developers responding to new changes and challenges. In the past twelve years, I have adapted to seven or eight generations of web browsers; four major versions of HTML (with a fifth on the way); the rise of static and streamed multimedia content; the rise, fall, and return of push-type technologies; and countless web plug-ins and frameworks. I am assuming that, for most of you, accessibility feels like just another one of these changes to cope with.

I'm not going to tell you that designing accessible web pages won't change the way you need to develop, but I can promise that the changes you'll need to make come with benefits. Something that has always been true for me in the process of change is that by striving for accessible content, I've had a framework that I can use to understand and successfully leverage new technologies.

One thing I know from experience is that if your background is in the graphic arts, you are worried that I'm going to tell you that you have to give up your creativity in exchange for accessibility. This is absolutely not the case! What I *will* do, however, is ask you to think about the visual arts in an expanded sense that reflects working with dynamic media and diverse audiences.

As creative professionals, we also like to be challenged, and these challenges are what make us more capable. Web accessibility provides the kinds of challenges that make us rethink the ways we "have always" done things. Here are some challenges to think about:

- What do our layouts look like for someone who can't see color? What about someone who sees color differently?

- How do we explain and present complex visual concepts without using imagery?

- How can we maximize the experience of a song to someone who cannot hear it?

> ### Accessibility Doesn't Have to Be Boring
>
> There is a perception that accessibility means creating sites with the appeal of boiled mush. Much of this perception is based on accessible development in the era before Cascading Style Sheets (CSS) support was widely available in web browsers. Sadly, some accessibility experts are still fixated on this style of design and perpetuate the myth. When we discuss accessibility, we are *never* throwing out visual design that is useful for sighted users. What we are doing is ensuring that the visual design doesn't express vital information that isn't available in any other form and building designs that step out of the way of users who can't use them. To see the creative visual power provided by CSS, take a look at css Zen Garden (http://www.csszengarden.com).

These are interesting questions to ask, and they are important ones to ask if you really want to understand the ten principles in Chapter 1, *Introduction*, on page 3.

These questions have interesting answers that we'll be looking at in later chapters, but before we get to these questions, we need to ask two more important ones: "Who is our audience, and what are their needs?" In the next chapter, we'll take a closer look at answering these questions.

Act on It!

1. How many customers do you have? If you could reach out to even a miniscule percentage of people with disabilities, how much could you expand?

2. Is usability a current goal within your organization? Is accessibility being treated as a part of this?

*Equality isn't when everyone gets the same thing; rather, it
is when everyone gets what they need.*

► Unknown

Chapter 3

A Brief Introduction to Disabilities

In the previous chapter, we looked at reasons why we should develop
accessible content for users with disabilities. To do this, we need to
learn a little about the types of disabilities and the needs of users with
disabilities. In this chapter, I'll describe some common disabilities and
the technologies frequently used to accommodate them.

In the most general sense, a disability is any unchangeable condition
where some aspect of everyday life is limited without the use of an
assistive technology or alternate means. Disabilities fall into four major
categories: visual, auditory, mobility, and cognitive. One chapter is certainly not enough time to develop deep expertise on disabilities, but
I'll show you some of the types of disabilities in each category, as well
as the assistive technologies that people with disabilities use. Within
each category, we'll also look at the implications that the disabilities
and assistive technologies have on web development.

3.1 Visual Impairments

Visual impairments are a major focus for us as web developers. I don't
mean to disregard the needs of those with other disabilities, but creating access for users with visual impairments touches on almost every
aspect of web development. The first thing we need to understand is
that blindness isn't the only kind of visual impairment. There are vision
deficiencies other than complete loss of sight, and each of them requires
us to look at different aspects of our content.

Blindness and Low Vision

Blindness is used to talk about two similar but distinct disabilities.
Total blindness is when someone has absolutely no light perception.

Visual Acuity?

Visual acuity (VA) is the measurement for clearness of vision. This is written as a ratio of two numbers where 20/20 is considered normal vision (6/6 if you're seeing it in the metric parts of the world). The first number is always the same, and the second is the individual's eye measurement. The meaning of this is fairly straightforward. Someone with 20/20 vision sees at 20 feet what a person with normal eyesight could see at 20 feet, while someone who is legally blind (we'll say 20/200) sees at 20 feet what someone with normal eyesight could see at 200 feet. These measurements can be made for corrected or uncorrected vision. Usually the number you will see mentioned by a particular person is their best level of vision with correction.

Legal blindness is when someone has a visual acuity of 20/200 or less. Both types of blindness are an inability to make visual distinctions.

To access the Web, many blind users use screen readers such as JAWS,[1] Hal,[2] VoiceOver,[3] or Orca.[4] Screen readers use text-to-speech (TTS) technology to speak screen text and text representations of graphical elements. Another option for accessing the text of web pages is a device that combines a braille keyboard with a refreshable braille display. These are less common than screen readers, however. See the sidebar on the facing page for one reason why.

Low vision is when someone's visual acuity is less than 20/70. Low vision can be genetic or develop later in life because of injury or macular degeneration. The degree of low vision may vary widely—some people can use magnification, while others might be able to perceive only motion or changes in the level of light.

Many low-vision users rely on screen magnification solutions, sometimes one included with an operating system but, more commonly, one available from a third party. Third-party magnifiers, such as Zoom-Text,[5] provide higher levels of magnification and reduce pixelation of magnified images.

---

2. http://www.yourdolphin.com/
3. http://www.apple.com/macosx/features/voiceover/
4. http://live.gnome.org/Orca
5. http://www.aisquared.com

Not All Blind People Use Braille!

You might hear the word *blindness* and immediately think about generating braille-ready content. Although many blind people can read braille text, even optimistic estimates put the number at less than half of the total blind population. This is partly because some cases of blindness are caused by another disorder, such as diabetes, where sense of touch is too weak to use braille. Other people simply can't pick up the braille language. Because screen reader use is much more common among users with visual impairments and creating high-quality braille is a specialized art needing considerable training, this book focuses on creating text alternatives rather than braille-ready translations.

As visual acuity moves toward the edge of legal blindness, magnification isn't always enough, and users with low vision might use the same assistive technologies as blind users.

Color and Contrast Deficiencies

Some users can see with normal acuity but can't see in color. Some see color but can't distinguish green from red, blue from yellow, or even dark shades of red from black. Still others cannot differentiate closely matched colors. On average, one in twelve of our users will have a hard time resolving color or contrast, so we need to be careful about our color choices.

Users with *color blindness* or contrast differentiation problems often change their monitor settings to use palettes that are clearer for them. They may also use alternative browser style sheets that override style settings for pages that are poorly designed. We'll discuss nuances of developing useful content for color-blind users in *Stoplights and Poison Apples*, on page 148.

Photosensitive Seizures

Some people suffer from *photosensitive seizures* when exposed to particular patterns that repeat or flash. These seizures are difficult to predict because the cause can be hard to identify—the trigger can come from sources ranging from video games to sunlight flickering through the leaves of a tree.

We'll look closer at the kind of flickering that's a potential threat to users with photosensitivity in *It's Not Polite to Flash the Audience*, on page 177.

Because of photosensitivity's unique nature, some accessibility experts consider it a fifth distinct type of disability. In terms of web accessibility, however, I look at photosensitivity as a kind of visual impairment because it's triggered by visual stimuli. That is not to say that I minimize the importance of eliminating flicker from web pages. Although accessibility in all forms is important, this is an area where we risk directly causing harm to our users if we don't take action.

What Visual Impairments Mean for Web Development

As I said earlier, visual impairments affect most aspects of web content development. All assistive technologies for the blind rely on text, so we need to add appropriate alternative text representations for all visual elements that have informational content. Alternative text is a big topic, and we'll look closely at it in *To Put It Another Way*, on page 158, and in *More Than alt= Can Say*, on page 163, as well as in small pieces throughout the book.

Video requires two approaches for accessibility. Although visually impaired users may be able to hear the soundtrack, they might miss important silent events on screen. In *Describe It to Me*, on page 186, we'll look at adding auditory descriptions to fill in the missing information.

Interface design is also impacted. Timed effects need to be adjusted or eliminated because it often takes longer to move through a page with a screen reader or braille display. Visually impaired users, particularly those who are blind, may not have an equivalent to a mouse interface, so we also need to ensure that our sites are navigable by keyboard.

3.2 Auditory Impairments

Auditory impairment includes more than just deafness, much as blindness isn't the only kind of visual impairment. Compared to visual impairments, auditory impairments give fewer issues to consider when we create accessible content. In fact, if your site doesn't rely on audio-based multimedia or sound cues, you may already be accessible with respect to auditory impairments.

Deafness

Deafness is the absence of all sensitivity to sound. If someone's sound sensitivity low enough, however, they may for all practical purposes be considered deaf. Unlike the notion of legal blindness, there is no official classification of "legal deafness" for people with extremely low sound sensitivity.

Deaf users rely on captioning and transcription of audio content. Transcription is a textual representation of audio, and captioning is the same for the audio portion of video and multimedia content. Captions are synchronized to the media and appear either as closed captions that the viewer can turn on or off as needed or as open captions that are always visible. Although all captions look like subtitles on the screen, not all subtitles are captions. Subtitles represent spoken content only, while captions also present other important sounds.

Speech-to-text converters automatically transform dialogue into text. General-purpose speech recognition is an evolving technology, however, and existing software isn't good enough yet to replace captioning and transcription as a primary assistive technology.

Hardness of Hearing

Mild to moderate loss of sensitivity to sound is referred to as being *hard of hearing*. Sometimes this can be corrected, but even with correction, sound may be difficult to understand. Some people also refer to themselves as being hard of hearing if they have *tinnitus* (buzzing or ringing in their hearing) or loss of tonal ranges. People who are hard of hearing usually use an amplification system with noise reduction to boost audio volume to an understandable level.

What Auditory Impairments Mean for Web Development

When the content we're creating makes no use of audio or sound cues, then there is nothing to do. If we *are* creating audible content, it should be produced clearly with minimal noise, and the user needs to be given control over the playback and volume. As usual, for any important non-text content, we need to create a text alternative. Plain audio files need accompanying transcripts, and video and multimedia with audio call for synchronized captions.

Creating good transcripts is one of the topics we'll discuss in *Describe It to Me*, on page 186. Synchronized captioning is a *big* topic that sits somewhere between fine art and deep magic. I won't be able to make you a master in this topic, but in *Words That Go [Creak] in the Night*, on page 181, we'll discuss the basics of captioning. *On the Cutting-Room Floor*, on page 190, will show you how to merge captions, audio descriptions, and video into a single product for the Web.

3.3 Mobility Impairments

A *mobility impairment* is any condition where there is a limitation or loss to the range of motion in one or more limbs. The area of mobility impairment represents a wide range of disabilities from relatively mild, like minor arthritis or minimal repetitive stress injuries, to severe, such as missing limbs or paralysis. The type of mobility impairment that a user has doesn't affect the way we create content as much as the technologies used to accommodate them do.

Mobility impaired users may employ alternative keyboard or pointing devices. Some of these are tuned for ergonomics, while others are completely reworked devices that use foot pedals, joysticks, or eye-gaze systems to harness available mobility. Because these devices are designed to use conventional keyboard and mouse interfaces, they appear as such to software applications.

Some people with mobility impairments choose to use speech recognition software such as Dragon Naturally Speaking,[6] MacSpeech,[7] or IBM ViaVoice.[8] Unlike the general-purpose speech-to-text systems mentioned previously, the user can tune these systems to the unique characteristics of their voice, which helps speech-to-text reliability.

What Mobility Impairments Mean for Web Development

The needs of users with mobility impairments don't usually have much of an effect on the types of media we use. Our interfaces are another story, however. The assistive technologies used by mobility impaired users are designed to mimic the input of a keyboard or mouse. The most critical issue posed by alternative devices and speech recognition is that they are often slower than conventional keyboard and mouse input. This means we have to eliminate unnecessary timing effects in our content. I'll say more about this in *It's Their Web—We're Just Building in It*, on page 126.

---

6. http://www.nuance.com/naturallyspeaking/
7. http://www.macspeech.com/
8. http://www.nuance.com/viavoice/

Some users also have difficulty with fine motor control, so we'll want to avoid creating small icons or tightly spaced navigation that these users will have trouble navigating. Because it takes more effort to navigate with these technologies, we should also keep our interfaces as simple as we can. In *Your Interface Has Some Explaining to Do*, on page 140, we'll look at ways to do this.

3.4 Cognitive Impairments

A *cognitive impairment* is any deficit or irregularity in the way a person's brain handles information. Because this definition is so broad, dozens of specific disorders fall under the umbrella of cognitive disability, including the group referred to as *learning disabilities*. The broadness of this definition also means this is the largest and most abstract category of disability. We can classify most cognitive disabilities as impacting perception or processing.

Perceptual Disorders

A *perceptual disorder* is an inability to clearly or correctly understand sensory information. This might appear as an inability to distinguish spatial relationships or to separate foreground from background. There can also be gaps in sensory perception where there is no loss in vision or hearing but there is an incomplete recognition or understanding of visual or auditory information.

Processing Disorders

Processing disorders are an inability to encode or decode information.

One processing disorder is *dyslexia*, a general term used to refer to reading disorders. One well-known form of dyslexia is character transposition, a *sequential processing disorder*. Dyslexics may also experience difficulty connecting words to sounds or distinguishing spatial properties of letters, such as *b*, *d*, *p*, and *q*, which differ only in orientation.

Aphasia is another family of impairments in language-processing capacity. Aphasia is an inability to produce or comprehend language and may manifest in many ways, including difficulty in forming or understanding spoken or written communication.

Some people can't process figures of speech or other idiomatic cues. This includes nonverbal cues such as gestures or facial expressions as well as figures of speech or slang. Someone with a perceptual disorder might well find these expressions confusing or take them as literal statements.

In all cases, someone with a perceptual disorder might use alternate presentations of information that don't rely on sensory or processing paths affected by their disability. For example, someone with a visual perceptual impairment or a processing disorder that precludes reading text would use a screen reader. Likewise, someone with an auditory perception or speech-processing disorder would rely on transcripts or captions.

Users with cognitive disabilities might also use other tools to prevent overload of their mental resources. Autosummarization software generates an abstract of a longer narrative that can be used to understand main ideas and evaluate whether the content is worth further effort. Highlighting systems shade a majority of the user's screen to prevent visual drift and focus attention on relevant information.

What Cognitive Impairments Mean for Web Development

Clearly written content with straightforward language is the key to providing basic accessibility for cognitive disabilities. We'll look at conventions for creating understandable text and the impact of idiomatic expressions in *Keeping It Simple Is Smart*, on page 84. To make content accessible for the audience with cognitive impairments, we also need to include more than one way to access information. We'll see more about this in *Multiple Access Paths*, on page 45. The other aspects we need to keep in mind, such as eliminating time limits and providing alternative text to make the content accessible to screen readers, are already aspects that need to be done with respect to the other categories of disability.

3.5 Multiple Disabilities

It is easy to fall into the trap of considering each of these classes of disability as being separate from one another. Some people have more than one disability, however. There are blind people with mobility impairments as well as deaf people with learning disabilities. This means we need to provide balanced accessibility solutions usable by people with multiple disabilities.

With some basic information about disabilities in hand, we're ready to keep our users with disabilities in mind and develop for them in a well-reasoned way. Keeping the needs of our audience in mind, we'll move on to keeping the needs of our project team in mind.

Act on It!

1. Try to get access to a few of the assistive technologies mentioned in this chapter—some of the URLs referenced have demo versions of the software technologies. Get a basic feel for what these technologies do.

2. Politely ask a friend or co-worker who uses assistive technology how it works and what kinds of things are irritating to them about web pages.

What's the use of a fine house if you haven't got a tolerable planet to put it on?
▶ Henry David Thoreau

Chapter 4

An Environment for Access

We want to build content that is accessible, but if possible, we also want the process to be as straightforward and painless as possible. If I could just wave a magic wand and make this happen...I would patent the process and sell it to you for a reasonable licensing fee. Unfortunately, I can't do that, but I can give some advice about how you can create a project environment where accessibility is an essential component of the project—one no more imposing than any other part of the development process.

In this chapter, we'll look at what we need to do to build this sort of environment. Most of the time, we aren't doing this on our own,[1] and in *Making a Team Effort*, we'll look at which people need to be at the table when we make our content design decisions and what they each need to have from (and need to contribute to) the team in terms of accessible design. The first thing this team will need to do is *Plan for Access*. During planning, we have our best opportunity to tune a project's requirements to include accessible design. One of these requirements will be to ensure that *Multiple Access Paths* to the content are created for users with a wide variety of sensory abilities. We will do this by understanding attributes of media and how we can use them in a way that doesn't overload our users.

Creating multiple ways to access information has its dangers, however. It is possible to end up succumbing to the "WET dilemma," where we Write Everything Twice. In *Don't Get WET*, we'll learn how to avoid getting WET by staying DRY as well as how to avoid one-off design decisions that can lead us astray.

---

1. However, sometimes we are. I have often worked alone on projects and worn many of the content development hats at once. I still recommend looking at *Making a Team Effort* and watching to make sure you're wearing the right hat at the right time.

Finally, we'll close the chapter with an introduction to some guidelines for accessibility. Although the guidelines will not be our primary focus as we work toward accessibility, we don't always have a choice in the matter, and it is important to be knowledgeable enough about them to use them as tools and to field questions that may be posed to us about them.

1 Making a Team Effort

*Let every man be respected as an individual and no man
idolized.*
▶ Albert Einstein, **The World As I See It**

Producing high-quality online content requires a wide variety of expertise in several domains working together. During project planning, it is important to tap this expertise from the beginning of the process. It looks like we'll need to assemble a team. The team should include representatives from each of the following groups:

- Project stakeholders

- Content creators

- User interface designers

- Visual identity designers

- Software developers

There might be some overlap in responsibilities here (especially if you're part of a small team), and it will be important for these members to be aware of which role's perspective they are taking at a given time. I'm a big fan of keeping teams lightweight, so I advise that this planning team preferably be small with no more than two delegates from each group unless specialized skills become needed. Because these delegates should be a representative of their specialization and act as the line of communication between the planning team and the other members of their group, one primary and one backup would be even better. Backup members are important—for this team to work, each group needs to be represented and be able to provide input to the process. Let's take a closer look at each of these groups and find out what they need to bring to (and take from) the table.

Project Stakeholders

These are the people who are behind the project vision. They have developed an idea that is going to be made real through the activities of this team, and as such they will need to take responsibility for leading the planning team.

Accessibility Requirements

The project stakeholders have the most abstract requirement for accessibility. They need to have a commitment to accessible design in their project vision and be ready to lead the other members of their team in making the same commitment. This means becoming informed about the higher-level concepts of accessible design and understanding which needs are and aren't being fulfilled by the team's content design process. More than anything else, the primaries need to know where the other teams are having difficulties in designing accessibly in order to help find solutions to those difficulties.

Accessibility Responsibilities

To create an accessible final product, the project primary needs to listen to the needs of the other members and do what is necessary to make sure those needs are met. If the content creators need a new tagging model implemented, the primary will need to verify that the software team makes the changes in a timely manner. If a dispute crops up between the interface design and visual identity teams, the primary will need to make sure negotiations are made and step in to push for agreement if necessary. It will also be necessary to make sure the other members are on track for meeting the project's goals, as well as noticing when the wrong goals are being promoted. (See the sidebar on the next page for more on this.)

Content Creators

The content creators will be responsible for creating the content assets necessary to meet the goals of the project. These assets may take the form of text, illustration, or other media that is meant to be essential content of the site. This contrasts with the interface and visual identity folks, who will be generating similar assets for navigational or presentational purposes.

Accessibility Requirements

The content creators will need the interface designers to generate one or more interfaces to their content that ensure a clear and accessible path for the audience. The graphic designers will need to provide a complementary set of formats for the content tag set to enhance the user experience without violating the separation of content and layout.

Beware the Resume Builder

I think that some of my favorite needs assessments for web content look something like this:

- XML/XSL
- Ajax/Web 2.0
- Flash/Breeze
- LAMP
- JSP/Velocity/Struts
- Buzzword compliance
- Fuzzy pink bunnies

I'd like to say I haven't seen any of these in a project content plan before, but sadly I've seen all of them...but the bunnies (which is unfortunate—the bunnies at least have the potential to add some humor to the content). Note that I'm not arguing for or against any of these technologies, but when I see technologies floating freely without connection to a content need, I get a little tense. I first suspect a Resume Builder has reared his ugly ladder-climbing head. These are the people who always seem to find a way to justify that the current project is "just the right fit" for whichever technology happened to most recently give the most hits on their favorite career search sites. As much as I'd like to recommend a not-so-friendly burying of the hatchet, this is the time to take the high road and drive planning focus back toward delivering a principled content plan. Once we have that, it will help to clearly determine what the *real* technology needs of the project are. If the Resume Builder continues to refuse to focus on the project goals, it may be time to find someone else for your planning team who is better able to represent the needs and capabilities of their specialty to the project.

In both cases, there will need to be a common determination of media standards to which all three of these groups adhere. The infrastructure developers will need to respond to tagging designs in a timely manner as well as provide appropriate interfaces for content acquisition.

Accessibility Responsibilities

The content creators will need to make the nature of their content clearly understood such that formal tagging and media standards can be designed and implemented to fit their needs. If these needs change, they will need to provide suggestions about how to meet these new requirements. With respect to media assets, the content experts need to provide proper descriptions for these assets that will be used to generate alternative representations through the use of alt and longdesc attributes, captions, or transcripts.

User Interface Designers

The user interface designers create the content layouts necessary to ensure a consistent and reliable way for the end user to interact with the content. For accessible designs, this may involve a number of alternative interfaces, targeted toward different populations, that provide multiple access paths while retaining a common navigational feel.

Accessibility Requirements

The interface designers will need to work closely with the subject matter experts and graphic designers to set media standards that properly convey the nature of the content without causing damage to the user interface. Infrastructure developers will be called upon to provide the back-end hooks and scripts necessary to make the user interface work and ensure that it can be modified to meet specific user needs. Interface and graphic designers will need to work closely in the development of alternate interfaces to retain a consistent user experience. To accomplish this, the interface designers will need consistently standardized style sheets from the graphic designers that take into account the content tagging structure that is designed in collaboration with the subject matter experts.

Accessibility Responsibilities

The interface designer will need to be deeply aware of user interface and accessibility best practices in order to ensure positive results in the final design. This can be achieved through alternate interfaces, but the default interface *must* be accessible. In creating these interfaces, the designer needs to keep in mind the vision as it is presented by the project primary and subject matter experts and ensure that end users are presented with the content in a way that is true to that vision in each interface developed.

Visual Identity Designers

Sometimes, in the world of accessibility, graphic designers get a bum rap. Although it's true that layout graphics hinder some users with visual or cognitive impairments, many users without disabilities also benefit from well-designed visual formatting. Great graphic designers understand that not everyone can use visual styling and rise to the challenge of working within the freedoms and constraints of the online environment. By mastering this balance, designers are able to produce flexible visual layouts that enhance content for a wide variety of users but politely step aside for users who cannot or do not want to use them.

Accessibility Requirements

The graphic designers will need documentation about the interface design to help them understand the limitations of a given interface and how that might impact their design or create the need for an alternate design. Along with the subject matter experts and the interface designers, the graphic designers will make contributions to and follow the project media standards such that they can design according to them. Infrastructure developers will need to provide the means by which graphic designers can store style sheet templates and media along with any appropriate metadata.

Accessibility Responsibilities

The graphic designers are usually the ones informed about any existing visual identity standards that need to be addressed and will need to make sure to meet them in an accessible manner. If the existing standards conflict with accessibility principles, the graphic designers, possibly with the project leads, will need to work with those responsible for the organization's visual identity in order to find an alternate presentation that ensures accessibility compliance.[2] The graphic designer will

---

2. This isn't necessarily as bad as it sounds. Often, the central visual identity people know there is a need for accessibility and may already have a working group to discuss this issue. If the project team has come up with a good solution to a problem on the overall identity front, that group may be receptive to incorporating the update into the identity standards or at least in suggesting further revisions toward that end.

need to create appropriate styles for the project's content tagging and document them in a shared style sheet. Any ancillary formatting assets will need to come with all the information needed to create appropriate alt attributes. (In many cases, if a design element requires longdesc, something has gone wrong. It may be that the item is actually carrying information that needs to be conveyed by the subject matter experts in the primary content.)

Infrastructure Developers

Here we find the database administrators, programmers, and business analysts that build the tools and frameworks necessary to get the content, design, and interface to the audience and make the connection between them and the realized vision of the project stakeholders. Without the developers, the content couldn't get into the world. (The developers should always remember, however, that without everyone else, there is nothing to send out there in the first place.) The developers also provide the tools to help everyone else get things done.

Accessibility Requirements

The content designers need to let the developers know what they want in a manner that allows for changes to be made consistently and appropriately to the databases, templates, and frameworks for which they are responsible. If workflow tools are requested from developers, they need feedback about how well the tools work, where they could work better, and how changes could be made for greater functionality. The other groups will need to provide information about their expectations of the final product such that the developers can build appropriate tests.

Accessibility Responsibilities

The infrastructure developer will need to meet the needs of other groups in a timely fashion. In part, this involves helping the rest of the group understand what solutions are available to them and what it will take to implement them. The infrastructure should follow good development practices and be well tested. If an appropriate content management environment is being used, access to tools for creating and storing content and metadata should be provided. If alternative textual output for media is being stored, developers will need to make sure tools exist to extract this information. Results of any output testing systems being used should be made available to the content and design teams.

Your Friendly Neighborhood Accessibility Coordinator

On more than one occasion, it has come to my attention that I need professional help. When the issue at hand is accessibility, the person to sit down with is your organization's accessibility coordinator or compliance officer. This person is your best bet for finding the right advice for difficult questions. If you're not sure who to ask, try checking with your organization's human resources department for a pointer in the right direction. I am fortunate enough to have Dr. Christy Horn, an extremely knowledgeable and experienced accessibility coordinator just down the hall, and I'd like to ask her a few questions:

Jeremy: *What is the role of the accessibility coordinator?*

Christy: *It is the role of an accessibility coordinator, who is more often than not referred to as an ADA coordinator, to ensure that all aspects of the environment whether they be physical, programmatic, or virtual are usable by people with disabilities.*

Jeremy: *What do you find to be the most common misperception about web accessibility?*

Christy: *I think that the knee-jerk reaction when I am talking about web accessibility is that it will require completely starting over. I always focus on what the purpose of the web page is. For instance, if you have your employment application online, as many companies do now, can a person who cannot use a mouse apply for a job? You may have aspects of the HR web page that are not accessible, but focus needs to be on the information one would need from the site and whether they can interact with the web site.*

Jeremy: *What mistakes do web teams commonly make in terms of accessibility?*

Christy: *Web development teams commonly make more work for themselves by making accessibility something they do as an afterthought rather than making it a design feature. It is much easier to design an accessible web site than it is to redesign a site to make it accessible.*

Jeremy: *When should a web developer consider consulting with the accessibility coordinator?*

Christy: *The consultation should occur in the planning process. What often happens is that we are asked to review a completed site. The conversation should take place during the design process, particularly* *because many of the basic issues can be taken care of easily at that point.*

Jeremy: *Are there any other thoughts or pieces of advice that you would like to share?*

Christy: *It has been my experience that many of the design issues that one needs to address to ensure accessibility also make the technology more usable by the rest of the population. The fact is that all people have different levels of visual, perceptual, auditory, and navigational skills. Accessibility requirements tend to make web developers attend to these issues in the design of web pages, making them more usable by everyone.*

Dr. Christy Horn is the ADA/504 compliance officer for the University of Nebraska and the codirector of the Center for Instructional Innovation. Christy has more than twenty-five years of experience designing accommodation and accessibility solutions, including the first computer lab for students with disabilities in higher education.

Keeping the Team Together

You've gotten a team together and are working on making this content a reality. Now you need to make sure this team stays together. (I'm looking at you, project leaders.) Here are some suggestions:

- *Meet regularly*: There will certainly be plenty of sit-down planning meetings, particularly early in the project. Most of the time, however, I encourage frequent stand-up meetings to pass along information and updates. Making these meetings stand-up encourages that people keep things short and to the point, reducing the need for a meeting to discover why nothing is getting done. In a team that represents diverse expertise, make sure everyone is available for the meetings or has a backup who will keep the entire team in the loop.

- *Keep a project wiki*: With a team that brings together different expertise, it is important to be able to know what kinds of issues the team is working on and share information. A wiki is an easy way to provide a central point to share this information.[3]

---

3. If your organization uses a tool such as Lotus Notes that allows the creation of a shared project database and everyone feels comfortable using it, then use that instead. The idea is to have a shared space, not be buzzword compliant.

- *Have an "off-site"*: Try to gather the team for periodic nonworking lunches where everyone can get to know one another. This goes a long way toward creating a respectful collaboration.

Selling Accessibility to the Team

It is possible that you might be the only accessibility advocate on your team. How do you convince others that accessibility should be a core objective if you're not the project lead? Try to be positive in the way you present accessibility—using the danger of a lawsuit is only going to put the team on edge and inspire defensiveness. Consider some of the reasons for accessibility mentioned in Chapter 2, *Why Be Accessible?*, on page 9. If these ideas are already complementary to the core objectives of your team, present them as such. If that isn't clear, make an argument for increasing the served audience or doing the right thing. If it comes down to it, point out the legal requirements—just try not to be accusatory about it.

Designing accessible web sites is a multidisciplinary effort. By bringing together expertise in as many of these areas as possible to pursue accessible development principles, the odds of success are increased. Every team needs a plan, however, and that's what we'll look at next.

Act on It!

1. Think about your current projects. What communication barriers may be keeping your project from producing accessible content? How could they be eliminated?

2. Learn more about keeping your team healthy. *Behind Closed Doors* (RD05) and *Manage It!* (Rot07) provide excellent views on working with and managing teams that get things done.

Plan for Access

It will not do to leave a live dragon out of your plans if you live near one.
  ► J. R. R. Tolkien, **The Hobbit**

One of the most common objections that I've heard about implementing accessibility is the cost is too high, and in many projects, there's some truth to this. If accessibility is delayed until the last stages before deployment, costs for retooling user interface and visual layout to separate content from presentation and meet accessibility requirements can be substantial. In truth, the high cost that gets assigned to accessibility is actually the cost of correcting a bad content design.[4] By planning for accessibility from the beginning, we can reduce this cost by eliminating one reason to rebuild. We'll also plan for a revision process that will provide a way to account for new content structures in a well-ordered manner.

Your Friend, the Style Guide

Whether it's a collection of pages on a project wiki or a more formal document produced by a planning team, a project style guide can be one of the most valuable products of the planning process. This guide sets forth the tagging and styling decisions made along with content production and media acquisition standards that reflect all of the production targets.

Tagging with Structure

The first step in producing accessible content is to abandon any ideas that might linger about combining content and presentation. It was a bad idea from the early days of the Web that only became worse. Fortunately, the World Wide Web Consortium (W3C) has worked to eliminate the vestiges of HTML that served only to provide visual formatting information and moved this functionality into the CSS standards.[5] This means your style guide will need to determine which markup is appropriate for the content at hand and handle the styling separately.

---

4. This cost has become high enough that some educators are placing accessibility considerations early in their web design curriculum. See Brian Rosmaita's work on Accessibility First at http://academics.hamilton.edu/computer_science/brosmait/talks/ for an example.
5. Unfortunately, with respect to standards compliance, the browser wars never really ended. The Web Standards Project (http://www.webstandards.org) can help you find your way through these and many other content-related issues.

We'll talk more about tagging for meaning in *Say It with Meaning*, on page 78. If you *really* want to emphasize the structure of your content, you could look at constructing a document type definition (DTD) for your project. See the sidebar on the following page for more details. One of the advantages of using a DTD is that you can abstract the tagging and layout decisions necessary for accessibility away from the content authors who can then focus on their primary goal—writing good content.

Documented Output Formatting

As output styles are generated, the style choices need to be consistently documented. I find it useful to base this document on the source tagging to ensure that everything is documented and that every element that needs to be styled has been styled. If you are working from a project language with a DTD, there should be a documented format for every output. For example, you might be targeting XHTML+CSS, WML, and PDF. In this case, there should be three documented styles (more, if you have multiple styles for XHTML+CSS). When documentation is generated for content authors, however, it is probably best to include only those styles that should appear in their content (as opposed to styles intended for use in the site layout and navigation).

Content Style

To reduce the load on your audience, your content should be clearly written in a consistent manner. To help achieve this, use the *other* kind of style guide. If your content is targeted toward a specific professional audience, a style guide may already be available. The American Psychological Association (APA), Modern Language Association (MLA), and American Mathematical Society (AMS), among others, have created well-known and widely used styles.

Your professional audience might have their own recognized style, and if so, your audience would benefit from its use. For more general audiences, the Associated Press (AP) style might be useful, as might the *Chicago Manual of Style*. Whichever content style is chosen, document it in your project style guide, and mandate that content writers use it consistently.

Media Acquisition Standards

When creating or acquiring multimedia assets, we need to ensure that they can be suitably represented across our chosen output formats.

Tagging from a DTD

There is an option above and beyond XHTML tags with class attributes. If you already know that you have plans for multiple output formats, you could define a tagging language by creating or extending a DTD. Ultimately, unless you have very simple needs, you are probably better off adopting an existing one such as DocBook (http://www.docbook.org) and extending it. Not only has much of your DTD testing already been done, but tools and documentation are probably already available as well. Using a custom DTD allows your content authors to write things like this:

```
<article>
  <title>My Fine Article</title>
  <author>I. M. Writing</author>
  <body>...</body>
</article>
```

rather than this:

```
<div class='article'>
  <div class='article-title'>My Fine Article</div>
  <div class='article-author'>I. M. Writing</div>
  <div class='article-body'><p>...</p></div>
</div>
```

The content can then be transformed using XSLT into any format you need to produce, including the second one shown here. This provides several advantages:

- Your authors work in a semantic format that doesn't burden them with implementation details.

- The author can't drop in one-off inline styles unless you allow for it. Don't allow for it.

- The format isn't encumbered with extra layers of tagging (the world of nested <div> tags with classes in XHTML).

- Revisions to styling have less widespread impact. When class=article-author becomes class=article-byline, changes exist only in the XHTML output filter and related style sheets rather than in every existing article.

Even if you use a DTD, you still need a project standard for the output formats. Although it can be advantageous to prevent exposure of these decisions to the content authors, they will still need to be understood among those who need to maintain the output filters. Additionally, you'll need to provide documentation of the DTD for the content authors.

The standards we create either need to represent a best average of the formats or be in a form that can be converted (preferably automatically) for each target. We will also need to provide appropriate data for alternative access.

By way of example, let's consider image assets. We might want to think about the following:

- Maximum image height and width
- Color depth
- Image file size
- Content meaning of the image and how it will be stored

For our example project, we would like to be able to print articles and send them to handheld users, as well as providing the articles online, so, ideally, we would be able to provide 300 dpi output that is still meaningful when scaled to 200 pixels wide. Additionally, where possible, we would like to be able to represent images in 16-level grayscale. Images will also need to be compressed in order to minimize bandwidth usage on the portable devices. In this case, we would also like the person responsible for acquiring the image to create alternate text for it (odds are, they have the best idea of how the image should be described). Because we're considering image assets, we won't need to consider subtitling or transcripts, but keep this in mind for video and audio assets. Once we've determined our standard, it might be useful to create a media specification sheet. The sheet should contain a simple and clear breakdown of the needs that have been determined for the media type, including the extra metadata that needs to be provided and necessary alternatives.

Revising the Plan

You'll need to revise your style guide from time to time, and it makes more sense to plan for it at the beginning. Once the initial brainstorming work has settled, you might even find it useful to introduce a formal revision process into your original style guide development. Each revision should go through four steps, discussed in the following sections.

Step 1: Add the Proposed Revision to a Master Revision List

Your project's master revision list should be the entry point for all suggested changes. The merit of a given change should not be a consideration for inclusion on the list. That will be decided later when the impact of the revision is analyzed. An example change request might be as follows: "Add tagging to represent cookbook recipes."

Step 2: Consider the Impact of the Revision

Either as an online process or during content team meetings, the master list should be reviewed frequently. You should ask "Does this change fit with our content identity?" and "Have we already defined an acceptable alternative to this?" and (of course) "What will it take to ensure that this change is made without breaking accessibility?" For our example, assume you're developing a lifestyle news site and your readers have a growing interest in cooking. The recipes would make an interesting addition to your regular content. It might be possible to create this content in the context of a normal article, but your team comes to the consensus that this is likely to be a growing feature and new tagging will be added for the recipe features. In terms of accessibility, the only issue that comes up is making sure that measurements and ordering of directions are expressed in a way that is screen readable. The proposal makes it to the next stage and should be marked as such. If the proposal is rejected, don't delete it. Instead, mark it for reference, and add comments. If the same idea shows up again, it is useful to know why it was rejected the first time and consider what, if anything, has changed.

Step 3: Find Specific Actions That Need to Be Taken

Here, you'll want to think about what the needs of this change are and document the needs as formal subtasks:

- Will new content need to be acquired for this revision?

- Will new tagging forms be necessary?

- Will the current navigation and search systems suffice, or will we need something new?

- Do we need a new layout for this content?

- Does this change require the use of multimedia elements that will require captions or transcripts to be generated?

- What information about using this new tagging needs to be added to the style guide?

- Will the new content require additional infrastructure support such as new database tables or interface layers?

For the recipe proposal, it is determined that content will be generated internally, but new tagging for recipe content will need to be designed. The recipes will be included with the rest of the articles, so navigation and infrastructure shouldn't be impacted; however, the graphic designers will need to ensure that the new markup is nicely styled. The content authors will also need to be informed of the changes to the style guide, including specific usages such as making sure to mark abbreviated measurements with expansions for screen readers to use.

Step 4: Assign Tasks to the Appropriate Parties, and Determine a Revision Deadline

The task assignment might be to a team leader or an individual depending on the size of task. If the team has the representatives recommended in *Making a Team Effort*, on page 29, this is probably a matter for that representative or their team to decide. The deadline could be a specific date or a milestone in the style guide that implies a date. Your content team decides that the recipe features should start to go online for the fall/winter holidays. To make sure the content writers have sufficient lead time, the tagging and styling changes are marked for version 3.4, which has a late July release schedule.

If you have a project wiki, it might be useful to add a space to document the stages of this process and the changes that result. Better yet, if you have access to a ticket-tracking system that supports subtasks (ask your software developers if you're not sure), it might be better to use that instead. It has already been designed for this kind of work.

With a plan for accessibility in mind, it's time to consider how to proceed with creating accessible content. One of the underlying principles of accessible design is to give the user more than one way to access information. Next we'll look at the idea of multiple access paths.

Act on It!

1. Consider a markup format suitable for your current project.
2. Take a look at css Zen Garden (http://www.csszengarden.com).
    - Examine the sample HTML source file. What are the advantages of not combining style information into the source? How would you design this differently?
    - Construct a style sheet for the sample HTML, and document it with comments. Does the tagging provide you with everything you need to create a style?

- Attempt to construct an alternate markup that would represent the same content as the sample file. If you're looking for an extra challenge, write a DTD for it.

3. Look at a relevant style guide for your current project. Are you creating content that conforms to that style? If not, consider whether the content across pages is consistent and clear to the reader.

| 3 | Multiple Access Paths |

*The sweetest path of life leads through the avenues of
learning, and whoever can open up the way for another,
ought, so far, to be esteemed a benefactor to mankind.*
> ▶ David Hume

There's more than one way to convey a message, and the right way to
do it depends on the user viewing our web sites. A user who is deaf
or simply has a visual learning preference will benefit from content
based on captioned video or illustration, while users who are blind will
need text narratives or audio to get to the essentials of the content
with which they want to interact. In all cases, being able to choose a
representation that works best is of value to our users. Ultimately, of
course, we want to be valuable to our users, so we need to give them
these choices about how they want to interact with our content. This
doesn't mean we should build virtual towers of Babel by providing so
many overlapping options that our content ends up becoming confusing
(read: useless) for everyone, however. What we need are multiple access
paths.

Multiple Access Paths

The concept of multiple access paths is a simple one. Where we have a
given piece of content that relies on a particular media representation,
we provide at least one alternate version that uses another representation. Ultimately, we would like to use as few paths as we can to cover
as many use cases as possible. Planning for multiple access paths isn't
simply a matter of putting several versions of something on the same
page. What we really want to look at is what we're trying to convey to
the end user with a piece of content. For example, we may be creating
a screencast for a piece of software that our users might be interested
in learning about. The purpose here would be to demonstrate a piece of
software, explaining how it works and why it might be a good thing to
take a closer look at. Let's consider cases where the screencast might
not be the best choice for some users and how we might reach them as
well.

For hard-of-hearing users, the voiceover component of the screencast
will be difficult or impossible to use. This is easy to solve, however,
because screencasts are ultimately video. If we add a subtitle track
for these users that captures the voiceover content, the screencast

becomes fully usable for these users. It doesn't take much more effort to accommodate vision-impaired users. If the commands used during the screencast are captured in a transcript, it is possible for these users to follow along with the steps in the voiceover. It would be better yet to interleave the commands with a transcript of the voiceover—the vision-impaired users would have a completely parallel access path to the content.

In some cases, it isn't sensible to create these kinds of alternate paths because removing one aspect or another misses the point. For example, a text representation of a Photoshop demo isn't generally a realistic idea. When this happens, it is generally sufficient to provide text describing the demonstration. This serves two purposes—it makes sure we don't create a "black hole" in our content where users with disabilities become lost, and it allows these users to do forward research for others who do have the sensory abilities needed to use the content. What we want to keep in mind, however, is that we need to build an interface to sensibly access the alternate paths rather than just heaping all of the options in one place, which might overload the users.

Avoiding Overload

When we provide multiple access paths, we need to be mindful of *cognitive load theory*. The idea behind cognitive load theory is that we have a limited amount of mental resources to devote to a task. Some load is caused by the nature of information. We can't do anything about this because the only way to reduce it is for the user to gain experience. Some load is generated by the environment, however. The things the user has to do and the presentation of information adds extraneous cognitive load. We *can* do something about this. Some information is made more understandable when complementary text and imagery are presented in parallel. This means the subtitles made available for some users may be beneficial to others that we hadn't specifically planned for.

Noncomplementary information, on the other hand, can create *interference* and makes our content harder to understand. This means our multiple paths need to be designed in a way that they don't stomp upon one another. If, for instance, you provide a subtitled video, the subtitles need to maintain synchronization such that if a user hears the audio, it matches up to what they see in the subtitles. If that match isn't there, their level of understanding is likely to be diminished.

Another form of extraneous load comes from inconsistency in presentation. When presentation varies across pages, the user spends mental resources on understanding navigation and interface—resources that we would prefer be used on understanding our message. This is taken care of by developing uniform interfaces. We've all used applications and web sites that make us stop and think before we know what to do. If we're on a site that shows us video and gives a link to a transcript, we wouldn't expect to see a transcript on some pages with links to the video.

Keeping Media Attributes in Mind

I *hate* the phrase "All other things being equal...." All other things are *never* equal. If they were, text would provide the same experience as video, and television wouldn't have killed radio. Some things are clear in a video that aren't in a verbatim transcript of its dialogue. If you listen to the Second Audio Program (SAP) on broadcasts that make it available, you hear audio descriptions of the things happening that aren't indicated by the dialogue. Similarly, subtitles often put musical notes on-screen during significant background music or around lyrics to indicate to deaf users that actors are singing the dialogue. It is clear that we need to consider the *attributes* of the media that we choose and provide extra information to compensate for attributes missing in alternative medias.

I've already given a brief example of how adding auditory description can mitigate some of the deficits of audio relative to video. Similarly, text descriptors of audio such as the musical note, [yelling], and [whispering] compensate for an inability to use audio. Both of these issues will be discussed *much* more in Chapter 10, *Video Killed the Something-Something*, on page 175.

What about interactive elements? This is a much more difficult issue. The first step is to understand whether the interactivity is a central part of the experience. If not, you may be able to get by with building a path around it. If it is essential, however, there's a lot of work to be done. Alternate control and response needs to be designed to allow interactivity without mandating sensory-specific capabilities. Some time ago, I worked with a group that based hiring requirements on a web site that used a drag-and-drop concept map. The concepts weren't visually oriented, but the interface was—at this point the accessibility problem clearly becomes a discrimination problem. This can be solved, however, by constructing a conventional text-accessible alternate.

This allows the same information to be gathered in a way that doesn't exclude one or more classes of user. The important point here is that I'm not saying the graphical concept map should be eliminated. There are other classes of users who might be unfairly hindered by having to address a completely text-based version, so the graphical version would be better for them. This is, after all, the essence of providing multiple access paths.

You need to be careful when you plan for multiple access paths, though. There is a *big* difference between designing a page that can be understood clearly by many kinds of users and designing a different page for every kind of user. Whenever possible, you should avoid writing multiple versions of the same thing. This point is important enough that we'll be covering it next.

Act on It!

1. Consider the web pages and applications you regularly use. Are there elements on the page that distract you from doing what you went to the site to do? Is it straightforward to get things done on the site? How would you change the page to make your work easier and minimize distraction? Make notes of these changes and ideas for your next project.

2. Watch a movie that you know well with the sound turned down and the subtitles turned on. Does the experience still work? How would you change the subtitles to better convey what's really happening? If the user couldn't see the video and had to rely on someone reading the subtitles to them, what else would you have to add?

4   Don't Get WET!

But better die than live mechanically a life that is a
repetition of repetitions.
► D. H. Lawrence, **Women in Love**

D.H. Lawrence wrote, "But better die than live mechanically a life that is a repetition of repetitions." Repetition is a definite problem that we need to keep our eyes open for in any project. Every repetition of a core idea that we add increases the number of changes that must be made for revision. If the project has codependent repetition, it gets even worse and starts to increase the change possibilities multiplicatively. This is particularly important for accessibility oriented projects where we rely on alternate versions of interfaces and content. We want to provide these features without branching out into a new career in duplicate revision. What can we do about this? Fortunately, most of the work is in learning to think in terms of one simple idea:

The DRY Principle
by Dave Thomas and Andy Hunt, Pragmatic Programmers

Every piece of knowledge must have a single, unambiguous, authoritative representation within a system. [HT00]

It sounds scary when it's put that way, no? That's why DRY says it more simply: "Don't Repeat Yourself." Although the DRY principle was originally written to describe a principle of software development, it's also pretty handy for building structured content. Many times, we repeat small ideas as a component of larger ones that we use to build our content. This kind of low-level repetition takes us down a dark path toward the worst-case scenario where we fall prey to the WET dilemma—that of "Writing Everything Twice." What we would like to do instead is develop a set of basic pieces that we can reuse in multiple places.

Building Abstraction

It would be a mistake to believe that keeping DRY means we'll be able to cut down on the number of styles and tags in our content system. We'll certainly remove plenty of each, but odds are good that we'll be adding even more. The reason is simple: we want a lot of really useful basics rather than a handful of overdeveloped ideas. The basics can be used in many places while maintaining a single definition. If we build a basic concept into several larger concepts, then we have to change it in several places every time. The first thing this means in the HTML+CSS world is being clear in our definitions. If <div class='article'> is our construct and we expect to see <h1>, <p>, <ul>, and so on, we should make sure to define the styles for subtags of <div class='article'>. Why? Ultimately, we want the style behavior to be independent from the rest of the document where appropriate. If we inherit all our styles, changes from above may adversely affect us in unexpected ways, so we would prefer to define everything we need to protect us from breakage. Keep in mind this doesn't mean you have to define *everything*. For example, you might want to inherit the base font-family from above, but it should be up to the lower-level style to make sure that necessary local adjustments such as relative size are made. It's also important to break apart styles when they're not naturally connected. For example, I recently worked with another developer who had defined multiple styles of the form "iteminfo," "itempeople," "articleinfo," "articlepeople," and so on. Fortunately, CSS gives us a way around this. If you define styles for "info," "people," "article," and "item," you can combine them pairwise for the same effect without duplicating the specific aspects of their category. With respect to accessibility, you might find it valuable to extract basic color information into a separate style sheet that can be swapped with another that is designed for higher contrast.

Avoiding One-Off Decisions

As a project develops, you're likely to run into a number of requests for "one-offs." These are the single-use features that people consider necessary for their content, and you need to decide whether they're right. One of three things could be happening here.

It's Really a One-Off

Sometimes the content is about a particularly specific idea that requires some new markup. You don't know whether this idea will show up again, but your general feeling is that it probably won't. This is the time to make a big decision: will creating the one-off be worth the trouble, and will it make maintenance difficult later? Further, will the change require significant time and additions to achieve cross-browser support and accessibility? To mitigate these, you'll want to keep the changes local to the affected page. Most of the time in HTML this means using <div> and <span> and CSS classes to define the one-off. I recommend doing this in a local-style definition. This keeps us from polluting our style sheet with one-offs and gives us an implementation to extract for the main style sheet if the idea *does* achieve common usage.

They've Found a Gap in the System

No markup system is designed for all things. It could be that the developer has stumbled onto a perfectly legitimate construct that isn't supported already but probably should be. This is often the case when new kinds of content are being developed that move beyond old assumptions. If you look at the history of support for multimedia in the HTML specs, you will find that these sorts of things do really happen, and it's important to think them through when they happen to avoid fracturing the system with multiple one-off solutions. This is the point in time to build up a proposed solution to present to the markup design team. If there is an unresolved debate about the right way to do this, it is reasonable to pilot the proposed change in the form of a local style, as mentioned earlier.

It's Time to Look Again

Most of the time, I've found that this is really what is happening. Sometimes the content developer becomes too wrapped up in the original view of an idea and visualizes a particular markup. When that markup isn't there or doesn't work as expected, change requests come in. The challenge is to help the developer see what they're really trying to say and how the existing markup styles can be used to express it. We'll go over an example of this thought process in *Layout and Other Bad Table Manners*, on page 117.

Using a Templating System

Although I want to believe that all of us have moved on to web frameworks with templating engines, I know this is not in fact the case. The route to accessible content is a really good place to make the leap if you haven't already. Templates allow us to formalize abstractions and eliminate repetitions. Some may even provide support for DTDs that allow a higher level of abstraction yet. If you're still working primarily with static pages, then eliminating redundancy will be nearly impossible. After all, each page will be stuck with repetition of basic container and navigation content. Even with basic templating systems such as SHTML, you're still able to template in only a very simple way. Do yourself a favor now, and move forward with a good templating system—preferably one that supports separation of data, interface, and presentation.

Act on It!

1. Are there one-offs in your current projects? Try to classify them across the three categories in this chapter. Find ways to eliminate the ones that don't need to be there.

2. If you don't feel comfortable with the templating framework you are using, learn more about it. In particular, focus on abstraction and accessibility features. If you aren't using one yet, *work on finding one!*

5	Guidelines for Accessibility

The best thing about standards is that there are so many to choose from.
► Andrew Tanenbaum, **Computer Networks**

As you work more with web accessibility, you will find yourself in discussions about various standards and guidelines for accessibility. It is good to be familiar with these guidelines because many test suites are based on them, and when a client or manager asks about issues pertaining to specific guidelines, it is important that you be able to openly and knowledgeably answer questions about them. It may also be possible when your team plans for accessibility that, by convention or by law, one of these sets of rules is chosen as a success criterion for the finished product. *Don't* occupy yourself with becoming a "rules lawyer." Remember at all times that our real target is to get things done and make it accessible to all of our users while we're at it.

Guidelines? We Don't Need No Stinkin' Guidelines!

In Chapter 1, *Introduction*, on page 3, I gave you ten principles for web accessibility and told you that they will usually guide you in the right direction. I still maintain that. Ultimately, however, there is a place for guidelines that are more spelled out than that, particularly once you understand the principles of accessibility and need to focus on details of compliance. It's useful to have baseline criteria that we can use to measure the quality of an accessible implementation. The important aspect to keep in mind is that (unless codified as law) guidelines are simply that—guidelines. In general, the guidelines give us a good set of best practices to work with. If you run across a situation where following the guidelines to the letter would cause a reduction in the accessibility of a site, it is probably best to bend the guidelines a little. Keep in mind that some of the existing recommendations are headed for ten years old and not everything in them is still entirely relevant. Some things are less of a problem than they once were, and some recommendations never worked as well as intended. The guidelines that are out there also don't usually give much insight into *how* to achieve accessibility. That's alright, though—the how is exactly why we're here. Let's quickly introduce the main accessibility standards of interest if you're working in the United States. We'll discuss each of them in more depth in Part V, *Understanding the Building Codes*.

In the Beginning...

...there was nothing in the way of guidelines for web accessibility, so we had to use known best practices from the software world and do our best. A few years later, however, when accessibility problems with the Web became a deep concern, the W3C formed the Web Accessibility Initiative (WAI) with the goal of bringing the Web to its full potential by working on usability for people with disabilities. In 1999, WAI responded with the Web Content Accessibility Guidelines 1.0 (WCAG 1.0). WCAG 1.0 has given much-needed guidance to many web developers as well as formed the basis for many international laws. As we close in toward its tenth anniversary, some parts of WCAG 1.0 have begun to feel a little rusty, but it is still a fairly decent model that I expect will continue to remain the gold standard of guidelines for some time. WCAG 1.0 and some thoughts about it are found in Chapter 14, *Web Content Accessibility Guidelines 1.0*, on page 245.

Trust Us—We're the Government

In many places, governments have written accessibility legislation that governs the creation and acquisition of technology. In the United States, that legislation is known as Section 508 of the Rehabilitation Act of 1973, as amended (29 U.S.C. 794d). I and many others, for obvious reasons, refer to it simply as Section 508. This legislation states requirements for computers, software, multimedia, and *web-based information and applications*, as well as a few other technology products. Fortunately, many of the Section 508 criteria sit parallel to guidelines in WCAG 1.0, so not everything will be different. Section 508, thoughts about its requirements, and its relationship to WCAG 1.0 are found in Chapter 15, *Section 508*, on page 263.

Not Your Father's WCAG

I'll admit that WCAG 2.0 hasn't been in the works for *that* long. The workgroup has been busy for quite a while, however—six years is a large percentage of the lifetime of the Web at this point. Part of the reason that it has taken so long may have something to do with arguments and controversies over the best direction for web accessibility. Some useful information is already appearing in the working draft, however, such as metrics for evaluating contrast and flash thresholds. As I said earlier, WCAG 1.0 still has a lot of momentum behind it and will for quite a while yet.

Because a lot of people are asking about WCAG 2.0, we'll describe it in Chapter 16, *Web Content Accessibility Guidelines 2.0*, on page 273.

The Same Story in a Different Language

On occasion I hear these strange stories about other countries and global economies and such, and they appear to be largely true. If we want to participate at the global level, it will be necessary to understand what the local standards are and how they differ from what we may or may not already know. Many other countries have developed national and regional guidelines and legislation regarding web accessibility. It is well beyond my knowledge what the specifics of most of these are, and they really fall beyond the scope of this book, but the W3C has compiled a list of links to policies at http://www.w3.org/WAI/Policy/. I'll also introduce some standards in other parts of the world in Chapter 17, *Meanwhile, in the Rest of the World...*, on page 291.

Act on It!

1. Determine which guidelines pertain to your work. This may be something that is already a policy in your workplace, so it wouldn't hurt to ask.

2. Take a glance at an overview of accessibility guidelines. Just a glance for now—I don't recommend getting too deep until you've learned more about the principles behind them. There are overviews of some major guidelines in Part V.

The test is to recognize the mistake, admit it, and correct it.
To have tried to do something and failed is vastly better
than to have tried to do nothing and succeeded.
▶ Unknown

Chapter 5

Testing for Accessibility

You may be asking yourself why we're looking at testing as a foundation for accessibility. After all, isn't testing something that is usually done at the *end* of the project? You would be right—testing *is* often saved until late in the game, and that is exactly why we're going to look at it now. In *Testing As a Design Decision*, we'll look at testing from the beginning to reduce accessibility costs.

As with any kind of testing, accessibility testing requires that you have a good selection of tools and techniques in hand to do the job right. In *Building Your Testing Toolbox*, I'll introduce you to a few tools that I have found useful when I test for accessibility. More options exist than we'll be able to cover, so keep your eyes open for alternatives that suit you better or tools not designed for accessibility that happen to get the job done. Get used to this idea. The world of accessibility of full of examples of creative repurposing—this is the part that I find fun about working in the area.

Tools will get us only so far, however. Automatic tools are incapable of ensuring that two content alternatives are *really* communicating the same idea. In *Getting Your Hands Dirty*, we talk about hand testing and how to bring in *real* experts on accessibility when the need arises.

6 | Testing As a Design Decision

Speed is irrelevant if you are going in the wrong direction.
▶ Mohandas Gandhi

Total cost of development is one of the most common arguments against accessible web design. Although accessibility has a measurable development cost, using the cost as a showstopper is a weak argument at best. The reality is that projects with high accessibility costs fall into one of two categories: projects with large amounts of media requiring text alternatives and projects that wait until the end of development to add accessibility. In the first case, the cost can't be prevented. Media-handling costs are always going to be proportional to the volume of media. On the other hand, the cost of refactoring is largely preventable.

It comes as no surprise that if we were to wire a house after finishing the walls, it would cost considerably more than wiring it beforehand. Why should it surprise us that the same is true of accessibility? The real cost of accessibility is the cost of building content twice—the first time that may or may not be accessible and the second time to repair it. Projects that commit to accessible development from the beginning and maintain it reduce the risk of an expensive accessibility crash session.

Testing from Day One

To ensure accessibility, we need to test for it. These tests should be happening from the first lines of code at the beginning of a project. The best solution is to follow a policy where all additions to a project are expected to be accessible when checked in. The development process looks like this:[1]

1. Build an initial version of the content.
2. Ensure this version passes accessibility testing. Check this copy in as the initial version in the project.
3. Incrementally add new functionality and styling to the content.
4. Verify that the new functionality still passes testing.
5. Once verified, merge changes into the project's master copy.
6. Repeat steps 3 through 6.

---

1. This process, particularly when discussing styles and scripts, is better known as *progressive enhancement*. A description of this and the related issue of *graceful degradation* is found in *Unassuming Scripts*, on page 220.

Let's see an example of this process in action. We'll look at a simple list of navigation links:

```
<ul>
  <li><a href="/">Home</a></li>
  <li><a href="/About/">About Us</a></li>
  <li><a href="/Contact/">Contact Us</a></li>
</ul>
```

That was pretty straightforward. But is it accessible? Sure. The markup is well formed and the links are descriptive in their own right, so we don't need to add title= attributes to the <a> tags. Let's check this in as version 1.

Adding Some Style

So far, this isn't a very attractive solution. It would be nice to style the list to add boxes around the items and a background tint. First we'll add a CSS class to the <ul> element:

```
<ul class='navigation'>
  <li><a href="/">Home</a></li>
  <li><a href="/About/">About Us</a></li>
  <li><a href="/Contact/">Contact Us</a></li>
</ul>
```

And then we'll define some styles:

```
/* Navigation List */
.navigation {
  width: 12em;
  padding: 0.75em;
  background-color: #07c;
}
/* Navigation List Item */
.navigation li {
  list-style-type: none;
  width: 100%;
  margin: 0.25em;
  border: 1px solid #ccf;
  text-align: center;
  background-color: #dc8;
}
/* Navigation Link */
.navigation a {
  color: #cb9;
}
```

We know that the new changes fall back properly for users who don't have CSS enabled because we already saw the work in the first version and our addition of a CSS class doesn't change that.

Our first testing step will be to run automated testing to catch obvious errors. We'll use WAVE 3.5[2] to run automated tests because it allows us to upload an HTML file rather than serving it from a URL. Here are the results:

- Accessibility Errors: 0

- Accessibility Alerts: 0

- Accessibility Features: 0

- Structural & Semantic Elements: 0

Great—we don't have any alerts or errors. This isn't really that surprising because the only thing we changed about the HTML was the addition of a class= attribute. The "Accessibility Features" and "Structural & Semantic Elements" counts are to point out features of the page that offer enhanced accessibility. None of the elements we're using has options to offer here, so we can just ignore them.

With automatic verification passed, we need to look at the web page and manually confirm that everything is correct—and here we have a problem. There are no images or scripts to turn off, and the page reads fine without the CSS.

That's our problem—the page reads well *only* without the CSS. Notice the background color of the list item (#dc8) and the link color (#cb9). These colors are very close to one another, which poses a contrast problem that we'll discuss further in *Thinking in Terms of Black and White*, on page 153. For now, trust me that this color combination doesn't make the cut. Let's change the link color to something darker such as (#333). Checking it again, the contrast problem is solved, and we can merge the changes while avoiding the Duck of Doom (see the sidebar on the next page for more on this).

Continuously testing in this manner prevents us from introducing inaccessible features that could result in a time-consuming and costly refactoring job later. For this to work, we need a good set of tools and techniques for testing our content. In the rest of this chapter, we'll look at what should be in your toolbox.

---

2. http://dev.wave.webaim.org/

The Duck of Doom

Accessible development is a team commitment, and if you choose to take a test-driven perspective, that commitment needs to include keeping the build clean. This means not letting any little "quick fixes" into the project that break accessibility tests. Errors should always be resolved before checking the related code into the master copy of a project.

The nature of development is that sometimes code with errors will get checked in. If this is an infrequent occurrence, so be it. Sometimes it starts becoming commonplace, however, and developers need to be reminded that they are accountable to the codebase. How you choose to do this is certainly up to you, but I have heard positive results of a team "mascot" that gets passed to the last person to break the build and stays with them until it happens again. I have heard of rubber chickens and toilet seats among other things—just keep it good-natured. My personal suggestion would be a "Duck of Doom."

Act on It!

1. Practice starting with a "bare-bones" site and progressively enhancing it with features. This is incredibly useful for having sites that are both feature rich and accessible.

2. Encourage your team to add accessibility to its testing regimen and to test early and often. Bring a duck if necessary.

7   # Building a Testing Toolbox

Man is a tool-using animal. Nowhere do you find him
without tools; without tools he is nothing, with tools he is
all.
> ▶ Thomas Carlyle, **Sartor Resartus**

We want to produce good work, so we'll need to have good tools. No single tool does everything we need for accessibility testing. We'll need a number of tools, some designed for accessibility testing and some general-purpose web design tools. Many of the basic tools that we need are collected in the Firefox Accessibility Extension (FAE),[3] a free extension to the Firefox web browser that acts as a launcher for a wide variety of accessibility-related tools. FAE is a useful and organized way to access the tools that I'll be mentioning. These are tools that I have found to be of high quality, but if you think you get the same or better results from other tools that you find to be more comfortable, by all means use them.

Keep in mind that these are tools for general accessibility testing. Throughout this book, tools for specific techniques and technologies will be introduced. For example, in *Thinking in Terms of Black and White*, on page 153, we'll look at tools for testing contrast, and in *PDF: Trying to Make Portable Accessible*, on page 210, we'll see tools for PDF accessibility.

Web Standards Validators

For content to be accessible, the first step is that it needs to be standards compliant. Assistive technologies need to be able to correctly parse our content for their users. Many assistive technologies have been designed with workarounds to handle invalid markup, but they work better when we design the content correctly from the start. To do so, we need to test all of our HTML markup as well as our CSS style sheets and news feeds.

W3C provides validators for all three of these. You can validate your page content with the Markup Validation Service,[4] which validates against all major versions of HTML, XHTML, and SMIL and against a few other formats.

---

3. http://firefox.cita.uiuc.edu/
4. http://validator.w3.org/

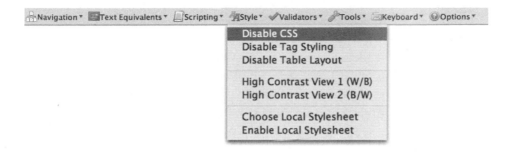

Figure 5.1: TURNING OFF STYLES WITH THE FIREFOX ACCESSIBILITY
EXTENSION

Markup validation tells you how well your pages conform to their document type definition (DTD)—the formal rules for the markup language.

The CSS Validation Service[5] validates CSS files and HTML files with included styles with selectable profiles for all versions of CSS as well as profiles for mobile, television, and Scalable Vector Graphics (SVG) usage. This points out improper usage including nonstandard selectors as well as selectors incompatible with your selected media profile.

The Feed Validation Service[6] is used for checking your RSS and Atom feeds. News feeds are a valuable tool for users, especially those with certain disabilities because they provide another access path to your content. In particular, feeds don't specify visual formatting conventions, which makes them appealing to visually impaired users. If you use FAE, the HTML and CSS validation services are available in the Validators menu on the toolbar.

Keep in mind that standards compliance is only one step toward accessibility. Sometimes this gets misunderstood as the only step toward accessibility, but nothing could be further from the truth. Although standards compliance is an important component, it is possible to create sites that are both compliant and inaccessible. We'll need other tests beyond these validators to test for accessibility.

Fallback Testing

The only things we can assume about our users is that they can send and receive text information. All of our content needs to be meaningful without the addition of images, style sheets, table layout, or scripting. To test whether our content falls back successfully, we need to be able to turn off any or all of these and verify that the page still makes sense. Although I have seen people do this by adding conditional switches to their web pages, I can't recommend that route. If the conditional switches aren't carefully placed, they may be changing the content in a way that isn't equivalent to what a user who has the technology turned off in their browser would receive. Also, alternative text for images can't be switched in this way. What we really need to do is turn off the technologies in the browser. FAE makes all of these options easily available from the Scripting menu and the Style menu, as shown in Figure 5.1, on the preceding page.

Conformance-Testing Tools

Many parts of WCAG and Section 508 are machine testable. Conformance-testing tools indicate the errors our pages have with respect to the *automatically* testable aspects of these guidelines. Each of the available tools has different strengths in what they test and how they present results. Cynthia Says[7] provides conformance checking against WCAG 1.0 as well as Section 508. In addition, it can give a basic report on the quality of alternative text for images. It isn't as useful for testing large sites, however, because it has a one-page-per-minute-per-site limit. The Functional Accessibility Evaluator[8] from the University of Illinois at Urbana–Champaign, shown in Figure 5.2, on the next page, is capable of evaluating an entire web site to two or three levels deep and can store combined reports of multiple sites into one report. UIUC is also the home of the Firefox Accessibility Extension; when I use the acronym FAE, I'm referring to the Firefox Accessibility Extension. Cynthia Says and the Functional Accessibility Evaluator are both available by clicking the Tools button in FAE.

I use both of the previously mentioned tools, but my current preference is WebAIM's WAVE Web Accessibility Tool.[9] I recommend the current

---

5. http://jigsaw.w3.org/css-validator/
6. http://validator.w3.org/feed/
7. http://www.cynthiasays.com/
8. http://fae.cita.uiuc.edu/
9. http://dev.wave.webaim.org/index.jsp/

Summary Report

Test Evaluation Summaries in HTML Best Practices Main Categories

	Status [1]	% Pass	% Warn	% Fail
Navigation & Orientation	Not Implemented	28	0	71
Text Equivalents	Complete	100	0	0
Scripting	Not Applicable	0	0	0
Styling	Partially Implemented	60	20	20
HTML Standards	Not Implemented	33	0	66

Test Evaluation Percentages in HTML Best Practices Subcategories

	% Pass	% Warn	% Fail	% N/A
Navigation & Orientation				
Document Title	50	0	50	0
Navigation Bars	0	0	0	100
Section Headings	0	0	100	0
Form Controls	0	0	0	100
Document Linearization	100	0	0	0
Data Tables	0	0	0	100
Frames	0	0	0	100
Access Keys	0	0	0	100
Text Equivalents				
Images	100	0	0	0
Embedded Objects	0	0	0	100

Figure 5.2: A SAMPLE REPORT FROM UIUC'S FUNCTIONAL ACCESSIBILITY EVALUATOR

development version, 3.5, rather than 3.0, which appears as an option in FAE. WAVE 3.5 provides text and outline views of the web page as well as a unique page view, where testing result icons appear next to the relevant page element (as shown in Figure 5.3, on the following page). This makes finding the point in a page where an error occurs easier. Additionally, WAVE shows where your page is providing particularly useful accessibility features in the icon interface.

I recommend using more than one of these tools for your automatic testing. Each tool interprets accessibility guidelines slightly differently, and using more than one gives better testing coverage. You will want to spend some time looking over the results that are given and interpreting what they mean.

Sometimes a tool will issue a failure for something that should really get a warning, such as duplicated alternative text. This is often a result of attempting to automatically verify something that should be checked by hand.

Figure 5.3: WebAIM's WAVE WEB ACCESSIBILITY TOOL OVERLAYS A PAGE WITH TESTING RESULT ICONS.

If, for example, you get a duplication warning because all your pictures have the alternative text "picture," the warning is really a failure. On the other hand, if an icon appears at multiple locations with the same alternative text, that would be correct. Ideally, the correct response from an automatic testing tool in this situation should be "Manually Test."

Similarly, some tools issue a warning or failure for not having anything to test. This is bad behavior on the part of the testing tool. Some tools will test for headers and summaries on tables, but they return a warning if no tables are found on the page. Obviously, this is a problem in the testing tool rather than in your content. You should learn the behavior of your tools well enough to know when this is happening.

If you choose to target the draft version of WCAG 2.0 as a goal for your projects, these tools will not work for you. It is likely that some of them will begin to support WCAG 2.0 after finalization, but that is likely to be a while yet. Until then, you're on your own for conformance testing beyond WCAG 1.0 and Section 508.

Media-Testing Tools

All of the visual elements of a page need to be checked for color use, contrast, flickering, and appropriate alternative text. Automatic tools can check for the presence of alternative text and some, such as Cynthia Says, attempt to measure alternative text quality. For actual media properties, a few web-based tools are available, but their limitations make installable desktop tools far more attractive. We'll spend much of our time in Chapter 9, *A Picture Is Worth...*, on page 147, as well as Chapter 10, *Video Killed the Something-Something*, on page 175, learning how to create and test accessible media assets.

Screen Readers

To verify that screen readers can correctly read your pages, you might want to have a screen reader on hand. Many of the manufacturers of the screen readers mentioned in Chapter 3, *A Brief Introduction to Disabilities*, on page 17 provide limited demonstration versions. The learning curve for a screen reader is somewhat high, however, so it may not be a practical testing solution. An easier to-learn solution is Peter Krantz's Fangs tool for Firefox.[10] Fangs translates a web page into text representative of what would be spoken by a screen reader. This is useful for verifying the ordering of pages, existence of alternative text, and other screen reader difficulties.

Commercially Available Testing Tools

Depending on the size of your project, you may prefer to purchase an integrated accessibility testing solution. These systems package customizable automatic accessibility testing and reporting with a centralized tracking and project management solution. LIFT Machine,[11] InFocus,[12] Deque Systems,[13] and WebXM[14] are well-known options in this market. All of these tools add some convenience and smart features beyond other accessibility-testing options. They do not, on the other hand, take care of hand testing any more than any other tool will. If you are looking for a high degree of support for your accessibility testing efforts, these tools may be worth considering.

---

10. http://sourceforge.net/projects/fangs/
11. http://www.usablenet.com/
12. http://www.ssbtechnologies.com/
13. http://www.deque.com/
14. http://www.watchfire.com/

That said, in their full "enterprise-ready" versions, some of them can also become quite expensive. If your project has the budget, by all means take a look at them. If you are already using another testing management system or issue tracker, however, many of the freely available tools do a fine job.

Although there are no completely integrated accessibility testing tools, I don't look at that as a disadvantage. With a wide variety of options, we can choose the best tools for our own usage and needs without being tied into an end-to-end solution with strong and weak points. The real point of tools is to make our lives easier by saving time and effort. The most important accessibility tests will be hand tests, as we'll discuss in the next tip. Hand testing can be time-consuming, however, so automating where we can is essential.

Act on It!

1. Install and experiment with the tools I just introduced. Try them on a variety of sites, and get used to their output.

2. Consider the ways you might integrate these tools into your existing test suites.

8	Getting Your Hands Dirty

*Handle your tools without mittens; remember that the cat in
gloves catches no mice.*
> ▶ Benjamin Franklin, **The Way to Wealth**

Most of the tools I mentioned in *Building a Testing Toolbox*, on page 62,
can't be run automatically. The output of most tools needs to be reviewed to ensure that their warnings and errors really are something
to worry about. Some matters of accessibility are also impossible to
test in an automatic fashion. Because we're working with content that
expresses ideas, we simply cannot replace a human reviewer—the attempts would be like turning loose control of a word processor document to automatic grammar, thesaurus, and spell-check tools without
reviewing them:

*The majority of the gear I mentioned in Structure a Difficult Toolbox can't
be sprint mechanically. The production of the majority gear wants to be
reviewed to make sure that their cautions and mistakes actually are
amazing to be anxious concerning. A number of substances of convenience are also not possible to examination in a routine style. Since we're
operational with substance that states thoughts, we just cannot substitute a person critic—the efforts would be like rotating not tied up man-
ages of an utterance computer text to routine syntax, lexicon, and spell-
check gears without appraising them:*

See what I mean?

Testing by Hand

Each piece of content needs to have the same basic verification done.
These steps are specifically tuned to HTML content, but the idea remains the same for *any* type of content you produce. Only the exact
techniques will differ.

Check the appropriateness of alternative text: You need to verify that
all of your alternative text representations are truly conveying the message of your content. This includes alt= and label= attributes as well
as transcripts and captions. You're not just looking to make sure the
representation is there—you want to make sure that the representation
is *good*. For more on writing good text representations, take a look at
Chapter 9, *A Picture Is Worth...*, on page 147, and also refer to Chapter 10, *Video Killed the Something-Something*, on page 175.

In the Firefox Accessibility Extension (FAE), introduced in *Building a Testing Toolbox*, on page 62, you can automatically view the alternative text for images by choosing Text Equivalents → Show Text Equivalents.

Turn off images: Does your content make sense with images turned off? Beyond whether the alternative text is appropriate, you need to know whether eliminating the images breaks page flow in a way that obscures the meaning of your content. FAE lets you turn off images with Text Equivalents → Hide Images.

Turn off style sheets: If your markup isn't written in a natural reading order and instead styled with CSS to place it in order on the page, it is inaccessible to anyone without style sheet support. You'll need to view the page with CSS turned off to test content reading order and flow. In FAE, you would select Style → Disable CSS. If you use WAVE 3.5, you can find out what the content would look like in a text-only browser by selecting TEXT View.

Check another screen size: Many users with visual disabilities don't use conventional screen resolutions. You'll want to make sure that the page is still usable if viewed at low resolutions. This may mean letting go of a few design decisions. If you have put effort into minimizing scroll, it may simply be impossible at low resolution. Your primary goal is to make sure that the content can still be accessed and understood at low resolution. To reset screen sizes, you can change your monitor settings, embed the page inside a <frame> for testing purposes, or use the Firefox Web Developer Extension,[15] which will allow you to set and select custom browser sizes.

Play unplugged: If you remember the ten principles for web accessibility from Chapter 1, *Introduction*, on page 3, you know that the only thing we can assume about our users is that their assistive technologies will provide them with the ability to send and receive text as if from a terminal screen and keyboard. Hide your mouse and work your way through the site to find out whether the process flows naturally. If you are particularly ambitious and patient, you can also try turning off your monitor and using a screen reader to navigate.

All of these techniques will give you valuable information about how well your accessibility efforts are going. Don't be fooled into thinking that this is all that can be known, however. It is easy to "slip" doing

---

15. http://chrispederick.com/work/webdeveloper/

these kinds of tests because, at the end of the day, we're effectively (badly) pretending to have a disability for testing purposes. Sometimes we need to consult with *real* experts on using the Web with a disability.

Involving Users with Disabilities in the Testing Process

No matter how experienced you become in web accessibility and using tools and assistive technologies for testing, you'll never be able to fully replicate the experience of real users with disabilities. Ideally, we want users with disabilities to have a voice in the process of designing accessible content. We can take two approaches.

Hold focus groups: If your content is already live or close to release, you can issue a call for participation to the users with disabilities who are or will be using your site. You'll want to inform your users of features in your content and give them some questions to think about as they review the site. When you meet with the users, you'll want to get answers to these questions as well as comments on what was easy or difficult to use and why. Focus groups are useful for getting information about your how real users experience your content's accessibility.

Bring in testers with disabilities: If you aren't already well into the development process, you can get more formal step-by-step feedback by recruiting testers with disabilities. You need to find testers who are indicative of your intended user base. For example, if your site is intended to provide retirement services to elderly persons, you wouldn't want to focus your recruiting on people in their 20s.

When you do bring in testers with disabilities, you'll need to keep a few issues in mind:

- Make sure the testing environment is appropriate to the needs of your testers. Your testing environment needs to be physically accessible. This includes obvious things such as ramp and elevator access as well as other issues such as making sure paths are wide enough and clear of obstacles.
- Be prepared to assist with arranging transportation and assuring appropriate parking arrangements if these are factors.
- Ask your testers about specific needs. Odds are that you are not an expert on your tester's disability. Mention the arrangements you have made, and ask whether there is anything you didn't consider. You're not going to sound stupid (and even if you do, it's far

better to sound stupid ahead of time than to keep yourself unin-
formed and have something go wrong).

- If the user is not bringing their own assistive technologies, make
sure the appropriate systems are set up and ready. This is another
area where you'll need to be in communication with your testers
to know what they need ahead of time.

- Compensate your testers! I shouldn't have to mention this one, but
I have heard of more than one organization that seems to think
testers with disabilities should be ready to jump for the opportunity to test pages for accessibility for free. Your accessibility testers
should be compensated the same way any other test group would
be.

Once you have your testers on site, you should run them through the
same testing protocols that you would use for users without disabilities,
with three questions in mind:

- *Which tasks couldn't be completed, and why?* If a tester with a
disability can't complete a task, you need to ask what is wrong
with the site. Some possibilities are that the interaction requires a
pointer action, critical information is not provided in an alternative form, or an unnecessary timeout blocked the user.

- *Did a task take unreasonably long to complete?* This one is difficult to assess without experience. Different users with different
assistive technologies will have varying task lengths. If some tasks
seem to take much longer than expected, you will need to look for
the subtasks that took longest and attempt to find out whether
they can be streamlined.

- *Was the user comfortable with the interface for completing the
tasks?* It's interview time. This is your opportunity to find out
where the interface was clear to the user and where it felt cumbersome. If you are recording interactions, it may be helpful to ask
the tester to work in a speak-aloud fashion, commenting on their
actions as they take them (note that this *will* affect task completion times, however).

For an in-depth discussion of the issues surrounding planning and
recruiting for live testing involving users with disabilities, take a look
at Accessibility in User Centered Design: Planning Usability Testing at
UIAccess.[16]

---

16. http://www.uiaccess.com/accessucd/ut_plan.html

Act on It!

1. Deconstruct a few web sites step by step. Do they stay clear and easy to follow?

2. Try "playing unplugged." It can be both terribly frustrating and incredibly educational.

Part II

Building a Solid Structure

Man did not weave the web of life—he is merely a strand in it. Whatever he does to the web, he does to himself.

► Chief Seattle, **Treaty Oration of 1854**

Chapter 6

The Structured Life

All web content is built around a framework of basic HTML, and that is where our look at accessible development will begin. Because we have very few guarantees about the nature of the hardware and software our users will use to view our content, we need to create markup that expresses as much information as possible about its meaning. In *Say It with Meaning*, we'll look at reading order, semantic markup, and micro-formats as ways to provide this information. Above all else, we're here to *communicate*, so we want to ensure that the words we use are under-stood by our audience. To do this, we'll discover that *Keeping It Simple Is Smart*. Originally, the Web didn't make these distinctions, and visual presentation was done with markup elements. In *Minding Your <p>'s and <q>'s*, we'll look at some of this nonsemantic markup as well as replacement solutions using CSS.

Hyperlinks are what makes the Web the Web. In *Linking It All Together*, we'll examine ways of making our links clear to our users as well as specific ways to use links to enhance the accessibility of our content. Accessibility applies to visual layout too, and we want to make our visual presentation appealing and useful for our sighted audience. In *Styled to the Nines*, we'll look at the basics of building layouts that work for a variety of users and devices. Web technology hasn't stopped evolving either. There are new specifications in process that intend to add new technologies and move the Web in new directions. In *Welcome to the Future*, we'll look at a few of these new specifications and their effect on accessible web development.

9   Say It with Meaning

Words are only postage stamps delivering the object for you
to unwrap.
> ▶ George Bernard Shaw

The only thing we can assume about our users is that they can send and receive text-based content. Often, the user will be using assistive technology software that parses the HTML, so we need to make sure it is standards compliant and designed with semantics in mind. Semantic content is based around expressing meaning rather than presentation specifics. Rather than thinking "This is 18-point bold sans serif text," you should be thinking "This is a second-level heading for a section."

The first step to creating semantic content is making sure markup tagging is correctly used. Before CSS was widely supported, there were a wide variety of formatting tricks based on conventional features of tags, such as the ability to indent a block with the <blockquote> tag. To make matters worse, many web design tools reinforced these tricks by hiding the actual tagging from the developer. For more on editors, see the sidebar on the next page.

A well-designed HTML document should be, for the most part, understandable to a human reader knowledgeable in HTML. Certainly, some constructs such as data tables are more difficult to comprehend, but the nature of the content in them should be clear.

Reading Order

Our HTML also needs to stay readable with style sheets and scripts turned off. The easiest way to do this is to tag the content in natural reading order. The default behavior of text browsers and many assistive technologies is to read the content in the order in which it appears. If you want to use CSS positioning to move things around later, that's fine—just make sure at all times that when the style sheet is turned off, the content still means the same thing.

For clarity and navigation, content should also be correctly nested. Unfortunately, HTML doesn't provide a <section> tag to make this easy.[1]

---

1. XHTML 2 plans to provide this element. See *Welcome to the Future*, on page 99, for more on upcoming technologies.

The Problem with WYSIWYG

People frequently ask which editors I prefer to use for building accessible web pages. They often stop asking when I tell them I prefer to use text editors such as TextMate and emacs. Although visual editors have gotten a little better over time, they have had a bad reputation for producing invalid source or using deprecated tags. I'm not against the concept of visual editors, but like with all code-generating software, you need to have a good understanding of the code the editor generates and what you can expect from it. Up to this point, I have not found a visual editor that gives me a level of control or quality to my liking—your results may vary.

We can simulate sections with <div> and headings, but we need to watch out for the ordering of the heading tags. Top-level headings should always be marked up as <h1> (don't worry about what it looks like—that's what CSS is here for). The next heading should be either <h2> for a subsection or <h1> for the next section. What it should *never* be is <h3>—it isn't correct to skip levels of headings. Heading tags are available to six levels deep. If you find you are running out, it is likely that either you are adding too many levels of headings to a document where nested lists might be a better solution or you are tagging a large document that should be broken up into smaller pieces.

Using Storyboards to Avoid Mixing Content and Presentation

When the time comes to design the interface or look and feel of a web site, I like to start with storyboards. Storyboards help me think about the look of a site without thinking about the preconceptions of specific markup and styling. Good storyboards should be simple drawings of the site that avoid preconceptions of implementation decisions. Many semantically bad markup choices originate in "throwaway" layouts that stick around for too long. Web layout tools make it easy to slip into table-based layouts or misuse block quotations or lists. For this reason, I recommend against using WYSIWYG web development tools to do these storyboards. Using these tools is invariably slower than simply sketching the design, and during this process, you want to be getting ideas down quickly rather than spending time catching up with a layout tool.

This is also a good reason not to use presentation tools such as Power-Point or Keynote. These tools also create a problem by providing interactions that are not reflective of the way a web interface would be designed.

Additionally, a peculiar psychology surrounds this practice—people are too tempted to hold on to these "real" views of the final product—either they assume the final design will look the same, or, even worse, someone attempts to reuse the storyboard code as it is in the actual implementation. I find it best to avoid this temptation and just stick to sketches on paper or a whiteboard. This can have other benefits as well. Recently, I designed a whiteboard layout for a site targeted toward elementary-school students. The look of the whiteboard storyboard worked out so well that we modeled the final site design on a whiteboard motif. This isn't an idea that would be used widely, but we wouldn't have thought about the direction if I had worked directly in a WYSIWYG tool. I can't speak for your results, but if you have difficulty working through a design, you may find it useful to use unusual media in design process.

Adding More Information with Microformats

Microformats are small specifications that use the class= attribute to add semantic information to HTML elements. This allows software tools to extract the information in the format to be presented in a different form or stored for future reuse. Additionally, because the format uses class=, the tagging provides plenty of information to allow customized styling with CSS. Adding microformats for accessibility is a relatively new approach. Because microformats contain a lot of semantic information and can be output in many ways, we give our users more options for accessing the information in the way most useful for them. Let's look at an example of how a microformat can add extra contextual information to our page—let's say we want to keep track of contact information for John, who will be helping us later in the book:

```
<p>John Q. Public<br/>
   1313 Mockingbird Lane<br/>
   Nowhere, XX, 99999</p>
```

This works—we have a name and an address—but we can do better. We know which parts of the address are first, middle, and last names as well as the meanings of the different parts of the address.

If we pass this on to the user, their browser can use extensions such as Operator for Firefox, which allows customization of microformat output[2] to access the information on their own terms. One of the benefits is that by extracting semantics and allowing for alternative presentations, the navigational load of the site can be reduced, which is important for users with disabilities. We *could* build spans with classes to describe this information better, but we don't need to—it has already been done for us. Here is how John's contact information would be marked up with the hCard microformat:[3]

```
<div id="hcard-John-Q-Public" class="vcard">
  <span class="fn n">
    <span class="given-name">John</span>
    <span class="additional-name">Q</span>
    <span class="family-name">Public</span>
  </span>
  <div class="adr">
    <div class="street-address">1313 Mockingbird Lane</div>
    <span class="locality">Nowhere</span>,
    <span class="region">XX</span>,
    <span class="postal-code">99999</span>
  </div>
</div>
```

Now we have all of the information about the contact stored in a re-usable semantic format for our users. For those of you with database experience, it should also be clear that using a microformat reduces the workload of deciding how to design output templates. Microformats are a methodology rather than a specific technology, however. I have described one of the formats provided by http://microformats.org/, but there are other forms to choose from like W3C's RDFa specification.[4]

Custom Formats

Even if there isn't a predefined microformat for our needs, nothing is stopping us from building an internal format of our own. Tools such as Operator, mentioned earlier, allow you or your users to add new handlers for parsing new formats if desired. John is a big music fan and wants to share information about his collection.

---

2. http://addons.mozilla.org/en-US/firefox/addon/4106
3. http://microformats.org/wiki/hcard
4. http://www.w3.org/TR/xhtml-rdfa-primer/

For each album, he'd like to have the following:

- Artist
- Title
- Year
- Label

And for each track of the album, he'd like to have the following:

- Title
- Length

This is straightforward—by convention, we can use <div> for blocks of information such as album or track and <span> for individual elements such as artist or title. All that's necessary to create the format is adding classes to indicate the type of information:

```
<div id='album-Koala-Grip' class='album'>
  <span class='artist'>Koala Grip</span>
  <span class='title'>Koala Grip</span>
  <span class='year'>2006</span>
  <span class='label'>Unsigned</span>
  <div class='track'>
    <span class='title'>My Little Jewel</span>
    <span class='length'>2:56</span>
  </div>
  <div class='track'>
    <span class='title'>Multiple Frenzy</span>
    <span class='length'>2:59</span>
  </div>
</div>
```

This is clearly a simplified format. We could easily add more information such as track numbers, song ratings, cover art, or the song itself. For the last two, we would need to assign classes for appropriate <img> or <object> tags, but the method remains the same.

Not all assistive technologies use semantic data at this point, but there is growing interest in using this kind of markup to provide clear contexts to users. I expect that tools such as Operator will continue to grow in popularity and that microformats will gain support in screen readers that can benefit from added information.

Act on It!

1. Examine the microformats described at http://microformats.org/. Look specifically for formats that work well with the content on your sites and how using them might be beneficial.

2. Develop a custom recipe format. Go through the steps of deciding what information needs to be contained in the format and how it will be marked up (pay attention to natural reading order). If you get stuck, feel free to refer to the RecipeML format at http://www.formatdata.com/recipeml/.

3. Use storyboards to describe a look and feel for the hCard and music collection formats. Use CSS to style the tag formats for a web browser based on your storyboards.

10 │ Keeping It Simple Is Smart

A vocabulary of truth and simplicity will be of service throughout your life.
▶ Winston Churchill

Using straightforward language is an easy way to increase the accessibility of content. Some cognitive disabilities can slow down language processing, and complex text makes content really difficult for these users. Screen readers have also been known to choke on unusual words and usage.

At some point, most of us have spent a lot of time in school learning about language grammar and vocabulary. I understand that some might like to justify the classroom time by attempting to inspire onlookers with impeccable locution utilizing esoteric nomenclature. Please don't. It just makes your content more difficult to read. Besides, when you spend time trying to sound smart, it works—you come off as someone trying to sound smart. Keep it simple and informative, and leave the $2 words for Scrabble. This doesn't mean you should "talk down" to your readers by oversimplifying, just that you should use conventional language to express yourself.

Some experts recommend writing to a late primary school level, and if you are targeting a general audience, this might be useful for you. Forcing the "fourth grade reading level" standard on all content, however, is complete nonsense. If you are writing content for researchers in subaqueous plaited container construction, then you should write to the level and conventions of that audience rather than to grade-school children. Your content should always be written to the needs of your users rather than to arbitrary guidelines.

Reading Level

Reading level is a way of measuring the complexity of text by looking at average sentence length and the average number of syllables per word. In general, these measures give a good idea of how difficult a page may be to read. You'll usually see references to the following measures:

- *Flesch Reading Ease* is a score where higher numbers represent more easily read text. In the United States, Reading Ease is used as a standard test of readability for documents and forms. The

Reading Ease of the section that you're reading now is 52.78, making it similar in difficulty to *Time* magazine.

- *Flesch-Kincaid Grade Level* represents the number of years of education required for understanding. For levels 12 and less, Flesch-Kincaid is meant to translate to a grade level in school. This section's grade level is 9.56, so a high-school freshman should be able to comprehend it.

Because these measures are widely used, they are often available in word processor software. Juicy Studio also has a tool that you can use to check the readability of a web page.[5] These measures give a benchmark for readability, but you shouldn't weigh them *too* heavily. Because these are simple formulas, they can be tricked easily. For example, even though *alligator* isn't a very difficult word, it scores high because it has four syllables. Many popular books have higher reading levels than expected for this reason.

Specialized Terminology

When writing technical text or any other specialized content, we need to pay attention to special words and usages. For example, the words *parse*, *script*, *method*, and *object* are common in texts about software development. They also have special meanings and connotations that a general reader might not be familiar with. If the terms should be common knowledge for your readership, there is nothing to worry about. If you have any doubts, however, it is best to define the terms on first use.

If you find yourself introducing a *lot* of new terminology, your users will find it useful to have a glossary available. The glossary shouldn't be a replacement for first-use definitions, though—jumping back and forth between the text and a glossary has a negative impact on the user's ability to understand. For software- or mathematics-related text, you should also make sure the meaning of any names are understood. This can be done with description in the narrative as well as by using names consistent with common practice (such as using i, j, and k as indexing variables).

---

5. http://juicystudio.com/services/readability.php

It's All Greek to Me

Use of multiple languages can cause accessibility problems. At this point in time, for example, screen readers are usually designed to work with a single language. By specifying the natural language of a piece of text, we can give the screen reader the opportunity to handle unusual text. Screen readers currently do little or nothing with this information, but they could use it to switch language patterns to handle the word or point out to the user that the word is in another language and spell it out.

You should specify a text's native language with the lang= attribute. The content of the attribute should be an ISO 639-1 language code.[6] For the page's primary language, add the lang= attribute to the <html> tag. Nearly all HTML elements can have a lang= attribute, so when you're just using a short passage in another language, you would add lang= to the <p>, <q>, or <span> tag containing the passage.

You don't need to highlight *all* foreign terms, though. When the word is commonly understood, like pizza or sushi, you don't need to call it out with a lang= attribute.

The Idiomatic Minefield

Overuse of idiomatic expressions can be like slapping your users with a 2-by-4. I feel fairly confident that you understand that I'm not *really* comparing idioms to explosives and that I would never suggest that using them is nearly as bad as hitting your users with a large piece of lumber, but it makes for a nice illustration. Idioms are valuable for putting abstract ideas into concrete terms, but they can also be confusing to our readers. If our users have cognitive disabilities that make it difficult to comprehend idioms or simply if they are unfamiliar with the idiom used, then using expressions can reduce comprehension of the text as a whole.

You should always be careful of using slang or idiomatic expressions that might not be understood by your audience, particularly if it doesn't in some way enhance the text as a whole. The same problem can apply to using humor, wit, or satire. Don't avoid these tools; just use them carefully and *always* in context.

---

6. A list of valid codes can be found at http://en.wikipedia.org/wiki/List_of_ISO_639-1_codes.

Giving Meaning to Abbreviations

Abbreviations and acronyms are nice shorthands for frequently repeated concepts or phrases. Not all of our users (or their screen readers if they're using them) pick up on these, however.

Abbreviations

Abbreviations are marked up with <abbr>:

<abbr title='expansion'>abbrev.</abbr>

where expansion is the full text abbreviated. Here's an example:

```
<abbr title='tablespoon'>Tbsp.</abbr>
```

<abbr> can also be used for unconventional types of abbreviation. For example, emoticons abbreviate concepts such as smiling or frowning. We might mark them like this:

```
<abbr title='smile'>:-)</abbr>
```

Acronyms

Acronyms are marked up with the <acronym> in a similar way to <abbr>:

<acronym title='expansion'>Acronym</acronym>

where the title= attribute is again an expansion of the acronym. For example:

```
<acronym title='Synchronized
            Multimedia
            Interaction
            Language'>SMIL</acronym>

<acronym title='ACRONYM:
            Concise
            Remark
            Ordered as a
            Name
            Yielding
            Meaning'>ACRONYM</acronym>
```

Some browsers and screen readers ignore the extra information in the <abbr> and <acronym> tags, but for those that do, specifying the expansions significantly increases the understandability of your text. For the users who can't or don't know how to access the expansion, it's a good idea (and good language style) to expand the acronym or abbreviation on first use anyway.

Language gives us an immense amount of power for communicating ideas to our audience, but that power also allows us to overdo it and lose our audience along the way. By keeping our language usage clear and well explained, we ensure that our users are more able to get the meaning we're trying to convey.

Act on It!

1. Find the reading level of a few of your pages. Compare them to reading levels for sites that you think have a similar readership. Do the numbers match reasonably closely?

2. Search your content for abbreviations and specialized terminology. Consider whether it might be obscure for your audience, and add extra information as necessary.

11 Minding Your <p>'s and <q>'s

When a subject becomes totally obsolete, we make it a
required course.
   ▶ Peter Drucker

Sometimes it seems like *semantic* simply means "use a bunch of tags."
The reality is that the tags you use with semantic markup need to convey *meaning*. We have already seen tags such as <abbr> and <acronym>
that allow us to clarify the meaning of our content.

HTML provides many markup tags that allow us to express meaning.
For example, <q>, <blockquote>, and <cite> let us refer to other sources
of information and clearly show from where that information came. A
full discussion of every tag in HTML is well outside the scope of this
book, but a good HTML reference will give you an overview.[7] Not all
tags are useful for expressing meaning, however. Browsers support a
wide variety of markup that isn't semantic in nature and may obscure
the meaning of your content, harming overall accessibility.

Fonts and Formatting

Before CSS support allowed us to style text, HTML had tags to do
the job. Most of these formatting tags overlapped in appearance with
semantic tags, leading to confusion about the difference (in fact, the formatting tags became more popular because they're shorter to type). The
formatting variants have been deprecated for quite some time, however,
in favor of semantic equivalents or <span> tags with a class= attribute
and an associated style. For example, the <font> and <basefont> tags
were deprecated (in 1998!) in favor of more powerful CSS properties,
such as font-family, font-size, and color.

W3C's deprecations with respect to text styling are a bit strange. Although <s> and <u> for strikethrough and underlined text were deprecated, <b>, <i>, and <tt> for bold, italicized, and fixed-width text were
not. I recommend avoiding all of these in favor of more semantic choices
such as <em> and <strong> for emphasis and strongly stated messages.
Figure 6.1, on the next page, shows appropriate translations from deprecated HTML to CSS along with a few possibilities for semantic tagging
choices.

---

7. Jennifer Niederst-Robbins' *Web Design in a Nutshell* [Rob06] is a particularly good
option.

Visual Form	HTML	CSS	Semantic
Bold	<b>	font-weight	<strong>
Italics	<i>	font-style: italic	<em> <var>
Underline	<u>	text-decoration: underline	<em> <strong>[8]
Strikethrough	<s>	text-decoration: line-through	<del>
Overline	None	text-decoration: overline	<ins>
Fixed width	<tt>	font-family	<code><kbd> <samp> <var>

Figure 6.1: VISUAL FORMATTING EXPRESSED IN DEPRECATED HTML AND IN CSS. ALSO SHOWN ARE POSSIBLE SEMANTICS COMMONLY REPRESENTED BY THE FORMATTING.

Framed!

Frames occupy a strange space in the HTML standard. Instead of being part of the main specification, frames are kind of "bolted on" to the side of it. Rather than defining part of a page, frames are a higher-level form for wrapping HTML pages in HTML pages. This makes them kind of a pain to manage in general but also creates a few accessibility concerns.

Because frames *are* an external container around normal page flow, it is much more difficult for someone in a nonvisual interface to interact with them. Some screen readers allow the user to jump between them, but this is like interacting with two separate windows (and for practical purposes, they kind of are). Links targeted from one frame to another also will not work when frames are disabled.

The official solution to these problems is to let the users know what is contained within a frame by adding a title= attribute and providing an alternative version of the content in a <noframe> tag. At this point, you're usually left with the option of Writing Everything Twice (No!) or using frames only to create floating navigation. Since we can do this with CSS, I suggest doing it that way and leaving frames out of the picture entirely—it's hard to think outside the box when you keep drawing them around yourself.

---

8. Be *very* careful when using underlines for styling text. Because links are conventionally marked with underlines, underlined formatting may be confusing for your users. Unless you are duplicating something like a legal document that cannot be changed, I recommend avoiding underlining entirely.

Gate Crashers

During the "browser wars," some tags appeared that never made it into standard HTML. Some, such as <applet> and <embed>, were first attempts at new technologies that were later formalized—in this case, with <object>. Others were presentation effects intended to sway developers and users to prefer one browser over another. Many times these effects weren't very good to begin with and were never officially adopted. Backward compatibility made some of them stick, however. As well as being generally irritating to most users, these tags are accessibility problems. The three that concern us are as follows:

- <bgsound> is a way to embed background sounds into pages. The first problem is that continuous background sounds can interfere with the output voice of a screen reader. The larger problem is that <bgsound> doesn't provide a method to turn the sound off other than turning off system sound—a completely unacceptable option for screen reader users. As we'll see in *It's Their Web—We're Just Building in It,* on page 126, it is also generally unacceptable to take control of the user's system in this way.

- <marquee> provides scrolling "ticker tape" text. This poses two problems. The user can't control the speed of the scrolling, so they may not be able to read the text quickly enough to understand it. Also, the marquee movement is generally choppy, so there is a possible threat to users with photosensitive epilepsy (see *It's Not Polite to Flash the Audience,* on page 177, for more on this).

- <blink> is the infamous leader of "bad tags." Like <marquee>, <blink> poses a real threat to photosensitive users. Some browsers have even modernized the blinking text effect by introducing a nonstandard text-decoration: blink; to CSS. Just Say No!

Most of these tags are deprecated or otherwise out-of-date, and I hope you haven't used them in quite some time. Often, however, we have to go into legacy pages from the time period where these were in common use. One of the first steps in updating old content should be to purge these usages.

Act on It!

1. Do some spring cleaning. Search through the sites you maintain, and eliminate deprecated tags from your markup, replacing them with appropriate tags and styles.

2. If you use frames, consider what would be necessary to eliminate them in favor of positioned <div> elements.

12 Linking It All Together

*Thus he goes, building a trail of many items. Occasionally
he inserts a comment of his own, either linking it into the
main trail or joining it by a side trail to a particular item.*
▶ Vannevar Bush, ***As We May Think***

Hypertext links are the heart of what makes the Web an interesting
environment for developers and users. Because links are so critically
important, we need to make sure they are used in a clear way that
doesn't obscure their intent. For sighted users, our links need to be
clearly distinct visually so they don't require large amounts of attention
and mental processing to find and understand. Similarly, we need to
prevent links from "hiding" when placed next to each other. For screen
readers, we should also provide extra metadata describing the nature
of our links. It isn't particularly difficult to do this, but we'll need to
keep a few things in mind.

Making Links Stand Out

For visual accessibility, links should "pop" on the page and clearly be
links. This can be done by assigning the link a clearly contrasting color,
by changing the font to make it bold or underlined (the de facto method
for representing a link), or both. In addition, it is good practice to use
the CSS :hover selector to give visual feedback to the user.

Links should also be spaced in a manner that makes the separation
between links clear. Consider the following:

```
<a href='#foo'>These Links</a>
<a href='#bar'>Look Like The</a>
<a href='#baz'>Same Link</a>
```

These links would appear to be one link in many cases. The biggest cue
would be that the underline, if used, continues under some words but
not others. If the links are separate concepts, you could add a separating character like a comma between them to reinforce the difference.
If you have added links to words in a sentence in a way that makes
them look like a single link, it's time to revise the text to clarify the link
usage.

Saying Where the Link Goes

The text enclosed in the <a> tag should give the reader a reasonable
idea of where the link will go.

In other words, you should avoid anything that looks like this:

```
<a href='#here'>Click Here</a>
```

As a general rule, if you have the word *click* in your links, something is probably wrong with the way you're writing your content. The user already knows that links are for clicking; what they want to know is why they should click that link and what to expect on the other side. Some accessibility advocates say that every link should have different text identifying it. Although I see the value in clearly labeled links, I don't buy going to that extreme. First, if I have the same link at multiple points on a page, I expect that it *should* have the same text. Second, the primary reason to structure the page this way seems to be so people can scan the links of the page without reading the surrounding context. I'm sorry if this seems harsh, but when I've already explained the links in the context of my page content, I don't feel responsible for providing context a second time for people who don't want to read it the first time. The *real* concept to remember is that the links aren't all "Read More" or "Click Here," which doesn't give any context to the user about the link function. We also have the option of providing extended information about the link definition to go with the surrounded text.

The title= attribute can be set for a link to give extra information to the reader about the nature of the content behind a link. Screen readers can be configured to make this option available, and browsers make it available as a tooltip for the link. Not all links need titles, however. If you find yourself writing a link title that simply repeats the text surrounded by the <a> tag, it is better to leave it blank. Similarly, if you find yourself writing long titles, it is a good sign that you need to revise your narrative. Link titles should generally follow the same rules as alt= attributes for images, as described in *To Put It Another Way*, on page 158. Let's look at an example from my blog where I had one link that doesn't need a title and one that benefits from it:

```
<li><a href='/static_pages/show/1'>About Jeremy</a></li>
<li><a title='Information about the design of this site'
       href='/static_pages/show/2'>Colophon</a></li>
```

In the first link, I didn't add a title because I think "About Jeremy" gives enough information to the user about what can be found on the other end of the link. For the second link, I wanted to give title information that the user could refer to if they don't know that a colophon gives information about the design of a piece of content.

Skip Links

Skip links allow users who cannot use pointer devices because of visual or mobility impairments to jump past complex or frequently appearing content like navigational elements. Implementing skip links is about as trivial as accessibility gets—all you need to do is place a target link early in the page and a named anchor where you want the user to be able to skip to:

```
<a href='#content'>Skip to Main Content</a>
<ul>
  <li><a href='/static_pages/show/1'>About Jeremy</a></li>
  <li><a title='Information about the design of this site'
        href='/static_pages/show/2'>Colophon</a></li>
  <li><a href='/articles/'>Articles</a></li>
  <li><a href='/galleries'>Galleries</a></li>
</ul>
<a name='content'></a>
<h1>My Fine Article</h1>
<p>Some content.</p>
```

It's as easy as that. The common use case, as shown, is to skip navigation. Skip links are also useful if you have lists of links, long tables, or complex image maps that the user might want to skip past.

Links are what the Web is all about. By keeping their purpose clear, we make our sites more accessible and increase the usability for all of our audience. Now that we know how to make our content understandable for our users who work in text browsers and screen readers, it's time to look at making it visually useful for our sighted users as well.

Act on It!

1. Make your links clear: check that your links are clearly separated, and add a title= attribute to links that can benefit from an extended description.

2. Improve navigation for your keyboard users by adding skip links wherever you have repetitive or complex content.

13 | Styled to the Nines

Style is the dress of thoughts.
► Philip Dormer Stanhope, 4th Earl
of Chesterfield, **On Education**

Now I've done it. I've pushed you to design semantic content and remove all of the visual presentation from your markup. Accessibility has made your page completely bland, right? Absolutely not. Using Cascading Style Sheets (CSS) to create a visual layout is perfectly compatible with accessible web development.

Some web accessibility "experts" argue that the only good page is a style-free page, but this perspective is weak at best. When we separate content from presentation, we allow our users to deactivate the style sheet if it helps them better understand our content. Additionally, if the style sheet is well designed, it can give visual cues that make our content more understandable for some users.

In short, when people want to beat your site black and blue (on a white background) in the name of accessibility, don't worry about them—they're reacting to a previous age of the Web when we couldn't independently style our content. That said, there are a few things to keep in mind when you design accessible style sheets.

Staying Flexible

To be accessible, our style sheets need to be ready for a wide variety of users. First up, you need to make sure your color choices make sense for users with color deficiencies. Information on making good color choices can be found in *Stoplights and Poison Apples*, on page 148, and in *Thinking in Terms of Black and White*, on page 153. Some sites choose to provide alternative style sheets that have been specifically tested for color and contrast. If you do this, you need to ensure that the interface to change the style sheet is clearly visible to the user. As an example, I remember one web site where the contrast control was displayed with paired gray shades that would have made it impossible for someone who needed high contrast to see it. You should ask, if you have put forth the time and effort to create a good color and contrast controlled layout, why not just use it as the default? Even for users who don't have color deficiencies, the added contrast is beneficial.

Speaking of alternative style sheets, some people insist that high contrast and zoomed layout style sheets be made available. If you are already providing multiple style sheet options, you probably should develop these. You should know, however, that the people who need extremely high contrast or zoom levels are probably already using assistive technologies that do these things for them better than a style sheet can. What is more useful for these users is to use relative units of measure such as ems or percentages in your layouts rather than fixed units such as pixels or points. Relative units adjust to the font or element size and make it more comfortable for user adjustment.

Our sites also need to be functional when the style sheet is turned off completely. This means you shouldn't use CSS to express content. For example, if you use list-style-image to set custom list bullets, you can't use them to give added information to the list because they aren't available without the style sheet. At the other end of the spectrum, if what you want to mark is the title of a section, you should be using a heading tag rather than styling a <span> with large bold type.

There is a reasonably well-known trick for coercing transparency from PNG images in Internet Explorer by marking them up like this:

```
<div class='transparent'></div>
```

and styling them like this:

```
<style>
  div.transparent {
    background: url(transparent.png) no-repeat;
                height: 100px; width: 100px;
  }
</style>
<!-- Some Evil IE Voodoo -->
<!--[if gte IE 5]>
<style type='text/css'>
  div.transparent {
    background: none;
    filter:progid:DXImageTransform.Microsoft.AlphaImageLoader(
      src='transparent.png', sizingMethod='crop');
  }
</style>
<![endif]-->
```

This method has a *major* problem—when CSS is disabled, there's no image at all! When the image *does* appear, it still doesn't have an alt= attribute because the image exists only as a CSS background. This is certainly not an accessible solution.

Fortunately, with improved PNG support in Internet Explorer 7, this particular problem should fade away, but be careful not to use other "solutions" like it. Some script tricks also rely on using the hidden property. Keep in mind that when the style sheet is turned off, the elements aren't hidden anymore. If you test each change as you make it, as recommended in *Testing As a Design Decision*, on page 58, these kinds of problems won't sneak up on you.

The Media Types Myth

You may hear recommendations to use the @media rule from CSS 2 to add device-specific accessibility to a web site. The idea behind @media is to add specific CSS styles that are present for different types of output device. This is actually a pretty good idea, but in practice, it has never been well enough supported to make it worth spending time on. Major screen readers haven't supported the added aural style sheet properties necessary to make @media aural work for their users. In a similar fashion, specialized TTY technologies for web accessibility never became popular because of speed constraints.

But at least @media lets us do something for our braille users, right? Not so much. It's important to understand that braille text is composed with a series of contraction rules. For example, contracted text of the previous sentence might look like this: [CAP]S[TH][ING] IMPORTANT TO U[ST][AND] IS T BRL TEXT IS [COM]POS[ED] [WITH] A S[ER]IES [OF] [CON]TRAC[TION] RULES. Each of the contractions, marked with [] represents one or two braille characters. This translation is difficult to generate automatically, so I *don't* advise doing the translation yourself unless you are experienced in braille (I'm not, so I don't). The important thing to know in relation to CSS media types is that even if you build a braille style sheet, all you would be doing is removing styles that wouldn't make sense in braille—the text doesn't translate any better than simply ignoring the style sheet.

I don't mean to demonize @media, however. The "print" media type is widely supported for providing a consistent printable version interface, and you can support compact display of pages on some mobile devices by using the "handheld" type. The only hazard is thinking of @media as a way to support assistive technologies.

Clearly, the mechanisms for tailoring our CSS for accessibility devices aren't ready for prime time, but we have seen that striving for semantic markup doesn't mean we have to give up on providing an engaging visual layout. By assigning styles to markup, the design options provided by the Web can be made available in an accessible manner. Just make sure your design choices don't obscure your content, and allow them to be turned off if the user requires it. Ultimately, we would like to have even more control over our markup and presentation. Attempts to improve the Web are being made, and next we'll look at how these attempts impact accessible web design.

Act on It!

1. Turn off the style sheets on your web pages, and make sure that the content is still understandable. If it isn't, try to convey the information provided visually in a secondary way.

2. Check your color usage using the tools described in Chapter 9, *A Picture Is Worth...*, on page 147. If the color usage poses a problem, look for an alternative that works. Often improving the contrast will take care of problems for color-blind users as well.

14   Welcome to the Future

The best way to predict the future is to invent it.
▶ Alan Kay

I'm a big fan of those classic news reels that predict what life in "the future" is going to be like. These films are always overly optimistic, predicting revolutionary rather than evolutionary change. The technologies we're going to look at aren't *that* far in the future (all three are under active development), but only time will tell whether they will turn out to be transistors or flying cars.

Even if they change radically before completion, looking at edge technologies is still valuable. These are major contenders in defining the future of the Web, and we should be aware of how they could impact the way we design content. It also gives us a chance to practice approaching new technologies with an eye on accessibility and evaluating them accordingly.

CSS 3 Speech

CSS 3's Speech Module[9] allows us to give guidance to screen readers as to how content can be best presented in audio to the user. For example, if we wanted to "highlight" links by marking them with a sound and speaking them in a female voice, we could do that:

```
a {
  voice-family: female;
  cue: url(linksound.aiff);
}
```

The only concern I have about this is that there is currently no convention for how links should be signaled with audio. I expect that these conventions will emerge fairly quickly, though. The Speech Module also lets us specify *how* something should be read. In *Keeping It Simple Is Smart*, on page 84, we looked at the <abbr> and <acronym> tags. A common problem with these tags is that they still don't necessarily read correctly.

---

9.   http://www.w3.org/TR/css3-speech/

With the CSS 3 Speech Module, we can specify that the screen reader should read the expansion of abbreviations and spell out acronyms like this:

```
abbr {
  content: attr(title);
}

acronym {
  speak: spell-out;
}
```

Speech styles can also be used to change the voice to reflect content. In Chapter 10, *Video Killed the Something-Something*, on page 175, we'll look at a dialogue. In the HTML transcript of that dialogue, we can define differences in the speakers to make it easier to follow:

```
.john {
  voice-family:  male;
  voice-channel: left;
}

.mary {
  voice-family:  female;
  voice-channel: right;
}

.roy{
  voice-family:  neutral;
  voice-volume:  soft;
  voice-stress:  moderate;
  voice-pitch:   high;
  voice-rate:    slow;
}
```

In this case, I give gender, position, and pitch information to differentiate the speakers. This is certainly an improvement over a single voice, where we have to pay attention to announced transitions in speaker. As speech engines improve, I can even see this being valuable for general audiences.

The CSS 3 Speech Module seems to be a clear win for developers and end users. The specification is still a working draft, however, so it could still change a little. Early support for the CSS 3 Speech Module is currently available in the Fire Vox voice extension for Firefox[10] and in the Opera web browser.[11]

---

10. http://www.firevox.clcworld.net/
11. http://www.opera.com/—voice support is currently Windows only.

XHTML 2.0

XHTML 2.0[12] is W3C's solution for future web development. It is still a very active working draft, so many changes can still be expected before the specification settles. The structure of XHTML 2.0 makes a few accessibility methods easier to implement.

The most obvious change is the addition of the href= and target= attributes to the core properties. This means anything can be a link as well as be linked to. This makes it easier to add things such as skip navigation without polluting our markup with a horde of named anchors— rather than linking to something next to where you want to go, you can link to it directly.

Specifying page structure has also been simplified in XHTML 2.0. With the addition of a <section> tag, keeping track of which heading level you're at becomes less important:

```
<body>
  <h>Top Level Heading</h>
  <p>Some introductory Text</p>
  <section>
    <h>Second Level Heading</h>
    <p>More Text</p>
  </section>
</body>
```

This is particularly useful in templating environments where each developer needs to know what their local top level is to maintain correct nesting. With sections and headings, that concern no longer exists.

Part of XHTML 2.0 that promises to be particularly useful for accessibility is the expansion of how the <object> tag is used. Let's present a video with two levels of graceful degradation:

```
<object src="video.mpg" srctype='video/mpeg'>
  <!-- If the video can't be played, try an image and transcript -->
  <object src="photo1.png" srctype='image/png'>
    Mary sits facing away at a desk, speaking on the phone.
  </object>
  <p class='mary'>You worry too much.  Everything's Fine!</p>
  <!-- More still frames and transcript text follow... -->
</object>
```

This feels much clearer than existing alternatives. First we present video—if that doesn't work, we provide a transcript with still shots.

---

12. http://www.w3.org/TR/xhtml2/

Then we give alt text for the still shots if they cannot be displayed. The only thing missing is a clear description of how the user could immediately default out the video without turning it off in the browser itself. The quality of alternative that be provided is also exceptional. Rather than being confined to plain text as with alt= attributes, this functionality allows us to specify richer, more semantic alternatives to our content.

XHTML 2.0 doesn't change accessible development in any earth-shattering ways, but it does provide some tools that try to make the job easier. It will be interesting to see where continuing progress of the development team takes the specification.

HTML 5.0

HTML 5.0, originally called Web Applications 1.0, is the result of discussions to update HTML by the Web Hypertext Application Technology Working Group (WHATWG).[13] The WHATWG work has been accepted as a starting point for an official W3C working group. Thus far, HTML 5.0 doesn't appear to add much in the way of accessibility support. Many of the new proposals pose problems for accessibility, however.

Because HTML 5.0 focuses on reverse compatibility with existing browsers rather than on a new specification, there is little focus on a DTD validation or well-formedness of code. Instead, correctness appears to be determined by browser behaviors. Allowing unstructured "tag soup" development without cross-browser standardization will make it significantly more difficult for accessibility technologies to successfully interpret content.

New tags introduced in HTML 5.0 are a bigger problem. At this point, the new <audio>, <video>, and <canvas> media elements provide fallback information primarily for older browsers to indicate where to go for the content, rather than for users who need alternative presentations.

The HTML 5.0 specification is in the early phases, with a tentative target of 2010 for an initial recommendation and estimates of five to ten years after that from WHATWG. This is clearly an incredibly long time frame in terms of web development, so I suspect other de facto solutions will appear in the meantime, and I hope accessibility will become more of a priority.

---

13. http://www.whatwg.org/

As much as we might like to look at the future as a place of revolutionary change, the reality is that we move one step at a time. The technologies we've looked at provide a good sample of where things are going, though. Ultimately how these technologies fare and whether they are adopted widely depends on *us*. As developers, the technology choices we make have a large impact. By knowing what functionalities we want, we become better adopters and implementers.

Act on It!

1. Download a copy of Fire Vox or Opera with voice extensions, and listen to the default voice processing of your pages. Experiment with using the CSS 3 Speech Module to alter the voice characteristics of your content. Can you make it read more clearly?

2. Form your own opinion on these technologies. If you find them useful, let the standards committee know that. If you think they can be improved, tell them how. As the developers who use these technologies on a daily basis, it is important for us to make our voices heard.

At a round table, every seat is the head place.
► German Proverb

Chapter 7

Round Tables

The topic of tables is a certain way to get a heated response from accessibility experts. Tables are particularly complicated for screen readers to work with, so it is easy for them to be the center of an accessibility problem. Further, tables are an infamous example of marking up content for visual intent rather than semantics since tables are commonly used as layout tools when they're intended to represent data.

Even data tables can be difficult to navigate for users with visually disabilities because they are intended to make complex information simpler through visual positioning, which is obviously a real problem for our visually impaired users. In *Setting the Table*, we'll look at adding header information to tables to make them easier to understand. When the table is complicated, we'll also need to add information to describe the layout of the data. This involves some unusual markup, which we'll cover in *Ah, <table>, I Hardly Knew Ye!*

As I said, the most common accessibility problem for tables is their use as a layout tool. This isn't the intent for the <table> tag, and CSS gives more freedom for layout anyway. It can be difficult to spot improper uses of tables at first, however. Once you get used to using tables for layout, it takes some mental retraining to break out of that habit. In *Layout and Other Bad Table Manners*, we'll look at eliminating layout tables and what can be done to patch layout tables in the meantime while you work on repairing them properly.

15 | Setting the Table

> *I do not literally paint that table, but the emotion it*
> *produces upon me.*
> ▶ Henri Matisse

Accessible web sites shouldn't use tables for layout, but what about tables for data? Tables are particularly problematic for screen readers because they express a lot of information briefly by putting it into a visual form. Tables can also be difficult for the rest of our users simply by being information dense. What we need to do is add extra information to our table to better describe it for our users. Fortunately, HTML gives us markup to do this. We'll be looking at a lot of markup that may be new to you in the next couple of sections, so we'll start with basics and add new information one step at a time.

Basic Tables

I'm confident that we're all familiar with basic HTML table structure, using the <table>, <tr>, and <td> tags. John wants to use a table to share information about his music collection. To start, he'd like to have the artist, the album name, and whether he has CD or MP3 versions of the album. The simplest way to do this is like so:

```
<h1>My Music</h1>
<table>
  <tr>
    <td>Artist</td>
    <td>Album</td>
    <td>Compact Disc</td>
    <td>MP3</td>
  </tr>
  <tr>
    <td>Magnetic Fields</td>
    <td>69 Love Songs</td>
    <td>Yes</td>
    <td>No</td>
  </tr>
  <tr>
    <td>U2</td>
    <td>Zooropa</td>
    <td>Yes</td>
    <td>Yes</td>
  </tr>
</table>
```

We could give a *lot* more information to our users as to what this table is all about, though. All we have right now is a grid layout for the data. It can be read in order, but we can give our users a lot more information. To start, that first row is different from the rest. It's heading information, and we should mark it up accordingly.

Getting Your <thead> On Straight

You may have seen the <th> tag that marks a table cell as a heading. We also have access to three other related pieces of markup to describe the structure of a table. The <thead> and <tfoot> tags are available to set header and footer sections for tables. When these are used, the main content of the table needs to be placed in <tbody> tags. Let's change our example to add these pieces:

```
<table>
  <thead>
    <tr>
      <th>Artist</th>
      <th>Album</th>
      <th>Compact Disc</th>
      <th>MP3</th>
    </tr>
  </thead>
  <tfoot>
    <tr>
      <th>Artist</th>
      <th>Album</th>
      <th>Compact Disc</th>
      <th>MP3</th>
    </tr>
  </tfoot>
  <tbody>
    <tr>
      <td>Magnetic Fields</td>
      <td>69 Love Songs</td>
      <td>Yes</td>
      <td>No</td>
    </tr>
    <tr>
      <td>U2</td>
      <td>Zooropa</td>
      <td>Yes</td>
      <td>Yes</td>
    </tr>
  </tbody>
</table>
```

<u>**Make Sure Your Tables are <table>s**</u>

One of the worst things we can do to a screen reader is send it a bunch of formatting text needlessly. This means we need to avoid doing something like this:

```
+-------------------------------------------------------+
|                        My Music                       |
+------------------+----------------+-------------+------+
| Artist           | Album          | Compact Disc | MP3 |
+------------------+----------------+-------------+------+
| Magnetic Fields  | 69 Love Songs  | Yes         | No   |
| Lifter           | Melinda        | No          | Yes  |
| U2               | Zooropa        | Yes         | Yes  |
+------------------+----------------+-------------+------+
```

This is really difficult to navigate and comprehend if you can't see it. Because it is plain text, there is no markup to navigate across and no context available to understand the values. Any "text tables" like these need to be converted into well-described HTML tables for accessibility.

Pay attention to the order of the sections. You can have only one each of <thead> and <tfoot> (and <tfoot> is optional). Both of these should come, in order, before <tbody>. You can specify as many <tbody> sections as you like, as long as the table follows the structure <thead> → [Optional <tfoot>] → <tbody> → [More <tbody> sections]. Yes, <tfoot> comes before <tbody>. Why? Well, once upon a time, the W3C said it would be that way—I never promised that HTML would always make sense.[1]

With header information specified, we've made it clear what is in the table and what we should expect to find in the rows that follow. It wasn't mandatory to put in a footer, but it's helpful for our sighted users who may be scanning from the bottom of the table. To be honest, I haven't had occasion to use multiple <tbody> sections, but you may find them helpful for organizing the table, particularly for scripted interactions. Headers and footers aren't all we can do, however. There is still a certain amount of effort in reading a table, especially for our users with screen readers, so we need to let them know what the table's purpose is.

---

1. The actual answer has to do with the lineage of HTML in the SGML tradition and various technical issues with printing tables. In other words, don't worry about it.

Labeling the Table

In the first version of the table, I used <h1> to give the table a title. This isn't really the best way to do this. In HTML, the heading tags imply the start of a section, which isn't usually the case for a table. A section usually has some introductory text, rather than going straight into a table. A better way to specify a title for the table is with the <caption> tag, which appears as the first markup after <table> (right before <thead>). For screen reader users, we can also add a longer description of the table with the summary= attribute. This is there to let them know whether they are interested in spending time navigating through the table. The summary should be brief and to the point, much like alternative text for images (which we'll look at closely in *To Put It Another Way*, on page 158). With summary and caption information, the beginning of our table now looks like this:

```
<table summary="Albums in John's Music Collection">
  <caption>My Music</caption>
```

Adding descriptive information to the top level of the table makes it much more understandable, but we still haven't looked at the actual data in the table. This is where it is most important to add structure for screen readers, and we'll be working on that next.

Act on It!

1. Build a data table with descriptive information. Some options might be a financial report or a metro schedule. We'll return to this table at the end of *Ah, <table>, I Hardly Knew Ye!*, on the following page.

2. Update your pages: add summary, caption, and heading information to your data tables.

16   Ah, <table>, I Hardly Knew Ye!

I drink to the general joy of the whole table.
  ▶ William Shakespeare,
      Macbeth, Act III, Scene IV

When we look at a table visually, the positioning of information into rows and columns lets us quickly understand relationships. Without positioning, tables can become daunting for visually impaired users who can navigate only one cell at a time with their screen readers. To make tables usable with a screen reader interface, we need to add information to connect the cells in a table to their context. The way we do this is by connecting table cells to their appropriate headers. We'll continue with the example of John's music collection, introduced in *Setting the Table*, on page 106.

Connecting Headings to the Rest of the Table

We can make it easier for users with screen readers by letting them know where they are in the table. For example, when the screen reader speaks "yes," is it referring to CD or MP3 format? We can clarify by setting the scope= attribute for the table headings. The scope can be set to row or col depending on whether your heading is a row or column heading.[2] For our table, the headings are by column, so that's how we'll specify scope:

```
<table summary="Albums in John's Music Collection">
  <caption>My Music</caption>
  <thead>
    <tr>
      <th scope='col'>Artist</th>
      <th scope='col'>Album</th>
      <th scope='col'>Compact Disc</th>
      <th scope='col'>MP3</th>
    </tr>
  </thead>
  <tfoot>
    <tr>
      <th>Artist</th>
      <th>Album</th>
      <th>Compact Disc</th>
      <th>MP3</th>
    </tr>
  </tfoot>
```

---

2. The HTML specification also lists rowgroup and colgroup as possible options. Browsers don't support these constructs, however, so it doesn't make much sense to use them.

```
<tbody>
  <tr>
    <td>Magnetic Fields</td>
    <td>69 Love Songs</td>
    <td>Yes</td>
    <td>No</td>
  </tr>
  <tr>
    <td>U2</td>
    <td>Zooropa</td>
    <td>Yes</td>
    <td>Yes</td>
  </tr>
</tbody>
</table>
```

With scope set, the screen reader now has the option of reading "Artist: Magnetic Fields, Album: Sixty Nine Love Songs, Compact Disc: Yes, MP3: No," which will be much clearer for the user than hearing "Magnetic Fields, Sixty Nine Love Songs, Yes, No" and having to remember that "Compact Disc" comes before "MP3." Speaking of those two columns, it would be better if we did a heading/subheading pair like this:

Media Format
Compact Disc MP3

This isn't an uncommon way to design a table but, if we do this, we'll need something more powerful to connect headers to cells.

Double Headers

We can define multiple headers for an entry in a table by setting the headers= attribute on a table cell. To make this work, we need to give each table heading an identifier with the id= attribute. The value of headers= is a space-separated list of these identifier values. This is a lot to keep track of—let's see how it looks in action:

```
<table summary="Albums in John's Music Collection">
  <caption>My Music</caption>
  <thead>
    <tr>
      <th rowspan='2' id='c1'>Artist</th>
      <th rowspan='2' id='c2'>Album</th>
      <th colspan='2' id='c3' abbr='Format'>Media Format</th>
    </tr>
    <tr>
      <th id='c31' abbr='CD'>Compact Disc</th>
      <th id='c32'>MP3</th>
    </tr>
```

```
    </thead>
    <tbody>
      <tr>
        <td headers='c1'>Magnetic Fields</td>
        <td headers='c2'>69 Love Songs</td>
        <td headers='c31 c3'>Yes</td>
        <td headers='c32 c3'>No</td>
      </tr>
      <tr>
        <td headers='c1'>U2</td>
        <td headers='c2'>Zooropa</td>
        <td headers='c31 c3'>Yes</td>
        <td headers='c32 c3'>Yes</td>
      </tr>
    </tbody>
</table>
```

I'll also take this opportunity to introduce the abbr= attribute. It gets cumbersome to keep hearing the phrases "Compact Disc" and "Media Format" when "CD" and "Format" work just as well. Now the row can read "Artist: Magnetic Fields, Album: Sixty Nine Love Songs, CD Format: Yes, MP3 Format: No."

You should have noticed that I played a bit of a trick with the headings. Headings should be read in the order they appear in headers=. If I had set headers='c3 c31', the appropriate response would have been "Format CD."

This brings up a matter of naming. There is no set rule for how you fill the id= attribute. I like *c* followed by the column and subcolumn numbers like in the previous example because it is particularly easy to generate with a script. It is certainly just as acceptable (and probably preferable for hand-constructed tables) to give descriptive identifiers. John is about to throw another twist at us, though—he wants to add track titles and ratings to the table. We can use the headers= attribute to describe the table cells, but this has become a pretty complex table now, and HTML gives us one more tool for this kind of complexity.

Axis: An Ally?

Adding track information makes things difficult because it means we have three dimensions to our data now:

- The collection of albums

- Each album, including which tracks it contains

- Information about the individual tracks

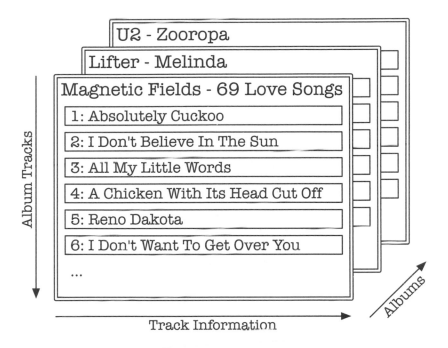

Figure 7.1: JOHN'S MUSIC COLLECTION IN THREE DIRECTIONS. THE AXIS= ATTRIBUTE PROVIDES ONE WAY TO NORMALIZE THIS INTO A TABLE.

Figure 7.1 shows one way of looking at this. We have two options at this point. First, we could create a table of albums information that links to tables that contain the track information. This would be the simplest (and in my opinion, the best) way to handle this situation. Let's say we're not going to do that—for whatever reason, John insists that it has to be one table.

This is where the axis= attribute comes into play. An axis is a cross section through the data in a table. Referring to Figure 7.1, we need to add two axes: one for the albums and one for the tracks in an album. Because the track information is a single row of data, there's no need for an axis. We're actually going to create one axis per album for track information to separate tracks from different albums.

Let's add *axis='albums'* to each album's title field and *axis='album#'* for each song and see where that takes us:

```html
<table summary="Albums in John's Music Collection">
  <caption>My Music</caption>
  <thead>
    <tr>
      <th id='artist' rowspan='2'>Artist</th>
      <th id='album'  abbr='Title'  rowspan='2'>Album Title</th>
      <th id='format' abbr='Format' colspan='2'>Media Format</th>
    </tr>
    <tr>
      <th id='formatcd' abbr='CD'>Compact Disc</th>
      <th id='formatmp3'>MP3</th>
    </tr>
  </thead>
  <tbody>
    <!-- The first album on the albums axis. This songs on this -->
    <!-- album will be put on the 'album1' axis.               -->
    <tr>
      <td id='a1artist' headers='artist'>Magnetic Fields</td>
      <td id='a1title'  headers='album' axis='albums' >69 Love Songs</td>
      <td headers='formatcd format'>Yes</td>
      <td headers='formatmp3 format'>No</td>
    </tr>
    <tr>
      <th id='tracktitle' abbr='Title' colspan='3'>Song Title</th>
      <th id='trackrating'>Rating</th>
    </tr>
    <!-- The First Song on the album1 axis -->
    <tr>
      <td id='a1t1title' axis='album1'
          headers='a1artist a1title tracktitle'
          colspan='3'>
        Absolutely Cuckoo
      </td>
      <td headers='a1t1title trackrating'>
        <abbr title='Four Stars'>****</abbr>
      </td>
    </tr>
    <!-- The Second Song on the album1 axis -->
    <tr>
      <td id='a1t2title' axis='album1'
          headers='a1artist a1title tracktitle'
          colspan='3'>
        I Don't Believe In The Sun
      </td>
      <td headers='a1t2title trackrating'>
        <abbr title='Four Stars'>****</abbr>
      </td>
    </tr>
```

```
<!--                                                      -->
<!-- 67 more songs in the first album on the album1 axis.  -->
<!--                                                      -->

<!-- The second album on the albums axis. This songs on this -->
<!-- album will be put on the 'album2' axis.                 -->
<tr>
  <td id='a2artist' headers='artist'>U2</td>
  <td id='a2title'  headers='album' axis='albums'>Zooropa</td>
  <td headers='formatcd format'>Yes</td>
  <td headers='formatmp3 format'>Yes</td>
</tr>
<tr>
  <th abbr='title' colspan='3'>Song Title</th>
  <th>Rating</th>
</tr>
<!-- The first song on the album2 axis -->
<tr>
  <td id='a2t1title' axis='album2'
      headers='a2artist a2title tracktitle'
      colspan='3'>
    Zooropa
  </td>
  <td headers='a2t1title trackrating'>
    <abbr title='Five Stars'>*****</abbr>
  </td>
</tr>
<!-- The second song on the album2 axis -->
<tr>
  <td id='a2t2title' axis='album2'
      headers='a2artist a2title tracktitle'
      colspan='3'>
    Babyface
  </td>
  <td headers='a2t1title trackrating'>
    <abbr title='Two Stars'>**</abbr>
  </td>
</tr>
  </tbody>
</table>
```

As I said, I prefer to break up the tables instead. This is a complex table to describe, and this should be your cue that it would be simpler for you and for your screen reader users to have the table split along one of the dimensions. Sometimes this just isn't possible, however, and on rare occasion you'll need axis=.

We've taken a data table from a simple undescribed grid to a complex multidimensional form with multiple navigation paths for our users. Data tables aren't the end of the story, however.

Layout tables are far more common and a far greater accessibility problem. Next, we'll be looking at these and how to avoid them.

Act on It!

1. Return to your data table design from *Setting the Table*, on page 106. Add scopes or headers to make the data more descriptive.

2. Redesign the axis implementation shown earlier to use separated tables. Consider which solution you find better in this case and why.

3. Build a small music database. Using a templating framework, automatically output versions of the database using scopes, headers, and axes.

17 Layout and Other Bad Table Manners

The greater the power, the more dangerous the abuse.
▶ Edmund Burke

When HTML first showed up, the emphasis was on communication of research between scientists. In that environment, the demand for visual formatting was low, so the few formatting needs that did exist were served with specialized markup tags rather than with a separate layout standard. When the Web became a major communications medium, these needs changed rapidly, and before a layout standard could emerge, designers were left to use whatever tricks they could find to generate their layouts. Often this involved (ab)using the <table> tag. The end result is that, in most cases, <table> usage has little to do with representing tabular information, leading to three problems:

- *Hard-to-manage layouts*: When you build pages that have layers upon layers of nested tables, the pages become progressively more difficult to maintain. Every change you make means altering one or more tables, hoping you haven't broken the layout somewhere and tweaking until it comes out right. Even if you use plenty of comments in your HTML,[3] this gets old quick.

- *Slower web pages*: Those tables don't come for free. Tables have a lot of markup, and that increases your page sizes. If you use spacer images to force a table layout, that also adds to the bandwidth use. Even after the page makes it to the browser, tables take time to process and display.

- *Less-accessible pages*: Screen readers and text browsers often have different modes for tables than for the rest of your content. This places an unreasonable burden on your users. We'll also see a little later that screen readers *linearize* tables, which may obscure the meaning of your content.

Fortunately for us, CSS came along and gave us freedom to format elements to our content while avoiding the worst of these problems. Now we can throw out most of our <table> markup and tag for meaning. (Just don't get *too* carried away—see the sidebar on the next page.)

---

3. If you have to sort through a lot of comments, you might want to take a closer look at what is happening. Comments are a good thing, but if you really *need* them to have an idea of what is going on, it probably means something has gone very wrong.

Sometimes a Cigar Is Just a Cigar...

...and sometimes a table really *is* a table. When we overfocus on staying semantic and avoiding visually oriented markup, sometimes we lose track of the real goal. I remember updating some older content, consisting of updating old layout to CSS and introducing semantics, when I came across a form asking for a rating from the user based on evaluation criteria:

```
<table>
  <th>
    <td colspan='5'>Please rate what you have just seen:</td>
  </th>
  <tr>
    <td>
      <input id='rating_1' name='rating' type='radio' value='1'/>
      <label for='rating_1'>This was missing X, Y, and Z.</label>
    </td>
    ...
    <td>
      <input id='rating_5' name='rating' type='radio' value='5'/>
      <label for='rating_5'>X, Y, and Z were all present
                            and of high quality.</label>
    </td>
  </tr>
</table>
```

Because tables have such a bad reputation for misuse, I looked at this markup and immediately jumped to finding an alternative solution. Then I stopped to think—this rating is part of a rubric giving evaluation criteria. A rubric is a table, and this question is simply looking at one row from it. The real problem was *I hadn't noticed that this content reflected tabular data*. Certainly the tagging needed to be styled and have deprecations removed, but the important thing is that this was essentially correct markup in need of cleanup, rather than misuse of the table construct. Make sure to keep an eye open—sometimes that old code is right after all.

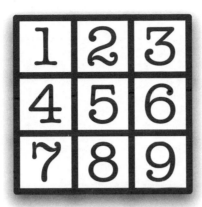

Figure 7.2: LINEARIZED READING ORDER FOR A 3×3 TABLE

If You Must Use Table-Based Layout

I've heard a *lot* of versions of "But I can't get rid of my table layout because of X, so how do I just make the table layout accessible?" I have yet to see a table layout that *can't* be replaced, but I've seen many developers who just don't want to mess with it. The truth is that table layout just isn't an accessible thing to do. I know it takes some work to get rid of it, but I don't find that to be a compelling reason to keep the table layouts. For large sites, however, making all of the updates might take some time, and we may need to do some temporary accessibility triage in the meantime.

When a screen reader or text browser processes a table, it often handles it in linearized form. The linearized form is the order that the <td> cells appear in HTML. For example, the table in Figure 7.2 reads as "1 2 3 4 5 6 7 8 9." To ensure minimal accessibility, any table layouts used would need to read correctly in linearized order.

Figure 7.3: BECAUSE OF TABLE LAYOUT, THIS PAGE COULD MISLEAD THE USER.

Linearization adds more limits to what table-based layout can do for us, though. Consider the layout in Figure 7.3. This layout is a real problem for users with text browsers and screen readers. Because our visually impaired users don't see the layout, they need to trace through in order. Let's follow along:

1. Listen to the heading information.

2. Verify that the order is correct.

3. Get bothered by a credit card advertisement.

4. Check the shipping type.

5. Activate Continue to go to the next part of the order.

6. End up on the credit card application page.

7. Get irritated and either:

   a) Back up a page and scan forward for the correct option (lucky us!).

b) Decide the checkout page is broken and go elsewhere.

c) Assume they're being harassed into a credit card and go else-where.

Not a pleasant outcome—all because of table layout. Get your table-based layouts linearized immediately, and update the markup with natural reading order and CSS as soon as you can. It won't be long before you can't imagine doing things any other way.

When a Table Isn't Really a Table

Table layout hasn't been used just for page layouts. Smaller elements on the page have been tossed into tables to give them a particular look as well. Most of the time, there are already other ways to mark these ideas up that make more sense. One of the most common cases of this seems to be using tables when the information is really a list.

Our Friend, the Definition List

Repeat after me, "A list is *not* a table!" So, why have we used tables as lists so often? I would guess that it comes from the ease with which tables could lay things out pre-CSS. Let's think about the roles in Figure 7.4, on the following page. I can already see the table:

```
<table>
    <tr><td>Interaction</td>
        <td>Nielsen</td><td>Norman</td><td>Raskin</td>
    </tr>
    <tr><td>Pedagogy</td>
        <td>Papert</td>
    </tr>
    <tr><td>Technology</td>
        <td>Kay</td><td>Minsky</td>
    </tr>
</table>
```

I don't like this at all. First, if you notice, this isn't even a well-formed table—our columns aren't consistent. Beyond the fact that this doesn't represent a table properly, it's also going to be ugly as sin. We could set colspan= if we wanted to be stuck maintaining the list by hand (I certainly don't) or push all the names into a single column to make it fit better. That strikes me as a warning sign. Why would we want to adjust our content to make the markup work?

That seems a little backward to me. Instead, let's think about this as a list. We have a list of roles and the people who fit their description. How about a definition list?

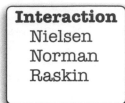

Figure 7.4: PEOPLE AND THEIR ROLES

```
<dl class='roles'>
  <dt>Interaction</dt>
    <dd>Nielsen</dd>
    <dd>Norman</dd>
    <dd>Raskin</dd>
  <dt>Pedagogy</dt>
    <dd>Papert</dd>
  <dt>Technology</dt>
    <dd>Kay</dd>
    <dd>Minsky</dd>
</dl>
```

This ends up being clear, meaningful (roles are defined by the people who fill them), properly marked up, and easy to understand in screen readers and text browsers.

Tables and Forms

Tables also show up when people try to give layout to forms. For a simple example, let's take a look at a storyboard for a login form in Figure 7.5, on the next page. Our first instinct might be to do something like this:

```
<table>
  <th><td colspan='2'>Please Login</td></th>
  <tr>
    <td align='right'>User ID:</td>
    <td><input id='userid' type='text' /></td>
  </tr>
  <tr>
    <td align='right'>Password:</td>
    <td><input id='pass' type='password' /></td>
  </tr>
</table>
```

Figure 7.5: A BASIC LOGIN FORM

A couple of problems jump out here, though. First, we have those align='right' attributes that mix formatting into our content, but that behavior could be easily moved into a style sheet. The deeper problem is that we're using all of this table markup for something that isn't particularly tabular. Let's look at what we're really trying to say here. The main <table> declaration is giving us a container for the rest of the form. That makes sense, but HTML already gives us one in the form of <fieldset>,[4] so let's use that instead. This means <th>, <tr>, and <td> all need to go. <th> is being used only to give a title for the form. Again, HTML already gives us that with the <legend> tag. The rest of the table layout is being used for formatting, so let's just get rid of it. Now we have this:

```
<fieldset>
   <legend>Please Login</legend>
   User ID:  <input id='userid' type='text' />
   Password: <input id='passwd' type='password'/>
</fieldset>
```

---

4. If you're not familiar with <fieldset>, <legend>, or <label>, their use is discussed in more depth in *Getting <form>al*, on page 130.

I don't like the "User ID:" and "Password:" text just hanging around like that, though. These are labels for fields, and we should mark them as such with the appropriately named <label> tag:

```
<fieldset>
    <legend>Please Login</legend>
    <label for='userid'>User ID:</label>
    <input id='userid' type='text' />
    <label for='passwd'>Password:</label>
    <input id='passwd' type='password'/>
</fieldset>
```

That's much nicer—the form is now described in terms of being a form rather than a table. This isn't to say that forms and tables should never mix. They just don't in this case because there's nothing tabular about a login box. Sometimes the form is oriented around tabular data, however. See the sidebar on page 118 for an example.

It takes work to break away from using tables as layout grids, but it is a powerful way of removing barriers to accessibility from your web sites. As we saw in our definition list and form examples, avoiding table-based layout can also make our code easier to understand and maintain. Speaking of forms, I dropped in a couple of tags back there that you may or may not have seen. Forms are another facet of our pages that need to be accessible, and it's time we discussed them, so that'll be our next step.

Act on It!

1. Ensure that any of your existing table-based layouts linearize correctly.

2. Purge your sites of table-based layouts. (You knew that was coming, didn't you?)

Chapter 8

The Accessible Interface

The interface we present to our users is as important as the accessibility of our content. If our users can't reasonably get to our content, it might as well not be there at all. One of the ways that users are often prevented from accessing content successfully is because developers have designed sites that try to control their users in an unreasonable way. It's always important to remember that *It's Their Web—We're Just Building in It*.

The default method of creating interfaces to interact with our users is the HTML form. In *Getting <form>al*, we'll look at the kinds of information we need to add to our forms to make sure our users can give us the information we're looking for, particularly if they're using assistive technologies. Next, in *Tickling the Keys*, we'll look at a couple of often-recommended methods for making forms more accessible and see that they may not be the best solution in most cases.

Simplifying our interfaces is the best thing we can do for all our users, including those who have special needs because of a disability. In *Your Interface Has Some Explaining to Do*, we'll finish up by looking at a simple way to get a basic benchmark for interface complexity.

18 It's Their Web—We're Just Building in It

Your master is he who controls that on which you have set
your heart or wish to avoid.
▶ Epictetus

We can't lose sight of the users for whom we are developing. Without users, there is very little point in what we do as web developers, so we need to keep them at the absolute center of our process. Unfortunately for us, users have their own ideas of what our site is for and how they'd like to use it, and unless we want to turn away readers or customers, we need to do our best to provide a good experience. Keeping users is a large task, but a big step is to never make our users feel like they're being pushed around.

As convenient as it might be to build restrictive interfaces that force the users to an action, it ultimately makes the user frame us as an adversary—not what we want our user community to see us as. This is particularly true when we look at our users with disabilities. The devices and technologies that they use to navigate the Web often have different dynamics. Forcing a particular pattern of usage makes their usage of the Web more difficult if not impossible. It's better for all concerned if we learn how to let go a little with our interface designs.

Don't Be a Control Freak

When a user requests our pages, we should treat this as being invited into their system, so we should do our best to be a good guest. Among other things, this means not taking control of their systems away from them any more than necessary. Certainly, some applications require the user to step through our pages in a specific order, but we need to keep them informed about what we plan to do.

One example is the pop-up window. Pop-ups should never be created without letting the user know it's going to happen, and pop-ups should always have alternatives for users of browsers that don't allow for them. Some people recommend just not using pop-ups at all, but I think that's a little too extreme—sometimes a pop-up is the cleanest interface choice. What we really need to be mindful of is that pop-ups are generated only as a response to a user request and that the interface clearly marks that a pop-up will result.

Media objects are another area where web pages often unreasonably take control from the user. Because our users may be reliant on screen reader technologies, it is critical to not "autoplay" media objects. Doing this creates cross-talk with the screen reader that makes the page unintelligible. As we'll see in Chapter 10, *Video Killed the Something-Something*, on page 175, we'll want to give the user plenty of options with respect to audio and video, so it makes more sense to let them start the media anyway.

Media also brings up one more control issue. Not only should the user be in control of starting events, but they also need to have the ability to stop them once started. For example, if a video file doesn't have a control set accessibly available, the user has no way to pause or mute it without actually turning down their speaker volume, which is again unacceptable for screen reader environments. Even more important to the user than control of their browser is control of their time.

I'm Sorry, Your Time Is Up

Part of giving control to the user is eliminating unnecessary timing effects. Two particular nuisances in this realm are timed page redirects and system timeouts. Consider the timed redirect:

```
<html>
<head>
  <title>This Page Has Moved</title>
  <meta http-equiv='refresh' content='3; http://.../' />
</head>
<body>
<h1>This Page Has Moved</h1>
<p>We're glad to see that you are interested in our page, "Giant
   Pygmy Weasels", but this page has been relocated to
   <a href='http://.../'>http://.../</a>.  Please update your
   bookmarks.  You will be automatically redirected to the new
   location in three seconds.</p>
</body>
</html>
```

There are a few control issues here. First, there's a presumption that the user bookmarked the page. More often, the user clicked an outdated link on another site. The real problem is that the refresh takes control from the user and forces an arbitrary time constraint on them. Even worse, this example uses a really short refresh time—three seconds. Odds are that the user will get just past "Giant Pygmy Weasels" when the refresh occurs.

Changing the refresh time isn't a great solution either. You can't guess how long it will take every user to read the page (they could be distracted by an angry weasel while they're reading, for example). At best, you could give a really long timeout that ensures that everyone has time to read the page, but at that point, it makes just as much sense to eliminate the timeout and tell them to click the link to the new location. That assumes that this kind of page makes sense in the first place.

A reality of the Web is that, if you do well, people link to your content, and even if you move the page, people will remain linked to the old location pretty much until the end of time. It's best to just cope with this and either automatically redirect at the server level or, if you can't do that, issue a <meta> style refresh with a time of zero.

This problem also applies to page or session timeouts. Some users need more time than others to process all of the content on a page or to navigate around a form and fill it in. Page timeouts may prevent our users from being able to read all of the content or being able to reasonably fill in a form. At the very least, the user should be given the ability to alter the amount of time that passes before an automatic session expiration.

We don't always have a choice about this, however. If a page is running a real-time event such as an auction or a test, the nature of the content prevents us from allowing the user to change the timing to fit their needs. All we can do in these cases is make sure that critical paths through the application are made as brief and simple as possible. In the case of tests with dramatic consequences, such as tests for educational or employment purposes, an alternative test method will probably need to be provided as an accommodation for users with timing problems on the Web.

Not taking control from the user is a key step toward web accessibility. When we take control of a user's system or time away from them, we may be preventing them from being able to interact with our site at all. Our users have individual differences that make it impossible to successfully force their actions to be consistent, so we need to let them decide. By giving control of the experience to the user, we allow them to come to our content on their own terms. This is especially important when we want interactions from our users, which we'll discuss next.

Act on It!

1. Check your sites for control-seizing operations such as unmarked pop-ups and media elements that autostart or have no user controls. Give control back to the user.

2. Eliminate any noncritical timeout effects from your pages.

19 Getting <form>al

A beautiful form is better than a beautiful face; it gives a higher pleasure than statues or pictures; it is the finest of the fine arts.
▶ Ralph Waldo Emerson

Many web pages wouldn't be very interesting or useful if they didn't allow for user interaction. The HTML <form> serves as our most basic tool for supplying interactivity to our web pages. This being the case, it's essential to make our forms accessible to all of our users. Look at it this way—when we put forms in our web pages, we're asking our users a question. This makes it our responsibility to make sure that our users understand clearly both what we're asking for and how we need them to respond.

Making the overall body of a form accessible is relatively simple—all we need to do is make sure we give some basic instructions at the beginning and ensure that the parts of the form are in a reasonable order. The depth of the instructions, of course, depends on the complexity of the form. If the form is a simple login or search form, you'll probably need to title it only "Login" or "Search." If the form is more complex, you may need a full instruction document. Putting the parts in order is also pretty simple—place the HTML in the order you want for the form to be read.[1] These parts—the bits and pieces of markup that actually make up the interface of the form—are the real accessibility challenge. Even so, making form elements accessible isn't all that difficult, and for existing pages, you probably already have much of the information you need. We'll just need to put it into the right form.

Sticking a <label> on It

Usually we don't leave form elements hanging around with no explanation at all—this isn't very usable for *any* of our users. Normally, we give some sort of description like this:

```
Username <input type='text' name='username' />
Password <input type='password' name='password' />
```

---

1. You may be tempted to use tab indexing instead of natural order to specify the form ordering. Take a look at *Tickling the Keys*, on page 137, to see why this isn't such a great idea.

This gives us a nice little title that we see next to the text input box. Hmm—"see" and "next to" are the two clues that not all is well with this. I want you to imagine a real label for a moment, say on a box of squirrels. It wouldn't make much sense to write "Danger! Box of Angry Squirrels" on the floor next to the box. It's much smarter to write it on a sticky note and put it right on the box where it can do people some good. This is exactly what the HTML <label> tag does for us.

The <label> tag wraps around descriptive text like a <span> and takes an for= attribute that specifies the element to which the label applies. We have two steps then—first we give a unique id= attribute to each of our form elements, and then we mark up descriptions of the elements with <label>. Our previous example becomes this:

```
<label for='user'>Username</label>
<input id='user' type='text' name='username' />
<label for='pass'>Password</label>
<input id='pass' type='password' name='password' />
```

It's as simple as that—like I said, you probably already have this information in your forms already, so it's just a matter of <label>ing it properly. Now we've associated the label text with the form element, so software such as assistive technologies can link the two together for our users. You may be wondering about the usage of id= and name=. When you submit a form, the value of the name= attribute is sent with the form to identify the data. In the browser, however, id= is the name for the element with respect to CSS, DOM, and references such as <label for='x'>.

Another issue to keep in mind about <label> is one of nesting. Some sources have suggested that you put the form element inside the <label> tag along with the descriptive text, like this:

```
<label>
  Username
  <input id='user' type='text' name='username' />
</label>
```

Don't do this—it doesn't work well in screen readers, and it doesn't make much semantic sense either. Labels *describe* forms; they don't contain them. We've kind of worked <input type='text'> to death here, and there are a lot of other types of form elements. Let's look at some examples of labeling the rest of them.

Text-Entry Elements

There are three types of form elements used to ask for a text response:

- <input type='text'>
- <input type='password'>
- <textarea>

All of these work as in the previous examples:

```
<p>We like to make our users feel like we're listening to them.
   Please feel free to send us your complaints and comments
   about this web site.</p>
<label for='comment'>Your Feedback</label>
<textarea id='comment' name='comment' cols='40' rows='10'></textarea>
<p>We really only care about what our subscribed users think, so
   please enter your username and password with your response</p>
<label for='user'>Username</label>
<input id='user' type='text' name='username' />
<label for='pass'>Password</label>
<input id='pass' type='password' name='password' />
```

No problems for our users here—no accessibility problems at least.

Buttons

HTML buttons, including <input type='submit'>, <input type='reset'>, and <input type='button'>, are as easy as it gets. These elements are self-labeled with their value= attribute. As long as you keep the value= descriptive, you're good to go (no "Click Me" here—I'm not Alice, and this isn't Wonderland).

Some people use <input type='image'> as a button substitute. This usage is *not* self-labeling, and <label> doesn't really make sense either. What we do for this is specify an alt= attribute that describes the content of the image. For more on alternate text, take a look at *To Put It Another Way*, on page 158.

Selection Elements

We also have three ways to ask our users to make choices:

- <input type='radio'>
- <input type='checkbox'>
- <select> and <option>

Radio and checkbox types get <label>s, just like the text input elements. The important point is that *all* of the radio buttons and checkboxes need a unique corresponding label. This means if you are doing a bunch of "Rate X from 1 to 5"–type questions, each question will have five labels (if you don't want the numbers to show up visually for each question, you can always assign visibility: hidden to the labels with CSS). Let's have a look:

```
<h1>Sam-Is-He's Breakfast Options</h1>
<p>Color</p>
<label for='colorRed'>Red</label>
<input type='radio' id='colorRed'   name='color'
                                    value='Red' />
<label for='colorGreen'>Green</label>
<input type='radio' id='colorGreen' name='color'
                                    value='Green' checked='yes'/>
<label for='colorBlue'>Blue</label>
<input type='radio' id='colorBlue'  name='color'
                                    value='Blue' />
<p>Food Choices</p>
<label for='foodEggs'>Eggs</label>
<input type='checkbox' id='foodEggs' name='food'
                                    value='Eggs' checked='yes'/>
<label for='foodHam'>Ham</label>
<input type='checkbox' id='foodHam'  name='food'
                                    value='Ham'  checked='yes'/>
```

Adding labels to <select> and <option> should seem pretty familiar as well at this point. We need to add an id= to <select> as well as a <label>, but like a button, <option> is self-labeled—this time by its contained text:

```
<label for='favWork'>Select Your Favorite Gaiman Work:</label>
<select id='favWork' name='favWork'>
  <option>Sandman: The Dream Hunters</option>
  <option>Death: The High Cost of Living</option>
  <option>American Gods</option>
  <option>Good Omens</option>
  <option>Coraline</option>
  <option>The Wolves in the Walls</option>
</select>
```

Hidden Elements

Hidden elements, marked up with <input type='text'>, exist only for internal use. They're not meant to be accessed by the user, so we shouldn't be doing anything to try to change that. Leave them hidden and unlabeled, and there should be nothing to worry about.

File Uploads

File uploads with <input type='file'> are a pain in the neck. This is true for all users, not just the population with disabilities. The browser just

When User Agents Grow Up...

Once upon a time, some browsers and screen readers didn't correctly handle forms if they didn't have some form of default text inside their input elements. Because of this, when WCAG 1.0 showed up, there was a recommendation to add default text to all form elements. What many people forget is that the recommendation starts with the phrase "Until user agents handle empty controls correctly...." It's considered appropriate to declare this a solved problem now; adding default text should no longer be looked at as an accessibility requirement.

Some argue that the default text should still be there for explanation. I disagree with this completely—that's what <label> is for, and it feels like a setup to populate form fields with defaults that will (probably) be the wrong input. The only time I agree with default text in form elements is either when it is likely to be the common choice (that is, the *default*) or when the form is being used to edit existing information.

kind of leaves us waiting with no feedback until the upload is complete, so sometimes file uploads act like a locked-up browser. There isn't much we can do to change this, so, unfortunately, the users with disabilities will have to suffer through their file uploads along with the rest of us.[2] Do make sure to put a <label> for the input element, though.

That takes care of labeling the parts of our form. The next thing we should take a look at is making sure the parts of the form are grouped in a way that makes sense.

Putting Your Eggs (and Ham) in One Basket

Let's return to the breakfast example from earlier. Take special note of the "Color" and "Food Choices" paragraphs:

```
<h1>Sam-Is-He's Breakfast Options</h1>
<p>Color</p>
<label for='colorRed'>Red</label>
<input type='radio' id='colorRed'    name='color'
                                     value='Red' />
```

---

2. *A note for browser developers:* Seriously, what's up with this? The interface for file uploads stinks. You know it, we know it, and our users *certainly* know it. We're not asking for miracles here, just a blasted (screen-readable) progress indicator—is that so much to ask?

```
<label for='colorGreen'>Green</label>
<input type='radio' id='colorGreen' name='color'
                              value='Green' checked='yes'/>
<label for='colorBlue'>Blue</label>
<input type='radio' id='colorBlue'  name='color'
                              value='Blue' />
<p>Food Choices</p>
<label for='foodEggs'>Eggs</label>
<input type='checkbox' id='foodEggs' name='food'
                              value='Eggs' checked='yes'/>
<label for='foodHam'>Ham</label>
<input type='checkbox' id='foodHam'  name='food'
                              value='Ham'  checked='yes'/>
```

Paragraphs? That doesn't seem right at all. Those are really another type of label for the group of options following them. Speaking of that "group," it would also be nice to show somehow that we really have two groups of options there, not just three radio buttons and two check-boxes. Enter <fieldset> and <legend>. The <fieldset> tag lets us put a group of controls together, and <legend> lets us give the group a name. Here's how we would use these on our food choices:

```
<fieldset>
  <legend>Food Choices</legend>
  <label for='foodEggs'>Eggs</label>
  <input type='checkbox' id='foodEggs' name='food'
                              value='Eggs' checked='yes'/>
  <label for='foodHam'>Ham</label>
  <input type='checkbox' id='foodHam'  name='food'
                              value='Ham'  checked='yes'/>
</fieldset>
```

That's much nicer. We can take this one step further, however. That heading is really a title for the rest of the form, and it would be nice to handle it the same way. Because <fieldset>s can be nested, this isn't a problem:

```
<fieldset>
  <legend>Sam-Is-He's Breakfast Options</legend>
  <fieldset>
    <legend>Color</legend>
    <!-- Color Choices -->
  </fieldset>
  <fieldset>
    <legend>Food Choices</legend>
    <!-- Food Choices -->
  </fieldset>
</fieldset>
```

Using <fieldset> and <legend> in this way to classify the parts of a form gives extra labeling information and makes it easier for our users to work through. We can also improve the favorite book example. I listed only a small fraction of Gaiman's works. If we added all of them, the list would quickly become difficult to navigate. We can help this some by using the <optgroup> tag to classify parts of the list:

```
<label for='favWork'>Select Your Favorite Gaiman Work:</label>
<select id='favWork' name='favWork'>
  <optgroup label='Comics'>
    <option>Sandman: The Dream Hunters</option>
    <option>Death: The High Cost of Living</option>
  </optgroup>
  <optgroup label='Novels'>
    <option>American Gods</option>
    <option>Good Omens</option>
  </optgroup>
  <optgroup label="Children's Books">
    <option>Coraline</option>
    <option>The Wolves in the Walls</option>
  </optgroup>
</select>
```

Adding these option groups again gives more information about the form element and makes navigating it a little simpler. Keep in mind that <optgroup>s can't be nested. If you think you need to, you might want to simplify your <select> options.

By adding labeling and structuring information to our forms, we have made them easier to navigate and understand, particularly for our visually impaired users. Ease of navigation and reduced complexity are important components of accessible interface design. Next we'll look at one attempt at simplifying interfaces that, unfortunately, isn't all it's cracked up to be.

Act on It!

1. Label your form elements (and your squirrels).

2. Clarify any complex forms you have by adding <fieldset>, <legend>, and <optgroup> as appropriate to large groups of elements.

20 Tickling the Keys

*It turns out that an eerie kind of chaos can lurk just behind
a façade of order—and yet, deep inside the chaos lurks an
even eerier type of order.*
▶ Douglas Hofstadter

It may surprise you to know that I'm about to tell you *not* to use certain accessibility features. The problem is that certain features, while being well intentioned, often cause more problems than they repair. Such is the case with the accesskey= and tabindex= HTML attributes. Both of these are frequently recommended as solutions for users who cannot use pointer devices and who rely on the keyboard for navigation. Both of these attributes also can cause major problems, so many people in web accessibility field (including myself) urge developers to use them extremely cautiously or preferably to not use them at all. Because they are commonly recommended, however, I'd like for us to take a look at them and understand how they are intended to work and what goes wrong with them so you can explain to managers or clients why they shouldn't be used.

Keys for Access

The accesskey= is supported by elements that can be "activated" such as <a>, <area>, <button>, <input>, or <textarea>. The key specified becomes a keyboard shortcut to activate the item or link by pressing a keystroke. This keystroke is implementation dependent but is usually one of Alt+<char>, Ctrl+<char>, or Cmd+<char>. For example, if we marked up a link like this:

```
<a href='comments' accesskey='c'>Read Comments</a>
```

the user would be able to jump to the comments page by hitting Ctrl+C. Not all is well with accesskey=, however. The first problem up is that we can assign pretty much any key to any element. This is a *big* problem for our users who might need to learn access keys for every site they visit. We could reduce this problem somewhat by using conventional access keys like those in Figure 8.1, on the next page, and by using the first letter of a command as an access key otherwise (such as using C for comments previously).

Key	Function
1	Go to the home page.
2	Skip to main page content.
3	Site map.
4	Site search.
9	Send feedback about the site.
0	Index of available access keys.

Figure 8.1: RECOMMENDED CONVENTIONS FOR ACCESS KEYS

The larger problem is that access keys can override system and browser keystrokes. Think about the example I gave before—we mapped C to comments. If our users can use only a keyboard, they may be prevented from copying a selection on the page (often mapped to Ctrl or Cmd+C). Even worse, we risk conflicting with keystroke commands for screen reader software—we could accidentally *reduce* accessibility with access keys! Some suggest using only numbers to reduce this problem, but even this may have problems for some applications. In general, I don't recommend accesskey because of overriding conventions on the user's system and difficulty predicting where conflicts might occur. If you *do* use accesskey=, I recommend keeping it to a minimum and testing thoroughly.

Put It on My Tab

When you press the Tab key in a web browser, the element focus should travel through all the elements on the page that can be interacted with in the order they appear in the HTML markup. This is called the *natural reading order* of the web page. This ordering can be adjusted by setting a tabindex= attribute with a value of 0–32767.[3] Here's a (really bad) example:

```
<a href='1' tabindex='1'>1</a>
<a href='3' tabindex='3'>3</a>
<a href='2' tabindex='2'>2</a>
```

With natural ordering, the tab would take you in the order "1, 3, 2," but with tabindex= set as shown, it would be "1, 2, 3." Tab indices also

---

3. Why 32767? Well, someone decided it would be based on a signed 16-bit value—that is, don't worry about it.

have problems, however. Anything that doesn't have a tabindex= falls through to the bottom of the list:

```
<a href='1' tabindex='1'>1</a>
<a href='4'>4</a>
<a href='3' tabindex='3'>3</a>
<a href='2' tabindex='2'>2</a>
```

This should read in "1 2 3 4" order as well. Another problem shows up when you work with templating environments. Let's assume import templates for a login form and a search form on the same page that have been independently indexed (I'll leave out the labels and IDs for brevity):

```
<input type='text' name='name' tabindex='1' />
<input type='password' name='password' tabindex='2' />
<!-- Other Page Content -->
<input type='text' name='search' tabindex='1' />
```

The tab order should be "Input Name, Input Search, Input Password"— clearly not what we would like to see happen. To get around this, we'd have to parcel our blocks of index values to each form, ranking them by priority and hoping everything goes well. This reminds me a lot of line numbering in BASIC. I *hated* line numbering in BASIC. A better solution is to just build your pages in natural reading order and let the browser handle the tabbing for you.

The accesskey= and tabindex= properties were well-intended attempts at making the Web better for the population with disabilities. Unfortunately, the reality of the situation is that the lack of a standard keyboard interface guideline and the ways that these properties actually behave in browsers prevent us from successfully using them to help our users most of the time. The behavior usually carries a risk of complicating the interface, which we don't want. I've mentioned the idea of simple and complex interfaces a few times now, so next we'll look at a simple way to see the difference.

Act on It!

1. Look at the menus of your web browser to see how many (few) keys there are that don't have the potential of conflicting with an access key. Do the same using the command reference for a screen reader.

2. Look at any areas where you may have already used tabindex=. If the indices are already in natural order, get rid of them to prevent updates from breaking your tab ordering. If the indices *aren't* in natural order, find a way of reordering your content to put it into natural order.

┌───┐
│ ┌─────┐   │
│ │ 21 │   Your Interface Has Some   │
│ └─────┘   Explaining to Do   │
└───┘

Man can alter his life by altering his thinking.
▶ William James

We want our users to be able to direct as much of their attention as possible to the work they want to do. For this to happen, we need our interfaces to be simple and easy to use so their efforts aren't mostly spent working through our interfaces. This is particularly important for our users with disabilities who, either because of personal limitations or because of the nature of their assistive technology, may already have some difficulties with navigation. We need to understand, then, what makes a user interface simple or complex.

There are *many* ways to determine the complexity of an interface, and most of them are well beyond the scope of this book to describe. I can, however, start you off with a quick and easy way of comparing two interface options as well as getting a feel for how much work a task is going to be.

Action Counting

The simplest way to go about evaluating an interface is to count the steps it takes to get things done. For example, to log in to a site, we might have a series like this:

1. Navigate to username input box.
2. Activate username input.
3. Type username.
4. Navigate to password input box.
5. Activate password input.
6. Type password.
7. Navigate to login button.
8. Activate login button.

That gives us eight steps for login. If the login form is the only thing on the page, we could optimize this a little by ensuring that the initial focus is on the username input box, verifying a natural tab ordering (in *Tickling the Keys*, on page 137, we see how *not* to do this) and making sure that pressing the Return key while the password input box is active submits the form without navigating to the login button.

Figure 8.2: A RUN-OF-THE-MILL WAY TO ADD A BOOK TO A CART

With these changes, a user familiar with the convention would go through these steps:

1. Type username.
2. Navigate to password input box (tabbing automatically activates).
3. Type password.
4. Press the Return key to log in.

So, we have a reduction of half the steps for a user familiar with the con- ventions of forms. This method is admittedly *very* simple and doesn't account for many factors such as switching between different input devices or the number of keystrokes typed. This kind of accounting should never be claimed as an attempt at a formal interface evaluation. If you need a heavier-weight tool for formal evaluation, I recommend looking into a method called GOMS (Goals, Operators, Methods, and Selection).[4] Nevertheless, action counting is still a handy way to get a quick, informal idea of the an interface's complexity.

---

4. For an introduction to the basics of GOMS as well as many other well-thought-out insights on user interface design, refer to Jef Raskin's *The Humane Interface* [Ras00].

Figure 8.3: A DRAG-AND-DROP SHOPPING CART. NOT ONLY DOES IT REQUIRE A POINTER, BUT IT'S ALSO MORE COMPLEX.

Comparing Two Interfaces

Action counting also lets us compare two interface options. Let's look at the shopping cart interface design mock-ups in Figure 8.2, on the previous page, and in Figure 8.3. The first is a conventional Add to Cart button, and the second is a Ajax-style drag-and-drop interface. We want to know which of the two options is simpler for our users, so let's count the actions for the two options and see how they compare. Let's start with the button interface:

1. Locate item to add.
2. Locate Add to Cart button.
3. Navigate to Add to Cart button.
4. Activate button.

Four actions—not too bad overall. How does the drag and drop compare?

1. Locate item to add.
2. Navigate to item icon.

3. Click and hold item icon.[5]
4. Locate cart icon.
5. Drag item icon to location of cart icon.
6. Release item icon at cart icon location.

Six actions—does this mean this navigation is "worse"? Not necessarily. It is certainly more complex, but it could be argued that it's more "intuitive" and hence worth the extra complexity. You just won't find me arguing that.

With information in hand to get you started on finding unnecessary complexity in your sites, we come to the end of our discussion of web interface accessibility and nearly to the end of our discussion of HTML accessibility. The last part of HTML to discuss is a *big* one, however—images, sound, and video. We'll be spending all of Part III getting up to speed on these issues.

Act on It!

1. Count the required actions for some of the common tasks on your sites. Do any of the tasks have a surprisingly high number of actions? What can you do to streamline the interface?

2. Look for more information about GOMS modeling, and apply it to the same interfaces. Note how formal evaluation compares to action counting.

---

5. You may notice that the drag-and-drop cart is also inaccessible because it relies on pointer input. We'll discuss this issue and how to work around it in *Higher-Order Scripts*, on page 224.

Part III

Getting the Perfect View

There are always two people in every picture: the photographer and the viewer.
► Ansel Adams

Chapter 9

A Picture Is Worth...

It's no secret that pictures are among the most powerful tools we have for communication. Images allow us to express complex ideas in a relatively small amount of space. We also know some of our users can't get the message we want to express through images alone. Many people are challenged by difficulties in differentiating colors. In *Stoplights and Poison Apples*, we'll explore some ways to know what our representations look like for our color blind audience as well as make sure we don't use color alone to express our ideas. We'll also learn how to understand the consequence of the contrast of our color schemes by *Thinking in Terms of Black and White*.

We also *must* provide another information access path for users who can't see our images at all. Alternative text representations are one of the fundamental building blocks of web accessibility, and we'll discuss using the alt attribute of images in *To Put It Another Way*. Sometimes an attribute worth of text isn't enough, however, and we'll need a few more techniques when we have *More Than alt= Can Say*. That covers the basic everyday issues we need to understand about providing accessibility for our image content, but, on occasion, a few oddities show up as well. To close the chapter, we'll discuss some of the more common anomalies in *alt.text.odds-and-ends*.

22 | Stoplights and Poison Apples

I have played hell somewhat with the truthfulness of the colors.
▶ Vincent van Gogh

As designers, one of our most compelling tools for conveying a message is color. Proper use of color enables us to easily and clearly evoke a perception in the mind of our viewer. The ways in which color is used provide a challenge, however, to the members of our audience who are affected by one of the forms of color blindness. Do you leave your users in the position of Figure 9.1, on the facing page? Less dramatically, consider this: without the ability to distinguish red from green, how would you suggest navigating a standard traffic light? Would you know whether to stop or go?

An Introduction to Color Blindness

First off, I need to confess to a little deception. In Figure 9.1, on the next page, I've simply changed the photo to grayscale. It illustrates the point, but it isn't fully reflective of how color-blind users would necessarily see the apples. Color blindness, rather than the inability to see any color, is the inability to distinguish differences between certain colors. Generally, we are concerned with three types: red-green color blindness, yellow-blue color blindness, and total color blindness.

Red-Green Color Blindness

The vision disorders protanopia, protanomaly, deuteranopia, and deuteranomaly are all associated with limitations to the ability to differentiate red from green. Some members of this group also experience a darkening or dimming effect where red becomes indistinguishable from black. Red-green color blindness is, by far, the most common form of color resolution disability at roughly 7–10 percent of the population, with a prevalence among men by a factor of 20:1.

Yellow-Blue Color Blindness

Tritanopia and trianomaly results in difficulty discriminating yellow and blue tones. Much rarer than red-green color blindness, yellow-blue color blindness affects less than 0.5 percent of the population with no discrimination between men and women.

Figure 9.1: ARE YOU FEELING LUCKY? BOTH APPLES ARE QUITE DELICIOUS—THE GREEN ONE, HOWEVER, HAS BEEN POISONED. HAVE A NICE DAY.

Total Color Blindness

Monochromacy is exceedingly rare and is marked by a complete inability to distinguish color hues and possibly by increased light sensitivity.

Prevalence of Color Blindness Types

In our natural environment, red and green often appear with one another. Because of this and of the higher likelihood of red-green color blindness, we're most likely to encounter difficulties in these ranges of the color spectrum. Because of the rarity of yellow-blue color blindness, fewer issues will occur, but we should be aware of them when we design in those color ranges so we can avoid color dependence and use appropriate contrast. The odds of encountering a user with total color blindness are extremely low. In fact, awareness of how pages look monochromatically is more likely to be a factor for users who deliberately view pages in monochrome because of contrast needs or equipment limitations.

Simulating Color Blindness

Although you can get some information by shifting your monitor settings to grayscale, the best way to check your style sheets and images for color blindness problems is to use a simulation tool. Several simulators are available for viewing web pages and images, so you'll want to try a few to find one you're comfortable using. The Colorblind Web Page Filter[1] translates web page style sheets and images to appear as they would to the various classes of color-blind users. Vischeck[2] (shown in Figure 9.2, on the facing page) is another option that exchanges fewer viewing options for a simpler interface as well as providing a Photoshop plug-in to check images during development.

The problem with web-based translation filters is that some parts of your content, such as plug-in media, won't be properly transformed. To get an overall view of the page as it would be seen by a color-blind user, you'll want to install a local simulation tool to perform a transformation on your local desktop. Sim Daltonism[3] for OS X and ColorDoctor[4] for Windows are two good options.

Color Keying of Information

The biggest challenge for color-blind users is the use of color-keyed information. Certainly for users who can clearly resolve the colors chosen, keying is a valuable tool. The key point is to pick colors that don't resolve too closely for the color blind. When colors *do* behave badly in a color blindness simulation, we have three options:

- *Change one of the conflicting colors:* Clearly, if possible, it is best to change the color scheme to avoid the color conflict entirely. This might still put a considerable burden on the user, however, who may still need to consider different values of the same hue in order to understand the color keying. For this reason, I prefer to add other cues in addition to preferring nonconflicting color palettes.

- *Add texture for clarity:* When texture is added to the color, it provides an additional visual cue to assist the audience in understanding the keying. This may also provide added content clarity for non-color-blind users. Actual texturing of the color doesn't

1. http://colorfilter.wickline.org/
2. http://www.vischeck.com/
3. http://www.michelf.com/projects/sim-daltonism/
4. http://www.fujitsu.com/global/accessibility/assistance/cd/

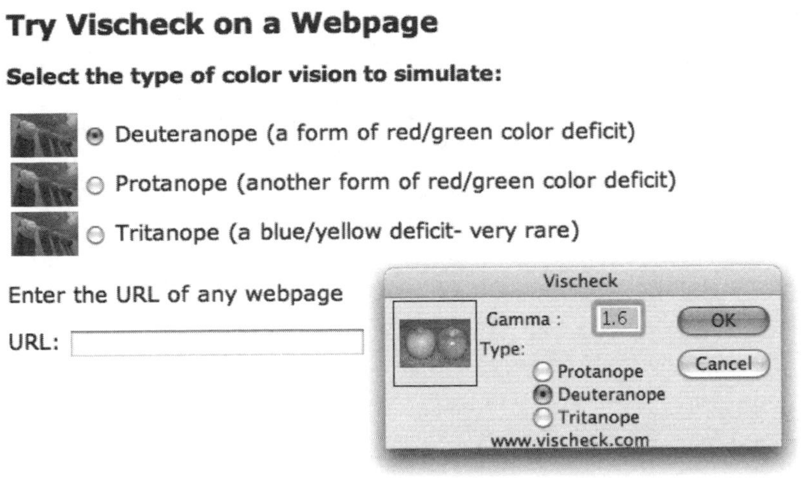

Try Vischeck on a Webpage

Select the type of color vision to simulate:

- ⦿ Deuteranope (a form of red/green color deficit)
- ○ Protanope (another form of red/green color deficit)
- ○ Tritanope (a blue/yellow deficit- very rare)

Enter the URL of any webpage

URL: [   ]

Vischeck

Gamma : [1.6]   (OK)

Type:
- ○ Protanope   (Cancel)
- ⦿ Deuteranope
- ○ Tritanope

www.vischeck.com

Figure 9.2: HTML AND PHOTOSHOP INTERFACES FOR THE VISCHECK COLOR BLINDNESS SIMULATOR

make sense in all situations, however. For example, if the color keying is used for navigation, then associated symbols or icons should be used to provide alternate cueing.

- *Add data information to the keying explanation:* If the color keying is used for a chart or another data application, adding summary information gives an alternate access path if the visual representation proves to be troublesome for the user.

Let's consider the progression in Figure 9.3, on the next page, of retooling a chart to minimize the impact of color keying. In sample A, the original color choices (red and green) don't resolve well when color information is removed. For fun, let's assume we can't change the colors outright. By adding a texture to one of the colors, as shown in sample B, the meaning of the chart is made clear. If we couldn't do that either (though I can't imagine why it wouldn't be possible to do either of these), we could just summarize the data for the user. Even if it's possible to change colors or add textures, this is still a good idea. We've done such in sample C, since it provides one more way for the person reading the chart to understand it.

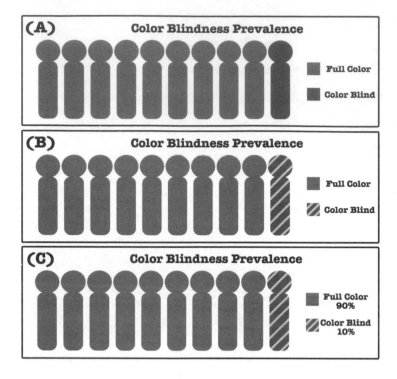

Figure 9.3: COLOR KEYING IN CHARTS: A IS UNACCEPTABLY COLOR KEYED, B USES TEXTURE TO IMPROVE THE CHART, AND C ADDS A DATA SUMMARY. OF COURSE, APPROPRIATE ALT TEXT SHOULD BE USED IN ANY CASE.

Act on It!

1. Use a color blindness simulator to review your web sites. Pay particular attention to images that lose their meaning and uses of color keying that don't provide other cues.

2. Consider items in your environment that employ color keying. What other information is available to describe your use of the item other than color? How would you redesign the item to reduce the need for color vision? For example, consider the traffic-light question posed at the beginning of the section. Some color-blind individuals rely on that traffic lights are standardized to read red, yellow, and green from top to bottom or left to right. Some regions are also beginning to consider the use of shaped lights to improve clarity.

23 Thinking in Terms of Black and White

Both of your socks should always be the same color—or
they should at least both be fairly dark.
▶ Dave Barry, **"A Conflation of Dunces,"**
Miami Herald, 1990.10.25

The color hues we design with pose only one accessibility issue. The *value* has at least as much, if not more, impact on our users' ability to comprehend our work. When color values are too similar, there may not be enough contrast for some users to differentiate between layout elements or resolve the content of images. Some forms of color blindness as well as low-vision disorders such as macular degeneration can lead to contrast resolution difficulties.

To illustrate the problem, let's take a look at a rainbow I've constructed and reduced to grayscale in Figure 9.4, on the following page. Notice anything wrong? If it weren't for the labeling and lines, would you clearly see seven colors? In my case, I can distinguish only two grays—one for green and indigo and another for everything else. Clearly, some pretty important information in this figure has been lost. So, what went wrong?

Luminosity and Contrast

To see what happened, we'll need a definition of contrast. In the Web Content Accessibility Guidelines 2.0 (WCAG 2.0), the W3C defines contrast in terms of the difference of the relative luminance of two colors. Relative luminance is essentially the brightness of the color, but not all of the components of a color are equal contributors to the brightness. For a given value, green contributes much more to brightness than red, and both contribute more than blue. To get a relative luminance value, the formula is as follows:[5]

Relative Luminance = (0.2126 * R) + (0.7152 * G) + (0.0722 * B)

To get *R*, *G*, and *B*, we need to transform the red, green, and blue components of our colors into sRGB like this:

$$R_{sRGB} = \frac{R_{8bit}}{255}, \ G_{sRGB} = \frac{G_{8bit}}{255}, \ B_{sRGB} = \frac{B_{8bit}}{255}$$

---

5. http://www.w3.org/TR/WCAG20/#relativeluminancedef

Color	Hex Value
Red	0xFF9999
Orange	0xFF9900
Yellow	0xCCCC00
Green	0x99CC99
Blue	0x99CCFF
Indigo	0x9999FF
Violet	0xCC99FF

Figure 9.4: THIS IMAGE WAS CONSTRUCTED WITH SEVEN HUES. KEY IN THE HEX VALUES IF YOU DON'T BELIEVE ME.

Then we can get R, G, and B like this:

If R_{sRGB} <= 0.03928, R = $\frac{R_{sRGB}}{12.92}$. Otherwise R = $\left(\frac{R_{sRGB}+0.055}{1.055}\right)^{2.4}$

If G_{sRGB} <= 0.03928, G = $\frac{G_{sRGB}}{12.92}$. Otherwise G = $\left(\frac{G_{sRGB}+0.055}{1.055}\right)^{2.4}$

If B_{sRGB} <= 0.03928, B = $\frac{B_{sRGB}}{12.92}$. Otherwise B = $\left(\frac{B_{sRGB}+0.055}{1.055}\right)^{2.4}$

These relative luminance values will always be in the range 0–1. In Figure 9.5, on the next page, I've added the luminance values for all seven shades. With these values in hand, it becomes possible to take a look at some relative contrasts. The contrast of two colors is simply a ratio of the lighter to darker relative luminance (with a scaling factor of 0.05 to prevent an unpleasant divide-by-zero problem). The formula is as follows:

Contrast = $\frac{L1+0.05}{L2+0.05}$

where *L1* is the greater (lighter) and *L2* is the lesser (darker) luminosity value of the colors being compared. This yields a contrast ratio in the range 1–21 where the higher the number, the stronger the contrast.

So, we now have the information we need in order to look at what happened, and I've added the relative contrast values to Figure 9.5, on the facing page. Hmmmmm—that's not good. With a contrast of less than 1.5 in all cases, it's really no surprise that the shades are hard to dif-

Color	Hex Value	Luminance	Contrast
Red	0xFF9999	0.4634	
			1.05
Orange	0xFF9900	0.4404	
			1.24
Yellow	0xCCCC00	0.5602	
			1.07
Green	0x99CC99	0.5226	
			1.09
Blue	0x99CCFF	0.5718	
			1.49
Indigo	0x9999FF	0.3678	
			1.15
Violet	0xCC99FF	0.4284	

Figure 9.5: ANOTHER LOOK AT THE RAINBOW WITH LUMINOSITY AND CONTRAST INFORMATION. CLEARLY, THIS COLOR SCHEME DOESN'T QUITE GET THERE.

ferentiate. Obviously, this color scheme isn't going to be something we would want to design our layouts around.

Some might say that this example seems contrived. After all, how often are seven colors from different parts of the color wheel chosen for a page layout? Probably not often, but remember that it only takes placing two noncontrasting colors next to one another to cause a problem. Note that all seven of the colors selected for the example fall into the classic web-safe palette, so we're not talking about strange or rare color options. Before any color pairing is finalized, it should be checked for adequate contrast.

Evaluating Contrast

Unless you're the sort of person who majored in mathematics in college, you're not looking forward to spending an afternoon plugging numbers into the luminosity and contrast formulas. I'm exactly the sort of person who majored in mathematics in college, and I certainly don't. Fortunately, we have a few other options to use for contrast checking. A simple way to make a snap judgment is to switch your display to grayscale or to a high-contrast mode, as shown in Figure 9.6, on the next page.

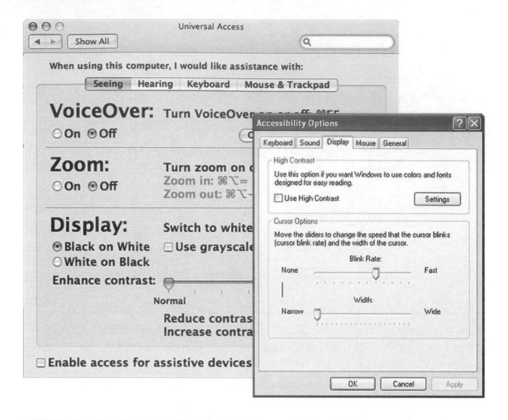

Figure 9.6: PREFERENCE WINDOWS FOR OS X AND WINDOWS XP TO ENABLE HIGH-CONTRAST DISPLAY MODES

This doesn't give the precise comparison formulas do, but if the matching doesn't look good here, it probably won't pass the formula anyway, and flipping modes is much faster than punching numbers. Another way to do a grayscale check is to use GrayBit,[6] which will transform a page, including images, to grayscale. Keeping in mind that not all plug-in–enabled media respects the system contrast settings and GrayBit doesn't convert *everything*, contrast settings and grayscale conversions may not completely work for a given page.

Although a number of tools are available to do color contrast checking online such as the one at Juicy Studio,[7] as of this writing they all appear to use an older contrast formula proposed in WCAG 1.0. This

---

6. http://www.graybit.com/
7. http://juicystudio.com/services/colourcontrast.php

formula also works well, but your results will be different from what you would get with the formula mentioned earlier.

When All Else Fails

I mentioned earlier that the rainbow scheme introduced in Figure 9.4, on page 154, wouldn't be a good choice for a layout. What if your content really *is* about the colors of a rainbow? It isn't possible to simply select different colors for contrast as it would be if their purpose were for layout. Unfortunately, for "normal" rainbows (those that someone without a vision impairment would recognize as a rainbow), it is essentially impossible to get to the 5:1 contrast ratio recommended by WCAG 2.0. Additionally, whenever an actual color is being referred to, as in the example, it is important to accurately represent it. What we need to do is understand what information is important to the end user. Certainly, in this case, it is important to know what the color codes used are, since the luminosity and contrast information provided rely on them. It is also nice to have the descriptive labels for the intent of the color. None of that information is directly related to the color usage, however. All that needs to happen is what is shown in the example— appropriate labeling was added to the image to allow someone who can't resolve the color and contrast (and via the magic of grayscale, I've made that happen for everyone) to get all the information without needing to resolve the color itself. Because the label color is *not* mandated, I chose to make it full white, which provides good contrast against all of the values present. Additionally, the important thing to remember is that the content needs to be accessible as a whole. It is certainly reasonable to place the relevant labeling and information in the surrounding text, if that works better. After all, the general gist of what's in the actual image is already available from the alt text, right? Right?

Act on It!

1. If you can, examine the colors produced for the hex values in Figure 9.4, on page 154. Even if you have no visual impairment, you may feel something looks "strange" about the combination of colors even without the grayscale reduction. If you pay attention to that feeling as you design, you will have fewer unpleasant surprises when you evaluate your proposed color schemes for contrast.

2. If you never have, spend some time browsing the Web with high-contrast settings turned on. Take note of what works and what doesn't. Keep these things in mind while you design.

24 To Put It Another Way

When someone tells you something defies description, you
can be pretty sure he's going to have a go at it anyway.
  ▶ Clyde B. Aster

In my experience, when most developers think about accessibility for the Web, the first thing that comes to mind is adding alternate text to their images. Although there is certainly more to accessibility than alt text, this first inclination is a good one. In 2006, the United Nations commissioned Nomensa to conduct a Global Audit of Web Accessibility.[8] The findings of this audit were that 93 percent of sites surveyed had inadequate text descriptions for graphical elements. That's a whole lot of untagged content, so we should probably get started.

Basics of Alternate Text Representations

Alternate text representations (alt text from here on out) are probably the easiest accessibility measure to implement from a technical standpoint. All you do is add the alt= attribute to all your <img> and <area> tags (and you have to anyway if you want valid HTML—alt= is a mandatory attribute on these tags):

```
<!-- Images -->
<img src='YourImage.png' alt='Alt Text Goes Here'/>
<!-- Image Map Areas -->
<area shape='rect' coords='0,0,75,75' href='somewhere.html'
    alt='Area Alt Text'/>
```

There you go. That's it. Well, not really. I only said that it was easy from a *technical* standpoint. The real work of alt text is determining what text needs to be in the attribute, and that's a "One moment to learn, a lifetime to master" kind of art.

Writing the Right Alt Text

The problem with writing correct alt text is that it often can't be done simply by looking at the image. Consider the photo in Figure 9.7, on the facing page. What should the alt text be? There are a lot of choices, depending on the context of the photo:

- It might be about clothing: alt='Action shot of a one piece jumper'
- Or about child development: alt='An infant learning to walk by cruising with a chair as a support'

---

8. http://www.nomensa.com/resources/research/united-nations-global-audit-of-accessibility.html

Figure 9.7: A PICTURE WITH MANY POSSIBLE ALTERNATIVE TEXTS

- To identify a specific person: alt='Aidan John Sydik'
- Part of my personal photo gallery: alt='Aidan playing in the kitchen'
- Perhaps I'm writing about web accessibility and talking about the context dependent nature of alt text: alt='A Picture With Many Possible Alternative Texts.'

Clearly the context matters. So does the length. The alt= attribute is meant to be a *brief* description as well. Something like alt='Aidan, a blond-haired toddler, wearing a light and dark blue striped jumper while standing against a green accented chair in a kitchen with hardwood floors that might need a bit of a sweep' would be far too long and detailed for normal alt text. Most of the time, the alt text should be no more than 40–80 characters or a couple of seconds when spoken. Odds are that it isn't suitable alternative text if it looks or sounds like a run-on.

<u>**It Isn't Called tooltip=**</u>

Some time ago, the makers of a couple of web browsers decided that it would be a nifty idea to add tooltips (those little text boxes that appear when you hold the cursor over-top of something) to images. In and of itself, this wasn't a bad thing. The problem comes from the fact that these browsers use the alt= attribute as the source for tooltips. This resulted in alt text being written as an extended description for users who could see the image rather than as a true alternative for users who couldn't. For supplementary information, the title= attribute should be used instead. This attribute is also the first choice in current browsers that display tooltips. This effect is not guaranteed, however—some browsers display the information in the status bar, while others don't display it at all.

Something alt text should *not* generally contain is the phrase image of.... When alt text is rendered, the image is generally identified as such, and what the user will get is something like "image: image of...," which is more than a little irritating, particularly in screen reader software. This should be avoided entirely unless, like the previous example, it is conceptually important that the image is an image. Similarly, words such as *photo*, *painting*, and *sketch* may be redundant.

We also need to avoid providing information in alt text that isn't otherwise available. For example, if I identify Aidan by name in the alt text but not in the narrative text of the content, I have actually tipped the balance the other direction and put the users who *can* view the image at a disadvantage. When this does happen, the extra information needs to either be removed from the alt text or be moved into the narrative as appropriate. We need to ask then, what if the image doesn't say anything not already covered in the text content?

If There's Nothing Good to Say...

Sometimes the alt text should be nothing. That doesn't mean not having an alt= attribute (remember, valid <img> and <area> tags always do). It means having the empty attribute alt=". There are two primary reasons to specify empty alt text, and both are found in Figure 9.8, on the next page.

Figure 9.8: SOME THINGS ARE BEST LEFT UNSAID. THIS SITUATION CALLS FOR EMPTY ALT TEXT.

- *Redundant images:* Sometimes the purpose of the image is already fully specified elsewhere, such as the shopping cart icon. It certainly doesn't make sense for the user to receive "Image: Cart View Cart," so it would be better to leave the alt text empty with the intention that the icon simply disappear if it can't be viewed.

- *Decorative images:* When a user is unable to view the nicely rounded corners, gradiated borders, spacers, and other images meant only to improve the look of a page, they probably don't care to be flooded with information about them via alt text. By setting alt=", you clarify that there is nothing useful to be said about the images and that it's OK to ignore them.

With regard to empty alt text, I have one specific warning for those who prefer to use WYSIWYG editors. In many cases, these editors do not allow you to enter empty alt text, instead leaving out the attribute entirely. Usually the editor will have a checkbox or option visible if empty attributes are an option. If you are unsure about your editor's behavior, open the generated HTML in a text editor, and check the actual code being generated (and take a look at the sidebar on page 79).

Responsibility for Alt Text

From my experience, the most common cause of bad or missing alt text is misplaced responsibility. I have watched (and participated in) situations where web developers are given text and images to put online. Usually no alternate text is specified for the images, and the developer is left to either ignore adding alt text (don't even think about it) or try to come up with some appropriate text. The problem is that the developer didn't create the content and doesn't necessarily have any reason to know what the correct alt text should be. What *should* happen is for the author to submit appropriate alt text with their content that clearly expresses their intended context.

Getting Rid of Images

At some point, there might be temptation to simply do away with images rather than write good alt text for them. In the big picture, this isn't a great idea. Although visually impaired users need text alternatives for images, other users benefit from explanatory imagery. Some developers choose the path of "text-only" versions of their pages. Don't make this mistake! To do this right, you would need to write alternative text content anyway—you would just be doing it the WET way. Take a look at *Don't Get WET!*, on page 49, if you don't know why that would be a Bad Thing.

Act on It!

1. Act locally. Take the time to add alternate text to your work if it isn't there already. If you are unsure of what a text should be, discuss it with the author of the content or image—don't add to the problem by generating bad attributes!

25 | More Than alt= Can Say

An image can say more than a thousand words, but which words are these?
▶ Taeke de Jong, **Naming Components and Concepts**

The text in the alt= attribute should be reasonably concise—ideally, no more than 40–80 characters. Sometimes an image says much more than can be summarized briefly, though. There are charts, diagrams, and other illustrations representing sizable amounts of content information, and fortunately for us, we have ways to manage longer alternative texts.

So Much to Say

If more needs to be said about an image than fits into normal alt text, we can place a longer explanation on a separate page and link to it with the longdesc= attribute. However, it's important to keep in mind that long descriptions are meant to be an *extension* to the alt text, not a replacement (alt= doesn't stop being a required attribute just because longdesc= is defined). Careful attention needs to be paid to the nature of the long description as well. Descriptions should still be reasonable in length and not contain any information needed by users who are viewing the image and not getting the long description. In fact, when I find myself getting ready to add a long description, I immediately stop and think it through. If the ideas presented by an image require that much alternative text to explain and the body text doesn't explain it, have I risked leaving my readers in the dark? Most of the time the answer seems to be yes, and revisions to the body text eliminate the need for a long description entirely. That said, sometimes it is the right solution, and here's what it looks like:

```
<!-- In The Main Page -->
<img src='YourImage.png'
    alt='Alt Text Goes Here'
    longdesc='YourImageExplanation.html'/>

<!-- YourImageExplanation.html -->
...
<p>Narrative Explaining YourImage.png.  Just be careful not to
   put anything here that non-alternative text readers might
   need to know.
</p>
...
```

The Honorable but Venerable "D Link"

Here and there you might see references to "D links." Back in an earlier era (that is, before longdesc=), some accessibility experts recommended adding a link marked "D" (or "d") immediately after images needing further alternate text description. This was a useful way to present the information in a conventional way for users who needed alternate description. In the here and now, however, this functionality is provided by the longdesc=, and the "D link" should receive its applause for a job well done and exit stage left.

That was simple enough. Long descriptions give us an opportunity to say a few more words about complex images. Just be judicious, and make sure they aren't covering for deficiencies in your body text.

Charts and Graphs

When it comes to needing a lengthy explanation of imagery, nothing beats data images. Consider Figure 9.9, on the facing page. The briefest it gets is this: alt='Pie Preference: 42% Peach, 28% Cherry, 16% Blueberry, 7% Key Lime, 5% Other. Sample Size 42. Error +/- 2%'. One hundred and seven characters is well longer than alt text should be, and ultimately, this is a very simple graph described as tersely as possible. If the graph is more complex, this won't do at all. We can use three strategies:

- *Minimize the content*: In Figure 9.9, on the next page, the heading "Pie Preference" could be moved into an HTML heading, and the sampling and error information could be moved into a paragraph just below the actual image. This would reduce some complexity
- *Rely on longdesc=*: Long descriptions are stored at a separate URL. This gives more freedom to mark up an explanation for clarity:

```
...
<h1>Pie Preference</h1>
<ul>
  <li>Peach:     42%</li>
  <li>Cherry:    28%</li>
  <li>Blueberry: 16%</li>
  <li>Key Lime:   7%</li>
  <li>Other:      5%</li>
</ul>
<p>Preference data is based on a sample size of 42 and has an
   error of plus or minus 2%.</p>
...
```

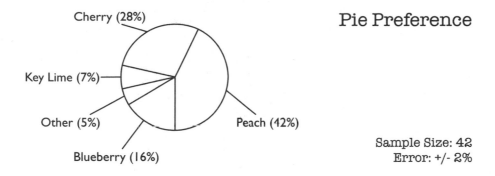

Figure 9.9: A SIMPLE PIE CHART

- *Explain it in the narrative*: Particularly for complex graphs, it is important to explain what the graph says and means in the body text of the page. If this is done well, it may suffice to say alt='Pie Preferences Chart representing the data discussed below'. If the narrative doesn't refer explicitly to the chart and all of its content is clearly described, it *might* even be reasonable to use an empty alt text (though it's probably better to explicitly mention it).

Which should you use? All of these—do what you can to make the content of the graph easily understandable by all of your users.

Sometimes You Don't Need an Image at All

For simple charts, there's another option. If you're comfortable with CSS and look at the right "obscure" tags, you could try to build your chart entirely in HTML. In a project where I was generating a simple histogram plot of user response data, I encountered two problems. First, the overhead of dynamically generating the image was a little higher than warranted—that is, it was too darned slow! Second, it was a slower process yet because I needed to feed raw data to the chart generator *and* do most of the same calculations a second time to generate alt text for the image. Not good. Let's consider the chart in Figure 9.10, on the following page. (No, the percentages *don't* total 100 percent. Such is the nature of rounding real data.) If you think about it, isn't that just a list of possible options and the response percentage for each?

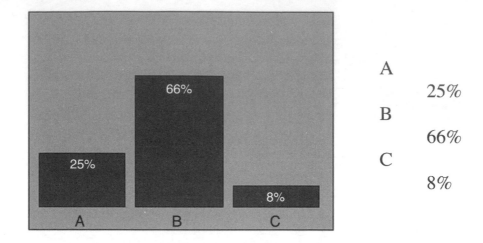

Figure 9.10: THE SAME DEFINITION LIST WITH AND WITHOUT CSS STYLING

If you think about it a little bit more, couldn't you think of the content as a list *defining* the percentage response for each option? Maybe it would look something like this:

```
<dl>
  <dt>A</dt><dd>25%</dd>
  <dt>B</dt><dd>66%</dd>
  <dt>C</dt><dd>8%</dd>
</dl>
```

Not bad. It certainly represents the content, but in a browser, it doesn't look anything like a chart. If we want to define this as a special class of list and build some CSS styles, we'll get there, though:

```
<style>
  .Chart {
    height: 250px;
    width: 360px;
    background-color: #8ad;
    border: 1px solid black;
    text-align: center;
    padding: 0px;
    margin: 15px;
    margin-top: 5px;
  }

  .Chart dl {
    margin-left: 25px;
  }
```

```
.Chart dt {
  display: inline-block;
  float: left;
  width: 90px;
  margin: 0px;
  margin-top: 210px;
  margin-left: 10px;
  padding-top: 4px;
}

.Chart dd {
  display: inline-block;
  float: left;
  overflow: hidden;
  width: 90px;
  color: white;
  background-color: #00a;
  border: 1px solid black;
  font-size: 0.8em;
  text-align: center;
  vertical-align: bottom;
  margin: 0px;
  margin-left: -90px;
  padding-top: 2px;
}
</style>
```

Of course, we'll need to reference the CSS in the HTML document. Here's the markup for the chart in Figure 9.10, on the preceding page:

```
<div class='Chart'>
  <dl>
    <dt>A</dt><dd style='margin-top: 150px; height:  50px'>25%</dd>
    <dt>B</dt><dd style='margin-top:  68px; height: 132px'>66%</dd>
    <dt>C</dt><dd style='margin-top: 184px; height:  16px'> 8%</dd>
  </dl>
</div>
```

Nice. Nicer yet, for those users who are using a screen reader, using a text browser, or simply browsing with styles turned off, the chart will render as a list of options and percentages like the one on the right side of Figure 9.10, on the facing page.

Of course, in a real application, this would probably be generated with a script, but since the heavy lifting is being done with the CSS, the scripting isn't particularly difficult.

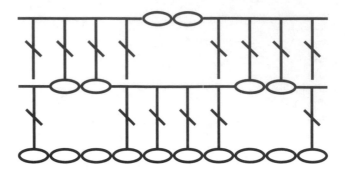

Figure 9.11: A SIMPLE FILET CROCHET DIAGRAM—A NOT SO SIMPLE ALT TEXT PROBLEM

Explanatory Diagrams

I won't pull any punches here—developing alternative text for diagrams explaining the steps of a process is usually a real pain. Sometimes even a lengthy narrative isn't quite enough to give the entire idea. Consider diagrams explaining the design of a circuit or device. The best solution possible may be to provide a general description of the purpose of an image and provide a high-resolution version that can be rendered into a raised line or braille diagram. In other cases, we can describe the diagram with a lengthy narrative, and we have two ways to do this. We can push the explanation out to a long description if it doesn't appear to be useful for everyone. As is often the case, however, it may be better to incorporate the explanation into the body text.

Consider Figure 9.11. With the resurgence of knit and crochet as popular crafts, the Web has been the obvious media to share pattern and tutorial information. This example of a filet crochet pattern is very basic—normally the pattern would be dozens if not hundreds of stitches wide and use many different shorthand symbols. In many cases, textual shorthands exist that can be used as the basis for our alternate text. For this example, the written shorthand for a crochet pattern looks like this:

Row 1: Ch 10. Row 2: SC, Ch 2, SC 4, Ch 2, SC. Row 3: SC 4, Ch 2, SC 4.

To be useful for the visually impaired, however, a couple of considerations need to be made. First, this shorthand is mostly composed of abbreviations. For best possible content accessibility, these should be marked up with <acronym> or <abbr> tags as appropriate and screen reader tested for understanding. For *all* users, it would also be considerate to add abbreviations to a site glossary. It is *not* necessary, however, for accessibility to expand all abbreviations that would be commonly understood in the content's context. Although "SC" might not be clear to the general public, it is understood as "Single Crochet" for anyone with minimal experience in the craft.

Act on It!

1. Try your hand at generating a graph entirely with XHTML and CSS. Better yet, if you're of the programming persuasion, build a library to generate them for you.

2. If your site already uses long descriptions, review them to ensure that they aren't providing a significantly different experience to that provided by imagery. If any of these long descriptions are old-school "D links," update them to use longdesc- attributes.

26	alt.text.odds-and-ends

The path of excess leads to the tower of wisdom.
▶ William Blake

Images can represent things that are neither purely informational nor completely presentational in nature. It is well worth our time to look at these kinds of images, because working with them doesn't necessarily fit into our general patterns and methods for image accessibility. Let's take a closer look at these areas and find out what we need to do about them.

Image Maps

Image maps have had a bad accessibility reputation. In the case of server-side image maps, this reputation is truth be told well deserved. Because server-side image maps require both vision and access to a pointing device, they are, by default, inaccessible. Client-side image maps, on the other hand, are effectively a list of links bound to a special visual representation. As we saw in *To Put It Another Way*, on page 158, the <area> tag requires the use of an alt attribute. We should still watch for two issues even after we've added appropriate alternative text to the image map, though. First, if the map has a lot of regions, it would be good to add a link, either before the map or as the first region, allowing the user to skip past the contents of the image map. Regions also need to be large enough so users with mobility impairments can accurately select them.

Text of Images of Text of...

The only guarantee we have regarding fonts on the Web is that we can use the CSS font-face property with any of the default values serif, sans-serif, monospace, cursive, or fantasy. This doesn't give us a lot of freedom, especially when we stop to consider that almost nothing is guaranteed about these fonts between platforms. There was a lot of talk about downloadable fonts for a time, but partly because of fears about the security risk to proprietary fonts, nothing really came of it. That lack of typographical support led many to take the route of opening an image-editing tool, setting up the font as they wanted, and exporting an image for inclusion on the web page.

This leads to a couple of problems. Obviously, if these images weren't given proper alt attributes, parts of the text would go missing. Another issue is that these images are often used as headers, but not given any semantic information to mark them as such. Again, this is easy. By adding the correct <h#> tags (yes, it turns out we *can* do that— headings are block-type elements), we can mark this correctly. The last major problem is less straightforward to solve. When images of text are magnified, they quickly become difficult to read because of pixelation and aliasing. The point of typography is to create a pleasing visual effect, but how can we achieve this consistently and accessibly?

Enter Scalable Inman Flash Replacement (sIFR).[9] sIFR allows us to replace short lengths of normal browser text with typeset text embedded in Flash media. The replacement itself involves a script function that checks for Flash and performs the substitution. The advantages is that when Flash isn't available or scripting is turned off, the system falls back to normal CSS styling. The process happens transparently to the user, and text remains text with respect to screen reading and browser selection. Figure 9.12, on the next page, shows an example of a "sIFRed" page.

Color Descriptions

Sometimes an image is meant to describe a color swatch. This is common practice for any content where a product is available in multiple colors or fabrics. I have been asked on more than a few occasions how we can successfully provide a complete text alternative for these swatches. To put it bluntly, we can't. This falls into the category of attempting to explain an almost purely visual concept. That doesn't mean we should drop back to a null alt attribute, however. For each swatch we provide, we also give a description of the nature of the color involved, any patterning used, and color codes or order numbers as appropriate.

For example, we might provide alternative text such as "Style 4242: Black and Green Plaid." This gives the user most of the information that we *can* give them. If they know they don't look good in green or hate plaid, this is not an acceptable choice for them. If they think this is a good choice, however, we have also provided a style number for them to use for future reference. This approach also allows someone who can't see the swatch to make choices based on information given to them. If the description of a swatch is complex, there is always the option of using longdesc—just make sure you're not getting *too* complex in your description.

---

9. http://www.mikeindustries.com/sifr/

THE GOTHIC TIMES

Geneva Plan Signed

New agreement creates Myriad opportunities for Fruitiger, sans-serifs

Vanden Keere, Mrs. Eaves wed in Baskerville

Use sIFR? (Requires refresh) no | yes | forget

Remove sIFR headlines

ed wisi. Cras ornare sagittis risus. Cras nisl neque, nonummy et, condimentum a, adipiscing ut, sem. Duis scelerisque ullamcorper elit.

Fusce aliquet aliquet sapien. Donec tincidunt eleifend odio. Morbi lorem. Pellentesque et massa elementum nisl commodo consectetuer. Sed eget quam. Nullam

Lorem ipsum dolor sit amet, consectetuer adipiscing elit. Sed ac urna. Sed rutrum lectus eu orci. Nulla mattis erat. Fusce scelerisque hendrerit wisi. Aenean imperdiet imperdiet nunc. Morbi tincidunt, mi vel posuere varius, mi est nonummy leo, eu volutpat leo massa sit amet turpis. Curabitur tempor auctor quam. Morbi dapibus. Vestibulum eleifend. Etiam eleifend sapien nec dolor. Proin porttitor felis a orci. Curabitur pellentesque urna a turpis.

Donec massa erat, vehicula ac, tincidunt vel, viverra nec, elit. Sed sodales, enim nec cursus auctor, dui ligula tincidunt augue, eget dapibus odio leo at dolor. Etiam tempor accumsan nisl. Nunc turpis mi, consectetuer pharetra, vulputate vitae, posuere id, lectus. Etiam auctor pharetra metus. Nullam eu urna ac

"THE QUEST TO ABOLISH THE SERIF SHALL CONTINUE."

Helvetica, Arial in Grotesque Accident

Maecenas rhoncus diam id metus. Aenean lacinia lectus sit amet diam. Vestibulum urna ante, mollis vitae, sagittis sit amet, aliquam nec, dolor.

Aenean ultricies tortor in nunc. Vestibulum quis lacus. Etiam lobortis gravida diam. Vestibulum ante ipsum primis in faucibus orci luctus et

Figure 9.12: SIFR ALLOWS ACCESSIBLE TYPOGRAPHY ON THE WEB. TAKE PARTICULAR NOTE OF THE SELECTED TEXT.

CAPTCHA'ed!

Completely Automated Public Turing tests to tell Computers and Humans Apart (CAPTCHAs) are a type of challenge posed to a user, often as an image to verify that a response is coming from a human rather than from automated software. An example of a typical CAPTCHA is shown in Figure 9.13, on the facing page. These systems create accessibility problems by creating content intended to be impossible to parse with software. The system is attempting to prevent access by automated "bot" software, but many assistive technologies are also software. I think we have a problem.

Some attempts have been made to create an accessible CAPTCHA, but this is unlikely to be successful. To beat automatic scanners, character or image recognition systems have to be difficult to read, and sound recognition systems have to be hard to hear. For either of these to have a chance of success, we are faced with the unacceptable option of eliminating alternative representations. Others have proposed logic puzzles or riddles as a potential alternative, but this shuts out some of

ALT.TEXT.ODDS-AND-ENDS ◀ 173

Figure 9.13: CAPTCHAS ARE MEANT TO BE DIFFICULT FOR SOFTWARE TO INTERPRET. UNFORTUNATELY THIS INCLUDES ACCESSIBILITY SOFTWARE.

our audience who have cognitive disabilities (as well as those who just aren't good at these kind of games). Ultimately, we would end up in a situation where we are offering many different varieties of CAPTCHA, each of which is made deliberately inaccessible in some manner.

Clearly attempting to build accessibility around CAPTCHAs isn't a lot of fun. The unfortunate punch line is—if we *did* manage to make it to the point of an accessible implementation—CAPTCHAs don't actually work very well. Many implementations have had gaps in the system and brute-force techniques such as image cataloging are very reliable in defeating the system. Worse yet, some neural network applications have been found to have higher rates of success at responding to CAPTCHAs than humans. My general advice is to not compete in this arms race and to try to select a different kind of validation system entirely.

ASCII Art

There is a long-standing online tradition of using text characters to create images. I'm referring to things like building a face like this:

Even though this is made up entirely of text, we need to treat it as an image. Doing this correctly will require the use of the <pre> tag, so we already have a way to separate it from surrounding content.

What we don't have is the convenience of the alt attribute, so we'll have to create a caption for the image, preferably before the image itself. Why before? Because we also should place a link before the block that targets a point just after it—screen readers will generally drop into character read mode for ASCII art, and we need to give a way to skip it.

In most cases, full-scale ASCII artwork isn't particularly common on the Web, but in the small scale, the emoticon is a very common case. Emoticons are the little "smiley" faces added to express emotion. I'm sure you've seen one or two of them ;). For small inline ASCII art like this, we can usually tag it as an abbreviation: <abbr title="Winking Smile">;)</abbr>.

Act on It!

1. Replace banner and heading images of text with a more functional alternative such as sIFR.

2. Add alternative text and links to skip any image maps you might have.

3. Bonus: seek fame and fortune—develop a CAPTCHA that successfully provides security to a site while maintaining accessibility (and good luck).

Chapter 10

Video Killed the Something-Something

Video is a great tool for presenting large amounts of information quickly in an engaging format. Not all of our users can access our video content, however, because of their impairments. They may be able to understand only the audio or video component of the content, and some users may not be able to safely view certain videos at all.

We'll start this chapter off by learning how to ensure that the videos we present aren't harmful to our users. In *It's Not Polite to Flash the Audience*, we'll take a look at the dangers of flickering video to users who have photosensitive epilepsy. Once we know that the video is safe to use, it's back into the land of multiple access paths.

If a picture is worth a thousand words, video is worth about 2 million per minute. We'll want to be a little more brief than that, so in *Words That Go [Creak] in the Night*, we'll look at writing good captions using them to provide an alternative to the dialogue and sounds of our videos. Users who have visual rather than auditory impairments need auditory descriptions to fill in the details of the video component. We'll look at creating these in *Describe It to Me*. With caption and auditory description scripts, we can also add full-featured transcript alternatives for video content.

Knowing how to write captions and auditory descriptions does little good until we connect them to the video for presentation. Wrapping up the chapter in *On the Cutting Room Floor*, we will look at common presentation formats as well as a tool that makes the job easier.

Not all web developers produce video content, and even fewer are directly responsible for creating captions or auditory descriptions. Even if you never produce alternative content for video, it is likely that you will be involved in deployment or testing, so it is important to have at least a working knowledge of how the process works and what makes for good alternative content.

27 It's Not Polite to Flash the Audience

*For thousands the world is a freak show, the images flicker
past and disappear, the impressions remain flat and
disconnected in the soul.*
   ▶ Johann Wolfgang von Goethe

We need to watch out for the presence of flicker when we add video and multimedia content to our web sites. Flicker can be anything from a strobe effect, the transition of color on a passing high-speed train, or even something as subtle as the movement of shadows on a light-colored surface. Flickering video certainly has the capability to be irritating or bothersome, but our foremost concern here is that flickering also has the potential to be severely harmful to our users.

Photosensitive Epilepsy

Photosensitive epilepsy results in seizures of varying nature and severity upon exposure to certain visual stimuli. The most common triggers are stroboscopic light, repetitive patterns, and flickering video. Some developers argue that photosensitivity is a relatively rare condition and minimize the importance of flicker prevention. In 1997, however, photosensitive epilepsy was brought to prominent public attention when the Pokémon episode "Dennou Senshi Porygon" was broadcast in Japan, triggering seizures in hundreds of viewers. Clearly, when large audiences are targeted, as we do on the Web, even relatively small percentages translate into large numbers of susceptible viewers. Even if the numbers *were* minimal, the importance of preventing potential harm to our users is still worth significant effort on our parts.

What Is Flicker?

Flicker is the rapid switching back and forth of any form of visual input from high to low brightness. With respect to photosensitive epilepsy, we are specifically concerned about flickering at a rate of 2–55Hz. The concept of flicker is often misunderstood, however. You may have noticed that video runs at a frame rate of 12–30 frames per second (12–30Hz). Does this mean we can't have video at all? Absolutely not. Although any kind of motion has the capability to flicker, motion itself is not, in and of itself, a concern.

Stumbling in International Competition

In June 2007, flicker struck again in a video meant to introduce the 2012 London Olympic Games. A segment in the video featured a multicolor flicker that went untested and caused seizures in some viewers. Fortunately, the impact was much smaller than the 1997 Pokémon incident, affecting fewer than a dozen people. I'm not as concerned about the reported numbers as by the potential damage, though—in the end, 23,000 people in the United Kingdom were put at risk of seizures caused by this video.

It's often easy to lose perspective and view photosensitivity as a minor factor that affects only a few people. It's never just a few people—a small fraction of percent of the total population still adds up to thousands of people. This perspective is also a pretty bad way to do business. At the time, London mayor Ken Livingstone had these comments:

- "If you employ someone to design a logo for you and they haven't done a basic health check, you have to ask what they do for their money."
- "Who would go into a firm like that again and ask them to do that work? This is a pretty basic thing."

These are important things to think about. As web developers, we make our livings by serving an audience. If we allow harm to come to that audience, we allow harm to come to ourselves as well.

The motion also has to have the previously mentioned back and forth switching. What we really need is a way of understanding whether the type of motion is potentially harmful.

The Flash Threshold

WCAG 2.0 gives us a way of measuring flicker, though it is anything but simple.[1] What we're really looking for are changes in brightness. For this we'll need relative luminance formula that we used for evaluating contrast in *Thinking in Terms of Black and White*, on page 153. This time, instead of looking for the difference of brightness by location, we'll be looking at it as time passes.

---

1. http://www.w3.org/TR/WCAG20/#general-thresholddef

A flash is defined as a sequence of two shifts in relative luminance of more than 10 percent. Both Dim → Bright → Dim and Bright → Dim → Bright are possible flash transitions. Three or more of these in a one-second period is the threshold for a flicker problem. When counting the number of flashes in an interval, it is important to remember that the flash components can overlap. This means that Dim → Bright → Dim → Bright → Dim counts as three flashes. There is also a *red flash threshold*, where the luminosity is assessed in terms of fully saturated red rather than fully saturated white.

Unfortunately, it gets more complex. Small flickering parts of the screen are not generally considered to be harmful, while larger ones are. The recommended metric is that if the total flashing occupies more than a quarter of the pixels in any 341×256-pixel rectangle anywhere on the display when viewed at 1024×768, there's a problem. I didn't react very well to that recommendation the first time that I read that, and I am betting that you aren't either. On first impulse, this looks very complex and difficult to measure. In this case, the first impulse is spot on—particularly because the 341×256 rectangle mentioned can be *any* subrectangle on the screen.

This is obviously the kind of evaluation that we do *not* want to do by hand. Luckily for us, the TRACE Center offers the Photosensitive Epilepsy Analysis Tool (PEAT).[2] PEAT analyzes a video file for flicker problems. For an analysis of a full web page, we need to create a screen-cast video of the page with a tool such as iShowU[3] or Camtasia[4] and analyze it with PEAT.

Wherever possible, it is best to simply avoid creating content that uses flashing elements. Beyond the risk of triggering a seizure, they distract the user and generally reduce usability.

When the Flicker *Is* the Content

What about videos of lightning or stroboscopic photography where flickering effects are an essential part of the content? There is very little we can do to change the nature of the content, but we can create an alternate path to the information. The video should be loaded in a stopped state, which is a generally good idea anyway, and a warning should be

---

2. http://trace.wisc.edu/peat/
3. http://shinywhitebox.com/
4. http://www.techsmith.com/camtasia/

added before the video that informs the user about its nature and that people with photosensitivity should not watch. Additionally, we need to provide a transcript of the video that gives the essential information presented in the video. More about transcripts will be discussed later in this chapter in *Describe It to Me*, on page 186.

Act on It!

1. Get a plan in place to have your video tested for flicker.

2. Try out the PEAT tool, and get a feel for how it works on a variety of videos. Note—if you have any suspicion that you yourself are photosensitive, *DO NOT TRY THIS!* (Not that I thought you would.)

| 28 | # Words That Go (Creak) in the Night |

We apologise for the fault in the subtitles. Those responsible have been sacked.
▶ Python (Monty) Pictures Ltd., **Monthy Python and the Holy Grail**

When we make video accessible for the hearing impaired, we do it by providing captions. It is not uncommon for people to mistake subtitles for captions. They *do* seem very much alike visually. Both are text displayed on-screen, either in an "open" format mastered on to the video and always visible or in "closed" format, where the user can control whether the text is visible. The content and intent of the text is where the two differ. Subtitles are meant to provide a translation of foreign language or clarification of mumbled words to someone who is able to hear the audio. Captions, on the other hand, provide an alternate representation of all relevant audio content.

Keeping It Relevant

What do I mean by relevant? What I mean is that, although we need to express the meaning of an audio segment, not every single background sound needs to be (or should be) captioned. We're looking for the sweet spot between too little and too much. Let's look at a caption set that misses the mark for relevance:

Too Little Information:

Don't worry, I'll be there soon.

You worry too much.

Everything's fine.

John.

John.

John.

Hello Mary.

Well, that's nice. It certainly represents dialogue. It doesn't do it very well, though. We have no indication of who is saying what, what their intonations are, or ultimately what is going on. It could be that I'm misleading you, since you don't have any video to go with this. Let's say that I'm not—let's say that the video for this is of a female character, holding a phone and turned three quarters away from camera (that is, you can't see her face). That tells us a little more but not enough to give us a good understanding of what's happening. We'll clearly need to add some more information for this to be a useful group of captions. We can also go too far in the other direction as far as information in captions is concerned:

Too Much Information:

Jeremy: *When we [book dropping] make video*

Jeremy: *accessible for the [cough] hearing*

Jeremy: *impaired, we [sniff] do it by*
[door opening]
[footsteps off camera]

Jeremy: *providing captions.*
[chair sliding]

For the video component, assume you are looking at me facing camera and lecturing. Here we definitely know what's going on in the room. It's enough so that we can put together a reasonable picture that I'm speaking to a room where a book was dropped, someone might have had a cold, and another came into the room and sat down. The more important question is, "Who cares?" Unless these off-screen noises somehow become important to understanding the video, omit them.

Synchronization

Another important aspect of captioning is that the captions be *synchronized*. That is, we want the captions to appear on-screen as closely as possible to the audio elements that are represented. This is particularly important for dramatic videos (see the sidebar on the next page for more on this) but also for informational videos where a significant time lapse can be distracting or otherwise have a negative impact on the viewer's ability to understand the video. If you've ever watched a badly dubbed foreign film where the voices are completely out of time with the actors, you know the effect to which I'm referring. Marking timecodes to use for synchronization is, of course, a long and tedious task.

Don't Spoil the Show

When the content being captioned has a dramatic element, we need to not damage these aspects when we caption it. This means not spoiling the plot or buildup by including important information in the captions that a viewer wouldn't normally have.

For example, we normally identify the speaker, if it isn't clear from the video. Sometimes, it is important to conceal the speaker's identity, however, if they aren't meant to be identified yet. When the identity of a speaker isn't intended to be revealed yet, the caption should still be identified but with something like "off-screen" or "*adjective*ing voice" with an appropriate adjective. That way you aren't ruining the surprise that the mysterious lady in black is really Roy, our hero's long-lost twin uncle.

Similarly, we don't want to ruin a buildup to a climactic event by spoiling the timing of a caption. When the killer is exposed, the winner announced, or the killer of the winner rewarded, the timing of the appropriate caption should match up extremely closely to when spoken in the audio track. If not, the dramatic effect in video of the announcement is lost. If the viewer in need of captions is watching with others who can hear the audio track, it is even more unpleasant for all concerned.

In *On the Cutting-Room Floor*, on page 190, you'll learn about a tool that will help make this a little easier.

Putting It Together

Now we have some basic rules for captioning:

- Every important spoken word should be represented by a caption. Ums, ahs, and other vocal effects that have no impact on the meaning can be ignored.
- If the speaker is unclear, identify them in the caption. If doing so would ruin the content, identify the speaker abstractly (something like "Off-Screen" or "Mysterious Voice").
- Describe any important background sounds, noises, or music.
- Disregard irrelevant background noises.
- Time captions such that they match correctly to video.

With these in hand, let's take a look at our examples from earlier in the chapter. We'll start with our "Too Much Information" example. This is easy to correct, since all we need to do is eliminate the irrelevant background noises. I'm also going to eliminate the repetitive speaker identifier. It wouldn't be harmful to leave it in, but caption space is somewhat limited, and we'd rather not fill it with unnecessary characters. I've also added rough timecodes that can be used to synchronize them with the video. Normally, the timecodes would be synchronized to fractions of a second, but we're not going to worry about that just yet:

Jeremy: *When we make video [00:45]*
accessible for the hearing [00:47]
impaired, we do it by [00:50]
providing captions [00:52]

Much better. We're now representing the essential characteristics of what is being said in a clear manner. What about our example of too little information? That requires interpreting the story as it exists with the audio available. We need to know which characters are speaking the lines and how they are being spoken. Let's take another look:

John: *Don't worry, I'll be there soon. [15:36]*

Mary: *You worry too much. [15:42]*
Everything's fine! [15:45]
[glass breaking over the phone][15:47]
[gunshot][15:49]

Mary: *John? [15:55]*
[Loudly] John? [15:58]
[Screaming] John! [16:01]
♪Suspenseful Music♪[16:04]

Voice: *[Snidely] Hello Mary...[16:07]*

That makes a significant difference. Instead of a series of disconnected phrases, we now have captions that give the whole picture of the audio track. As we can see, captioning is as much art as science, and there are a lot of decisions to make when creating good ones. We have just scratched the surface of this art, and it can take years or more to reach mastery at captioning. If you are generating a lot of captioned audio, it is likely that you will want to bring in a captioning specialist with experience in reinterpreting audio as text.

> **Unattended Video**
>
> Unattended web cameras that provide frequently or continuously updated content are essentially impossible to make truly accessible. When we work with one of these, we should provide a general description of what is being captured, such as "Live video feed of the site of our new building." This does *not* apply to attended cameras at live events, however, because nothing prevents providing alternate content. See the sidebar on page 200 for more information.

At this point, you may be wondering about creating an alternate page with the caption information for people who can't access the video. If you *have* thought about this, I applaud you for it—you're beginning to think accessibly. Hold off on the thought for now, though. If you're going to provide that alternate script, the captions aren't quite enough. We also need the information that we'll look at in the next tip.

Act on It!

1. Watch some captioned video with sound turned on. Try to get a feel for what the captioner is looking for in the soundtrack.

2. Try writing captions for a short piece of video with captions turned off. Watch again with them turned on, and note the differences.

| 29 | Describe It to Me |

Let these describe the indescribable.
▶ Lord Byron

Captions take care of presenting video with audio for the hearing impaired, but we also need to look at what we need to do to video for the vision impaired. Auditory descriptions are our tool of choice for creating an alternate path to essential visual information. Auditory descriptions are voiceovers that can be presented as an alternate audio track or dubbed onto the primary audio channel. In the television world, you might periodically see a reference to Second Audio Program (SAP) along with the closed caption, stereo, surround, and other notes at the beginning of the show. If you turn on SAP with your set, you should hear the auditory descriptions for the show. When we create these for our videos, there are similar rules to those of captioning with regard to relevance.

Saying What Needs to be Said...

...and no more is our rule for auditory descriptions. Where possible, we want to interleave the auditory descriptions with the primary audio content. This means we need to get in the essentials rather quickly and avoid describing every little detail of the scene. In the previous tip, we looked at and corrected some poorly written captions. Like a visually impaired user, we didn't have any of the video context to add to our understanding of the story. Because we can't actually look at the video of John and Mary's story (if for no other reason that it doesn't actually exist), we'll need to improvise a little. Let's take another look at the story, with a narrator filling in the gaps:

John: *Don't worry, I'll be there soon.*

Narrator: *Mary sits back, taking a drink.*

Mary: *You worry too much. Everything's fine!*

Narrator: *Mary jumps, drops the phone, and picks it back up.*

Mary: *John? John? John!*

Voice: *Hello Mary...*

Narrator: *The lights go out in the room.*

What we have now is dialogue added into the audio that captures the essential blocking information as it would have appeared in the original screenplay for our scene. Something that you might notice is that the timecodes for the narrator are sometimes very close to the spoken dialogue. Unlike captions, when we work with auditory descriptions, we are adding an alternate representation to a channel that is already in use. Many times we'll be lucky and find gaps in the audio where we can insert the narration. Other times, we may have to fade down a piece of background music to make room. In the worst case, there is no place to fit the description, and we may have to edit in a pause to fit the auditory description. This can be difficult with preproduced content, but if we're producing new content, it may be more straightforward. There are examples of video where no reasonable pause will take care of the problem, however, and we'll need to be a little more creative.

When There Is Too Much for Auditory Description to Say

Certain kinds of technical content may require more auditory description than can be reasonably inserted into a pause in the audio. One option is to master an alternate copy of the video with long narrations inserted at appropriate points. I don't like this option, but sometimes that is the best we can do. For web-based video, we have another option, however. We can take the long content description and call it out from another location in a manner similar to long descriptions for images as discussed in *More Than alt= Can Say*, on page 163. Let's look at an example where we might want to use this technique:

Jeremy: *Not bad. It certainly represents the content, but in a browser, it doesn't look anything like a chart. If we want to define this as a special class of list and build some CSS styles, we'll get there, though.*

Narrator: *Jeremy writes on the board*
.Chart {
text-align: center;
height: 230px;
border: 1px solid black;
background-color: #8ad;
...

I refuse to go further—that road leads only toward pain and suffering. Our day certainly has gone wrong at this point, hasn't it? Especially when you stop to consider that this is *spoken*, so we're actually looking at something like "dot capital 'c' chart open brace new line text hyphen align colon." It's long-winded *and* nearly useless to our audience. Let's approach this from another direction. Being read the code by a narrator without fine-grained navigation or speed control isn't likely to be very useful anyway, so let's take the code description out of the video entirely. Instead, we can extract the code example out to a separate page that we'll call "Example 1." Then we would add an explanation to the introduction that points the user to the code examples. That done, let's give the auditory description another try:

Jeremy: *Not bad. It certainly represents the content, but in a browser, it doesn't look anything like a chart. If we want to define this as a special class of list and build some CSS styles, we'll get there.*

Narrator: *Jeremy writes Example 1 on the board. Please pause and review the code.*

Now we have a way to get the viewer to the code and let them review it at their own pace before returning to the video. As a matter of form, we should make sure that, with notification, the code opens to another window so the viewer doesn't lose their place in the video.

Extra-Strength Transcripts

If you consider the example of our friends John and Mary earlier in the chapter, you should notice that we have pretty comprehensively described all of the essential content of the video. This makes sense, because we have a complete script with all of the dialogue and blocking. Since we have it anyway, why not put in a little more effort to put it together into a stand-alone transcript that we can provide alongside the captioned auditorily described video as another alternate path to the content? This is, in fact, nearly trivial if we have the original script that the video was created from, rather than having to work backward from a finished video. When we combine the dialog from our captions with sound information from our auditory descriptions into a stand-alone transcript, we get something like this for users who can't access our video at all:

John: *Don't worry, I'll be there soon.*

Mary: *[sitting back, taking a drink]*
You worry too much. Everything's fine!
[glass breaking and a gunshot are heard over the phone]
[Mary jumps, drops the phone, and picks it back up]

Mary: *John?*
[Loudly] John?
[Screaming] John!
♪Suspenseful Music Plays♪

Voice: *[Snidely] Hello Mary…*
[Lights go out in the room.]

In the last two tips, we've learned what the essential characteristics of captioning and audio description are. As with captioning, auditory description is a topic that runs deep, and there are many people who have devoted their careers to it. If you are producing more than a small handful of videos, you may want to seek these professionals out and consult with them about your projects. If you need to develop only a small amount of video, then you may want to handle it yourself. Either way, we eventually need to combine all this information into something that we can publish for our users. In the next tip, we'll learn about tools and formats to get the rest of the way there.

Act on It!

1. Try writing auditory descriptions for a short piece of video (that has auditory descriptions) with the second audio program turned off. Watch again with them turned on, and note the differences between your version and theirs. Try this experiment a few times to get a feel for what is being done.

2. Find a piece of video that is captioned and auditorily described. Try your hand at generating a full-scale transcript for the video (or at least a few minutes of it).

30 On the Cutting-Room Floor

Batteries not included, some assembly required.
▶ Unknown

Once we have created good captions and auditory descriptions that clearly describe our video content, we're only part of the way there. We need a way to combine these with their video asset to present them to our users. Unfortunately, our methods for connecting alternative representations to video aren't as simple and straightforward as they were for static images. There are many ways to go about synchronizing the final content depending on the format we are using, and each has different benefits and drawbacks. Let's take a look at some of the more common formats and how we can use them to connect our captions and descriptions for the clip about John and Mary from the previous two tips.

A Cornucopia of Formats

The format you select will depend largely on your targeted media format. Each one has a preferred captioning format, and there has been little standardization across media players. Even SMIL, described later, relies on implementation-specific technologies. If you intend to support multiple formats, it may be preferable to use an internal format and then use text- or XML-processing tools to convert it to the appropriate format when needed.

The commonalities between formats are greater than the differences, however. All of them require the same pieces of information for each caption:

- The timecode at which the caption occurs
- For spoken words, the current speaker, if it has changed or is otherwise unclear
- The text of the caption representing spoken words, sound effects, or music

With this in mind, let's take a look at some formats.

Simple Subtitling Formats

A family of similar subtitling formats is available that is simple to produce captions in, but the group provides very little in the way of formatting control and no capacity for auditory description inclusion.

A Matter of Quality

Because captioning is a completely alternate access path to a piece of content, it needs to be correct and of high quality. There is a fair amount of debate out there as to what the quality standard should be, however. Some captioning firms make a "99% correct" guarantee. We need to ask ourselves what that really means and whether that is a good measure of quality.

Often, the correctness mentioned is in terms of misspelled or incorrect words. There are two major problems with this. First, there are a *lot* of words in a piece of captioning, which means that small percentages compound. This sidebar, for example, contains 230 words. If 1 percent of them were wrong by this standard, that would mean three words are either incorrect or misspelled. Would you consider this book to be of high quality if one word per paragraph were incorrect?

A second issue is that not all words are equal. Certain parts of a caption *must* be spot on, or the whole caption is worthless. If we caption "John and Mary seem to be in trouble" as "John nd Mary seem be in trouble," the caption is a little difficult to understand but is still effectively functional. On the other hand, if we caption "We find the defendant not guilty" as "We find teh defendant guilty," we have a serious problem.

The common aspects are that they use blank line–separated blocks that may or may not include a caption number, a separated timecode range, and multiple lines of captioning. The general format looks like this:

```
[caption number for some formats]
[starting timecode][separator][ending timecode]
[first caption line]
[second caption line]

[next caption begins after a blank line]
```

Although there are differences in the variations, they can generally be translated back and forth with simple text replacement. The SubRip[5] SRT format and SubViewer[6] SUB formats are two commonly used variants of this type. The variant that we're going to look at is the one

---

5. http://zuggy.wz.cz/
6. http://www.dado.be/subviewer.Asp

used to caption Google Video content.[7] This variant does not use caption numbering and separates start and end timecodes with a comma. Here's our example with John and Mary:

```
00:15:36.000,00:15:39.000
John: Don't worry, I'll be there soon.

00:15:42.000,00:15:44.000
Mary: You worry too much.

00:15:45.000,00:15:46.500
Everything's Fine!

00:15:47.000,00:15:48.500
[glass breaking over the phone]

00:15:49.000,00:15:51.000
[gunshot]

00:15:55.000,00:15:57.000
Mary: John?

00:15:58.000,00:16:00.000
[Loudly] John?

00:16:01.000,00:16:03.500
[Screaming] John!

00:16:04.000,00:16:06.500
♪Suspenseful Music♪

00:16:07.000,00:16:09.000
Voice [Snidely]: Hello Mary...

00:16:12.000
```

Take note of the "blank" timecode at the end. If this isn't placed, the last text caption would stay on-screen until the end of the video. Although the caption before it *should* last only the specified length, some software that uses these formats ignores the end timecode and holds the caption on-screen until replaced by the next (a behavior that should normally result only from leaving the end timecode blank). To ensure that it behaves, I usually add a blank timecode at the end to make sure the caption doesn't stick around for the rest of the video. As I said earlier, this type of format gets the job done in a simple way. On the other

---

7. http://video.google.com/support/bin/answer.py?answer=26577

hand, the price of simplicity is that we have very little control over the presentation of the captions relative to other formats.

SAMI

Microsoft's Synchronized Accessible Media Interchange (SAMI) format is the method of choice for working with captions if you're targeting Windows Media Player as your video output format of choice. SAMI provides an HTML-like format with some CSS styling as well as the ability to specify multiple language captions. The form of CSS that is available in SAMI is limited, allowing only basic alignment and font-styling selectors to the <p> tag. Additionally, CSS classes are permitted only to specify language alternatives.

In the SAMI version of our example, I have chosen to provide English and Spanish captioning, identified as ENUSCC and ESCC, respectively. Each caption, identified by the <sync> tag, uses the start= attribute to specify the timecode. Rather than a format based on hours, minutes, seconds, and fractions of a second, SAMI uses milliseconds from the beginning of the video as its synchronization time. Let's see it:

```
<sami>
<head>
  <title>Title Goes Here</title>
  <style type="text/css"><!--
    P {text-align: center;
       font-family: sans-serif;
       font-size: 1.5em;}
    .ENUSCC   {Name: English; lang: en-US;}
    .ESCC     {Name: Español; lang: es;}
  --></style>
</head>
<body>
  <sync start=0>
    <p class='ENUSCC'> </p>
    <p class='ESCC'> </p>
  </sync>
  <sync start='936000'>
    <p class='ENUSCC'>John: Don't worry, I'll be there soon.</p>
    <p class='ESCC'>John: No preocuparte, yo estará allí pronto.</p>
  </sync>
  <sync start='942000'>
    <p class='ENUSCC'>Mary: You worry too much.</p>
    <p class='ESCC'>Mary: Te preocupas demasiado.</p>
  </sync>
  <sync start='945000'>
    <p class='ENUSCC'>Everything's Fine!</p>
    <p class='ESCC'>&iexcl;Todo muy bien!</p>
  </sync>
```

```
<sync start='947000'>
  <p class='ENUSCC'><i>[glass breaking over the phone]</i></p>
  <p class='ESCC'><i>[cristal que se rompe sobre el teléfono]</i></p>
</sync>
<sync start='949000'>
  <p class='ENUSCC'><i>[gunshot]</p>
  <p class='ESCC'><i>[tiro]</i></p>
</sync>
<sync start='955000'>
  <p class='ENUSCC'>Mary: John?</p>
  <p class='ESCC'>Mary: &iquest;John?</p>
</sync>
<sync start='958000'>
  <p class='ENUSCC'><i>[Loudly]</i>John?</p>
  <p class='ESCC'><i>[en alta voz]</i>&iquest;John?</p>
</sync>
<sync start='961000'>
  <p class='ENUSCC'><i>[Screaming]</i>John!</p>
  <p class='ESCC'><i>[griterío]</i>&iexcl;John!</p>
</sync>
<sync start='964000'>
  <p class='ENUSCC'><i>&#9834;Suspenseful Music&#9834;</i></p>
  <p class='ESCC'><i>&#9834;Música Suspenseful&#9834;</i></p>
</sync>
<sync start='967000'>
  <p class='ENUSCC'>Voice <i>[Snidely]</i>: Hello Mary...</p>
  <p class='ESCC'>Voz <i>[Snidely]</i>: Hola Mary...</p>
</sync>
<sync start='972000'>
  <p class='ENUSCC'> </p>
  <p class='ESCC'> </p>
</sync>
</body>
</sami>
```

We finish the caption sequence with blank caption as we did with the simple subtitle format. Because SAMI doesn't specify a finish timecode, however, this is a required step to clear out the last caption rather than a move to ensure compatibility. SAMI has the advantage over simple formats by supporting HTML <i> and <b> for formatting the caption text.[8] For more information about the SAMI format, including which tags are available for formatting, you can look at the MSDN article "Understanding SAMI 1.0."[9]

---

8. I've been asked whether it bothers me that subtitle formats use formatting-oriented tags rather than something more semantic. Not so much. The captions themselves are presented in a visual manner, and I provide transcripts that are tagged semantically.

9. http://msdn2.microsoft.com/en-us/library/ms971327.aspx

QuickText

If you distribute your video in one of Apple's QuickTime formats, you will need to become familiar with the QuickText captioning format. QuickText provides formatting via braced parameters such as {italic}, {bold}, and {plain}. Each of these parameters is active until another parameter changes it—in other words, if you apply {bold} in one caption and {italic} in the next, that caption and everything following it will be bold, italicized text until you issue {plain}. As we have seen before, a final timecode is entered to turn the last caption off. Unlike other formats, however, a second timecode is placed at the end that specifies the length of the video. This second timecode is used to create a text track of the same length as the video being captioned. Let's take a closer look:

```
{QTtext}
{font: Helvetica}{justify: center}{size: 18}{backcolor:0, 0, 0}
{timescale: 30}
{width: 320}{height: 120}
[00:15:36.00] {italic}John:{plain} Don't worry, I'll be there soon.
[00:15:42.00] {italic}Mary:{plain} You worry too much.
[00:15:45.00] Everything's Fine!
[00:15:47.00] {italic}[glass breaking over the phone]{plain}
[00:15:49.00] {italic}[gunshot]{plain}
[00:15:55.00] {italic}Mary:{plain} John?
[00:15:58.00] {italic}[Loudly]{plain} John?
[00:16:01.00] {italic}[Screaming]{plain} John!
[00:16:04.00] {italic}[Suspenseful Music]{plain}
[00:16:07.00] {italic}Voice [snidely]:{plain} Hello Mary...
[00:16:09.00]
[00:30:00.00]
```

There are two ways to use QuickText. The first is to embed the text track into the video directly. This method requires QuickTime Pro but results in a single distributable file. To do this, you would do the following:

1. Open the QuickText file in QuickTime.
2. Select the entire track, and copy it.
3. In the video to be captioned, use Edit → Add to Movie to overlay the text track.
4. Go to Window → Show Movie Properties. On the Visual Settings tab for the text track, change the vertical offset to match the height of your video.
5. Save or export a merged copy of the video.

If you would prefer to keep the captions and video in separate files, you would want to use SMIL to merge the QuickText captions.

SMIL

The Synchronized Multimedia Integration Language (SMIL) format is
W3C's solution for a variety of multimedia composition problems including that of adding captions and audio description to video. SMIL is
not a purely stand-alone format, however, because it does not specify
a standard underlying format for its pieces. For example, in the SMIL
version of our example, I specify an MPEG 4 video stream, MP3 audio
for the primary audio and auditory description tracks, and QuickText
for the captioning. These media features may or may not be available
in a given implementation. A certain problem is that the two predom-
inant SMIL players, QuickTime and RealPlayer, support incompatible
captioning formats (QuickText and RealText, respectively). This means
that, if you choose to support users of both players, it will need to be
done through the use of two SMIL files. Here's what the QuickTime one
would look like:

```
<smil>
<head>
  <meta name="title" content="John and Mary" />
  <layout>
    <root-layout background-color="black"
                 height="300" width="320" />
    <region id="video" background-color="black"
            top="0"   left="0" height="240" width="320" />
    <region id="text" background-color="black"
            top="240" left="0" height="60"  width="320" />
  </layout>
</head>
<body>
  <par>
    <!-- Video Track -->
    <video src="JohnAndMaryVideo.m4v" region="video" />
    <!-- Audio Tracks ->
    <switch>
      <audio src="JohnAndMaryAudio_ENUS.mp3"
             system-language="en" />
      <audio src="JohnAndMaryAudio_ES.mp3"
             system-language="es" />
    </switch>
    <!-- Auditory Descriptions -->
    <switch>
      <audio src="JohnAndMaryAD_ENUS.mp3"
             system-language="en" />
      <audio src="JohnAndMaryAD_ES.mp3"
             system-language="es" />
    </switch>
    <!-- Captions -->
    <switch>
```

```
        <textstream src="JohnAndMaryENUS.txt"
                    region="textregion"
                    system-captions="on"
                    system-language="en" />
        <textstream src="JohnAndMaryES.txt"
                    region="textregion"
                    system-captions="on"
                    system-language="es" />
      </switch>
    </par>
  </body>
</smil>
```

There are a couple of features of the file to point out here. First, we have a lot of power in SMIL to specify where the video and captioning are placed. Second, we have the SMIL-specific tags <switch>, <par>, and <seq> (not used in this example). The <switch> tag is used to provide alternatives based on player settings. In the example, it is used to provide multilingual audio and captioning. We also have the ability to control whether the components are played in parallel (<par>) or sequentially (<seq>). Obviously, for captions, we want them in parallel with their associated video, but we may want to separate the video into pieces for production, so <seq> can be used to present the pieces in order.

Timed Text Authoring Format (DXFP)

DXFP is a W3C solution for the distribution and transfer of timed text information. DXFP is intended to be usable as a portable transport format between tools or as a distribution format. In particular, the timed text committee mentions DXFP as a possible standard format for SMIL text tracks. There seems to be very little activity in the direction of actively supporting DXFP in SMIL implementations, but there is one implementation that we'll find *very* useful. In Adobe Flash CS3, a captioning component is included that utilizes DXFP captions. We'll look at this again in *The Many Faces of Flash*, on page 232. For now, let's see how the format compares to what we've seen before.

```
<?xml version="1.0" encoding="UTF-8"?>
<tt xmlns     = "http://www.w3.org/2006/04/ttaf1"
    xmlns:tts = "http://www.w3.org/2006/04/ttaf1#styling"
    xml:lang  = "en">
<head>
  <styling>
    <style id="defaultCaption"
           tts:fontSize     = "12"
           tts:fontFamily   = "SansSerif"
```

```
            tts:fontWeight     = "normal"
            tts:fontStyle      = "normal"
            tts:textDecoration = "none"
            tts:color          = "white"
            tts:backgroundColor = "black"
            tts:textAlign      = "left" />
      </styling>
    </head>
<body style="defaultCaption" id="thebody">
  <div xml:lang="en">
    <p begin="0:15:36.00" end="0:15:39.00">
      <span tts:fontStyle="italic">John</span><br/>
      Don't worry, I'll be there soon.</p>
    <p begin="0:15:42.00" end="0:15:44.00">
      <span tts:fontStyle="italic">Mary</span><br/>
      You worry too much.</p>
    <p begin="0:15:45.00" end="0:15:46.50">
      Everything's Fine!</p>
    <p begin="0:15:47.00" end="0:15:48.50">
      <span tts:fontStyle="italic">[Glass breaking
                            over the phone]</span></p>
    <p begin="0:15:49.00" end="0:15:51.00">
      <span tts:fontStyle="italic">[Gunshot]</span></p>
    <p begin="0:15:55.00" end="0:15:57.00">
      <span tts:fontStyle="italic">Mary</span><br/>
      John?</p>
    <p begin="0:15:58.00" end="0:16:00.00">
      <span tts:fontStyle="italic">[Loudly]</span>
      John?</p>
    <p begin="0:16:01.00" end="0:16:03.50">
      <span tts:fontStyle="italic">[Screaming]</span>
      John!</p>
    <p begin="0:16:04.00" end="0:16:06.50">♪Suspenseful Music♪</p>
    <p begin="0:16:07.00" end="0:16:09.00">
      <span tts:fontStyle="italic" >Voice</span><br/>
      <span tts:fontStyle="italic" >[Snidely]</span>Hello Mary...</p>
    <p begin="0:16:12.00" end="0:55:28.16"></p>
  </div>
</body>
</tt>
```

For the most part, there's very little new to say about DXFP. The style and span information is very much like other captioning formats we've seen. The real benefit of DXFP is the direct support from Flash and the promise of future support in SMIL clients.[10]

---

10. Apple, Microsoft, and RealNetworks are all contributors to the recommendation, so the situation is hopeful.

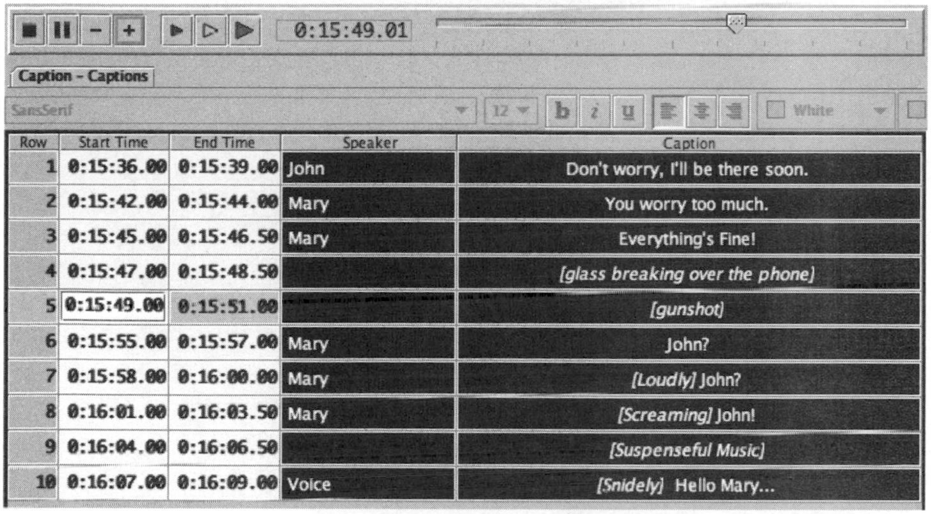

Figure 10.1: CAPTIONING WITH WGBH NCAM's MAGPIE

I've left an important question unanswered until now: "How do we collect all of these timecodes?" Stepping through the video and writing timecodes down in a text document, spreadsheet, or directly into a subtitle format is one option—and I have met people who do this.

MAGpie to the Rescue

You didn't think that I'd *really* leave you there to count timecodes for the rest of your life, did you? In reality you will want to use a subtitling or captioning tool. WGBH's National Center for Accessible Media (NCAM) provides an excellent choice called MAGpie.[11] MAGpie, shown in Figure 10.1, provides a convenient interface for adding captions to video as well as provides tools for recording auditory descriptions. An added benefit is that it stores the information in an internal format that can be exported to plain text for use with simple formats, SAMI, SMIL for QuickTime and RealPlayer, and W3C's Distribution Format Exchange Profile (DFXP), a complex format that can be used with NCAM's CC for Flash,[12] to caption Flash videos.

11. http://ncam.wgbh.org/webaccess/magpie/
12. http://ncam.wgbh.org/webaccess/ccforflash/

Live Broadcasts

Controversy surrounds the issue of live audio and video webcasts. For accessibility, these need to be captioned and transcripted, and ideally, it should be done live with the webcast. For some content providers, this may not be possible, however. If you are a small shop with a small budget, this might qualify as an undue burden. You will want to be absolutely sure of this before you decide against live captioning—that is, talk to your legal counsel. Even if you can't provide live captioning, it is essential that the captioning be added and transcripts be made available as soon as possible after the initial broadcast.

Another issue that comes with real-time captioning is that accuracy of captioning is necessarily lower. This is an understood factor of working in a live environment where there is no time to review and edit the captions before sending them. Before the video is archived for future viewing, however, the captions should be error checked and edited for correctness and clarity.

Extracting Existing Captions

If you are working with large amounts of content that have already been produced as videotape or DVD, it may be possible to extract existing caption work for reuse. You can do this by using caption decoder hardware or a subtitle OCR tool such as SubRip,[13] but keep in mind that this can be a complicated and time-consuming process. It is far better to obtain the original captioning information if at all possible.

We have just covered a *lot* of information about making video accessible. It will take some time to absorb everything that I've said here and put it into practice. I recommend that, before you try to set forth on any major project, you practice with small pieces of video, no more than five or ten minutes at most to get a feel for how the process works.

Oh, and if you were wondering—it turns out that, after a long series of ups, downs, wild plot twists, and mistaken identities, everything turned out well for our friends John and Mary, and they lived happily ever after. Well, *mostly* happily.

---

13. http://zuggy.wz.cz/

You see, Mary is a web developer, and although her web *pages* are fine, she has a pile of scripts and embedded content that aren't doing as well. It's certainly less exciting than gunshots and shattered glass—but much more likely.

Act on It!

1. Try adding captions to short pieces of video using some of the formats described to get a feel for the process.

2. Repeat the first exercise using MAGpie.

Part IV

Putting on Some Additions

Chapter 11

Not All Documents Are Created Equal

We often need to deal with the situation of moving non-HTML content onto the Web, and of course, we need to do it accessibly. The *most* accessible thing we can do is provide the content in HTML. This isn't always as easy as it sounds, however. When the document you're converting to HTML wasn't created with accessibility in mind, the HTML output you get from exporting it may require quite a bit of cleanup work. Although you can't entirely eliminate the cleanup, there is less work involved when the original document is created accessibly. In *Back at the Office*, we'll look at the basics of writing office suite documents that are more ready for conversion to accessible HTML.

When you already have print-ready documents, it is often desirable to use PDF to put them online. Because the document is already finished, it is less appealing to put effort into an HTML alternative, so you might prefer to make the PDF accessible. This decision requires some understanding of what it takes to add accessibility features to the document, and in *PDF: Trying to Make Portable Accessible*, we'll go through the issues involved so you can determine the best route for your project.

A key concept that I would like you to take from this chapter is that most of the basic accessibility principles that are covered in the first three parts of the book haven't changed. We're still looking at the same types of issues and creating solutions using the same basic techniques. The big change is that because we're working with a different document format, the execution of the technique will differ somewhat. As you become more experienced, you should become comfortable applying accessibility principles to many media formats beyond HTML.

31	Back at the Office

*The brain is a wonderful organ. It starts working the
moment you get up in the morning and does not stop until
you get into the office.*
▶ Robert Frost

It is common to receive documents for web placement that were designed in a word-processing, spreadsheet, or presentation application. In most circumstances, we *won't* want to put these online directly. Besides the problem of assuming that the audience has the same software as we do on their system, concerns about harmful macros cause informed users to skip the content if they can. Conversion to HTML should be our preference at all times for office suite documents, but we can do a few things to make the conversion easier.

General Specifics of Accessible Documents

The first steps we need to take with office suite documents are universal across format. We should check all our documents for correct color and contrast usage as described in *Stoplights and Poison Apples*, on page 148, and in *Thinking in Terms of Black and White*, on page 153. If video is embedded in the document, we should either caption it as described in Chapter 10, *Video Killed the Something-Something*, on page 175, or provide an alternate version. Finally, and this shouldn't be surprising, we need to make sure all the informational images in the document have alternative text descriptions.

In OpenOffice.org[1] and the Windows version of Microsoft Office,[2] alternative text is added by selecting the image and opening the picture properties under Format → Picture. In OpenOffice.org, we can find alternative text settings on the Options tab, and in Microsoft Office, it is the only option on the Web tab. Both are shown in Figure 11.1, on the facing page.

Where possible, we would like to continue to reenforce semantic document design. Word processors provide some functionality to do this via styles.

---

1. http://www.openoffice.org/
2. http://office.microsoft.com/ (Alternative text editing is not available in the Macintosh version of Office.)

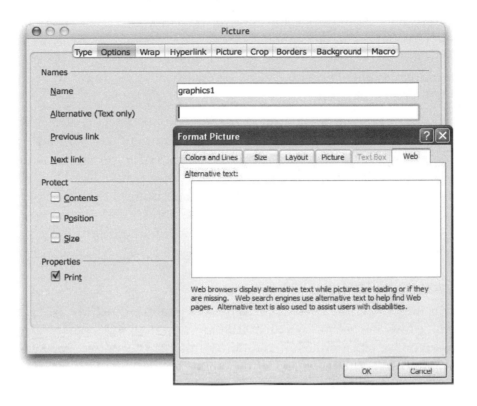

Figure 11.1: ADDING ALTERNATIVE TEXT IN OPENOFFICE.ORG AND MICROSOFT OFFICE (WINDOWS ONLY)

Using consistent styles rather than ad hoc formatting simplifies document creation and makes the document easier to work with after the fact. When it comes time to export the content for the Web, style usage will result in cleaner code. Both OpenOffice.org Writer and Microsoft Word provide a wide variety of built-in styles as well as functionality for defining custom styles in their formatting palettes.

Presentation software poses a different challenge for accessibility. Unlike word processor and spreadsheet documents, presentations represent information *and* a specific way of viewing it. When you produce accessible versions of the presentation for the Web, you need to take a couple of extra steps. First, you need to make transcripts or captions available for any attached spoken audio of the presentation. The other matter is one of presentation. When a presentation is viewed without synchronized audio or captions, in-slide transitions make the presentation less navigable and more difficult to follow. When you place presentations online, you should use a version that has had the in-slide transitions turned off.

You won't always have control over the creation of the documents to be converted. To get accessible document, you may need to make the people who produce them aware of a few issues of accessible document design including color choice, clarity of content, and use of semantic styling in document creation. The document authors often have an easier time when they're provided with templates that have predefined palettes and styles for use on submissions of content targeted for the Web.

Exporting to HTML

Exporting to HTML should be as easy as using the Save as HTML option, but as always, there's a little more to it than that. The HTML produced by office suites is notoriously messy and full of markup intended to duplicate the original document formatting. This HTML will usually need some rework to be what you need for your site and should *always* be checked for accessibility. In particular, any usage of tables will need a fair amount of work to add table headings and the other descriptive aids described in Chapter 7, *Round Tables*, on page 105.

If possible, you might want to have multiple office suites available that handle the same document types, such as OpenOffice.org in addition to Microsoft Office. The various strengths and weaknesses of HTML generation from each differ, and for a given document, you may find that one produces significantly better results.

It's also tempting to put PDF versions of these documents online. Keep in mind that this also has a few problems. First, you're now assuming your audience has a different piece of software, so you shouldn't provide critical path information this way. Second, you will still need to go through most of the accessibility steps mentioned earlier for PDF as well. Finally, as shown in *PDF: Trying to Make Portable Accessible*, on page 210, PDF accessibility isn't necessarily going to make the job easier.

External documents provide challenges to accessibility for the Web, but in general, the principles we use for general web accessibility serve us well when handling these documents. As I said in the beginning of the chapter, it is often simpler to provide HTML wherever possible, but when an external format is necessary, there is much we can do to make that format as accessible as possible.

Act on It!

1. Work through a few HTML conversions from office suite documents with a specific eye toward accessibility.

2. Develop some templates and styles to streamline the process of placing office suite documents online.

3. Educate people responsible for content submission about the use of templates. Some content authors will discover that they prefer to work without worrying about styling the document.

---

32 PDF: Trying to Make Portable Accessible

What gunpowder did for war, the printing press has done for the mind.
  ▶ Wendell Phillips

Adobe's PDF format has become the de facto standard for distributing print type documents on the Web, and it is looking more and more likely that PDF is on the way toward ISO standardization in the near future. PDF won't be going away anytime soon, so we'll need to make sure our PDF content is as accessible as the rest of our web content.

The good news is that if we're comfortable with HTML accessibility, we already know quite a lot about creating accessible PDFs. All of the lessons learned earlier about accessible content design apply directly to PDF accessibility. The difference is in the execution.

There is also some bad news, though—that difference in execution is a *big* one. Because there are so many ways to create PDFs and some are easier to make accessible than others, PDF accessibility is an abstract art, with many changing dependencies. The tools to make PDF accessible can also be a little obtuse, so it won't be quite as straightforward as web accessibility. We'll proceed by assuming that PDF is our only option (though we'll finish off by looking at exporting our PDFs), so our first step is finding out what we have to work with.

Getting Your Bearings

There are a wide variety of tools and techniques for creating PDF output, but most of the time, the PDFs generated fall into three categories:

- *Scanned image*: PDF may be a collection of scanned page images. These PDFs are not at all accessible with screen readers unless some optical character recognition (OCR) work is performed. Because the pages are rendered as bitmap images, they also do not scale well for users who need to zoom in on the page. If you cannot select the text in your document, odds are you're working with scanned pages.

- *Untagged text*: Some PDF output methods directly embed text into the PDF. If the document is entirely text (no images that need alternate text), you *might* be accessible, but this is uncertain—

you would need someone expert in screen reader use to navigate through the PDF to know for certain. Depending on the way the PDF was generated, the PDF text may not be read correctly, so this is clearly a concern. If you can select the text in the PDF, you know it's there. To know whether it's tagged, you'll need to understand what *tagged* means.

- *Tagged PDF*: Tagged PDF is an extension introduced in PDF 1.4 (Acrobat 5) to embed a text-only representation of the PDF content inside the PDF file. These tags are similar to HTML tags that describe the structure of the document. We'll look at creating and editing tags shortly, but first we need to know whether we already have tags. In Acrobat,[3] you can find out whether the document is tagged under File → Properties. The information we're interested in is the bottom line, Tagged PDF. If it says Yes, then we're looking at a tagged PDF. If it doesn't (or if the tagging is incomplete), we'll have to add it ourselves.

For the rest of this section, we'll be starting from the most labor-intensive case and go through the steps of working with a scanned image document.

Obtaining Text for Scanned Images

The first step will be to see where we're at with a basic accessibility check. The basic check is Advanced → Accessibility → Quick Check. With a scanned image, Acrobat will tell us that our document doesn't appear to have any text and suggests that, if it is a scanned image, we can use Document → OCR Text Recognition → Recognize Text Using OCR to add text automatically, so let's do that.

The Recognize Text dialog box contains a few options, as shown in Figure 11.2, on the next page. The one we're most concerned about is PDF Output Style, which tells Acrobat what *kind* of OCR we want. If you want Acrobat to convert the page images into text, you can pick Formatted Text & Graphics. This is also useful for verifying how well the OCR process is working. If you want the PDF to retain the look of the scanned document, Searchable Image will do that, embedding invisible text blocks in the page while retaining the scanned page image. Be warned, however—OCR is a tricky art, and conversions are usually less

---

3. Although there are many tools for working with PDF, I find Acrobat to be the most useful for accessibility-related tasks. I'll be speaking specifically about Acrobat Professional CS3, though the steps I give should apply to most recent versions.

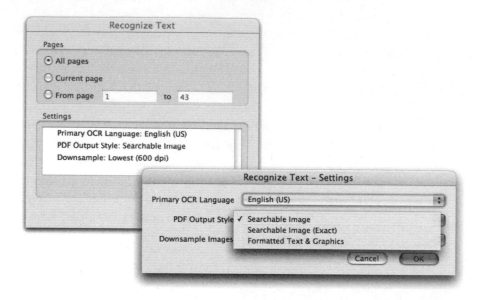

Figure 11.2: USING OCR TO RECOGNIZE TEXT WITH ACROBAT

than perfect. You will probably need to spend some time correcting the output before it's what you want. Let's run Quick Check again. Now Acrobat tells us that the document isn't structured and that the reading order might not be right. What it's actually trying to say is that we don't have PDF tags yet.

Adding Tags to the PDF File

Acrobat can add tags with the action Advanced → Accessibility → Add Tags to Document. After you select this, Acrobat will take over for a while and come back with a recognition report. This report points out aspects of the document that still pose accessibility problems. The most common problems are text that doesn't have a language specification and figures with no alternative text.

Odds are that most of the errors you will see in the accessibility report are from missing language specifications. The report is easier to read if you take care of these first. The language for the entire document can be set on the Advanced tab in File → Properties. If we need a different language setting for a region of the tagged text, we can add that as a property of the tag later.

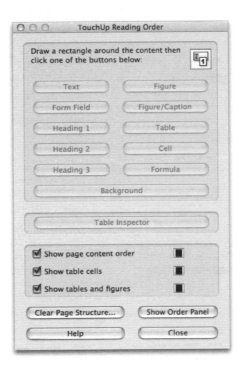

Figure 11.3: WE CAN USE THE TOUCHUP READING ORDER TOOL TO ADD AND ADJUST TAGS.

Figures that don't have alternative text need to be handled one of two ways. If the figure is a decorative image, we'll want to mark it as background (the equivalent of alt=", as described in *To Put It Another Way*, on page 158). For this, we'll need to use Tools → Advanced Editing → TouchUp Reading Order tool, shown in Figure 11.3. If you select the figure and click Background, the object should be marked as decorative content. This is also useful for scanning artifacts that don't convey meaning. You may also have to delete a <Figure> that matches the background artifact. For this, we'll need to know how to edit tags.

The Acrobat Tag Editor

By selecting Show Order Panel from the TouchUp Reading Order tool and selecting the Tags tab, we get the tag editor, shown in Figure 11.4, on the following page. Editing markup in a tree view leaves a little to be desired, but we'll need to make do with what we have. In the editor we

Figure 11.4: THE TAG EDITOR ISN'T NECESSARILY CONVENIENT—BUT IT'S WHAT WE HAVE.

can reorder tags by dragging them around,[4] add or delete tags, or alter the properties of an existing tag. Tag properties are where most of our accessibility work will happen.

By selecting Properties from the Tag Editor's Options menu, we arrive at the TouchUp properties dialog box, shown in Figure 11.5, on the next page. These are the options we're most concerned with:

- *Actual text*: Sometimes text tags are incorrect because of an OCR failure or misspelling. We can place the corrected text here.

---

4. You may have noticed that several of the accessibility steps I've mentioned require the use of pointer input, and this is an accessibility concern in its own right. The topic of accessibility in authoring tools is an important one but beyond the scope of this book. If you are interested in this topic, you might want to look at WCAG's Authoring Tool Accessibility Guidelines at http://www.w3.org/TR/WAI-AUTOOLS/.

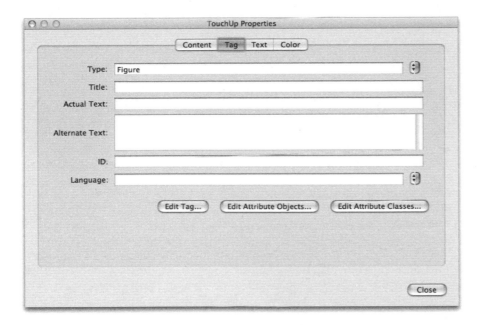

Figure 11.5: THE TAG TOUCHUP PROPERTIES DIALOG BOX IS WHERE MUCH OF OUR ACCESSIBILITY WORK WILL TAKE PLACE.

- *Alternate text*: This is the place where we can add descriptive text for figures in the PDF file that are informational in nature.
- *Language*: If a piece of tagged text is in a different language than the main body content, it should be specified as a tag property.

The amount of work needed to adjust the tags will vary considerably depending on the properties and length of the PDF you are using. If the tags are poor to start with, it will take longer yet. In fact, if the tags are bad enough, you might want to start over by selecting Clear Page Structure from the TouchUp Reading Order tool and selecting and tagging by hand.

Done? Not Quite.

Even after we've been through all of these steps, there's still a little more to do. We need to verify our PDF. The accessibility checker performs some nice tests, but PDFs really should be tested by an actual user with a screen reader to verify that there aren't any subtle problems with the tagging. (Unfortunately, the built-in tool won't do the trick. See the sidebar on the following page.)

Acrobat's Screen Reader

Acrobat comes with a built-in screen reader, available by selecting View → Read Out Loud. If you use this feature to check the PDF tagging, you will notice that it doesn't react to your changes. At this point, it appears that the built-in reader ignores the tagging and reads embedded PDF text instead. To verify your tags, you'll need to export tags and check manually. In a future release, I hope this issue will be resolved and we will be able to use Acrobat's accessibility features to verify PDF's accessibility features.

We can do a little bit of checking before we bring in our tester, though. Exporting the PDF with File → Export → XML 1.0 allows us to do a basic View Source on the PDF tags. If you just want to verify the text substitutions, File → Export → Text → Text (Accessible) will give you the appropriate plain text. Be warned—none of the changes you make to the output files can be reimported into the PDF.

Is All of This Worth It?

At this point, you might be wondering whether it would be better to simply convert the PDF to HTML. This depends on a few things. If you're committed to providing PDF, then obviously this isn't an option. If HTML is a viable option, you might find that easier to implement, however. The third option is to provide both. Before you remind me not to get WET, let me point out that PDF tagging already screams of nearly writing the document a second time anyway, particularly if the automatic tagging doesn't work out well.

Another consideration is that not all of your users will have the ability to work with PDF, tagged or not. If the information in the PDF is critical to the value of your site, working with an HTML representation may be the best solution. Ultimately these are decisions that you will have to weigh project by project.

PDF is here to stay, so we'll need to make sure we use it in an accessible way. Whether we use PDF accessibility features directly or export the document's contents to provide an HTML alternative, understanding accessibility tools for PDF allows us to provide the information in these documents in a more useful way for our audience.

Act on It!

1. Grab a PDF (preferably one you didn't create), and walk through the steps of adding accessibility features.

2. Run OCR on a scanned image PDF using both Searchable Image and Formatted Text & Graphics to get a feel for the differences.

3. Use PDF tools to build a few HTML versions, and decide for yourself whether you find it best to work directly in PDF or build an HTML alternative.

It is the framework that changes with each new technology and not just the picture within the frame.
  ► Marshall McLuhan

Chapter 12

Scripted Responses

JavaScript has grown to be an essential component of web development...except that it isn't really—there are many times it isn't even an *available* component of web development. JavaScript suffers from a bit of a chicken-and-egg problem. Not every browser supports scripting, and those that do have no guarantee that it'll be enabled. This leaves us in the position of needing to create sites that are completely functional without JavaScript and enhance themselves with scripting for people who can use it.

There's an old Irish proverb that says it's far better to make a good retreat than to take a bad stand. This is exactly how we need to treat our scripted interactions, and the notion of scripts that step aside without taking the site's functionality with them is the topic of *Unassuming Scripts*. We'll also discuss the philosophy of progressive enhancement and how it lets us provide the best possible experience for both audiences. JavaScript has become a powerful language at this point and has been around long enough that some developers have attained deep expertise in the language. These developers have begun to step to the next level and stretch our notion of what JavaScript is useful for. In *Higher-Order Scripts*, we'll briefly look at what this means for accessibility—and some of the news may be very good indeed.

The thing we *won't* be doing in this chapter is learning JavaScript. I'm not one of the deep JavaScript experts that I mentioned, so I won't pretend to be. If you want to develop a good understanding of the depths of JavaScript, I recommend David Flanagan's *JavaScript: The Definitive Guide* [Fla06] and Jeremy Keith's *DOM Scripting: Web Design with JavaScript and the Document Object Model.* [Kei05]

33   Unassuming Scripts

User-centered design means understanding what your users need, how they think, and how they behave—and incorporating that understanding into every aspect of your process.

    ▶ Jesse J. Garrett, **The Nine Pillars of Successful Web Teams**

JavaScript puts us in a tough position sometimes. It gives us the opportunity to enhance user interactions with our site. At the same time, we don't know whether a given user has scripting available or whether it's enabled when they *do* have it. Further, even if the scripting is there, we still have to remember that we can assume only that our users have access to some equivalent to keyboard access.

Ultimately we need our scripted pages to satisfy three properties:

- Scripts should be designed with the same separation of concerns that we use for styles.
- Pages can't rely on the presence of a specific input device.
- The page needs to function without scripts.

First up, let's see how broken separation of concerns indicates a likely accessibility problem.

Signs of Script Problems

How do we know whether scripts are causing an accessibility problem? The obvious test is to turn off scripting in our browser and load our site. If it doesn't work anymore, we have a problem. Similarly, if we block unrequested pop-up windows and essential functionality disappears from our site, scripts are killing our accessibility. There are also a few common bad smells we should watch for that regularly show up in the source of pages with accessibility problems.

Pages that maintain the separation of concerns necessary for accessibility also usually keep their code in a separate resource. This means seeing a lot of <script src='...'> elements, usually nicely grouped together. On the other hand, if we find reams of inline code scattered through the file, odds are good that the page doesn't function well if those scripts don't run.

The best signs of scripting gone wrong are a horrible group of three bad habits that showed up in the early days of JavaScript, and all three of them hang around the anchor element:

- `<a href='...' onclick='[intensely long script here]'>`: Long scripts inside event handlers isn't a direct accessibility problem in its own right, but like massive inline script blocks, it's a good sign that the script is too tightly bound to the content for the page to function properly without it.

- `<a href='javascript: func(...)'>`: This one is wrong on so many levels that it's painful to even bring it up.[1] First up, a JavaScript function isn't a location, so it has no business at all being in an href= attribute. This also makes the worst assumption possible—if JavaScript isn't available, this link is either going to do nothing or send the user to a malformed URL. Either way, it's Bad News for your users.

- `<a href='#' onclick='...'>`: The "empty" href='#' attribute shares the previously mentioned problem of assuming the presence of Java-Script. The underlying intent of the # is a bit more subtle, however. This link construct executes the event handler and then activates the URL assigned to the href= attribute. At some point, someone noticed that by targeting the blank named anchor, href='#', the browser wouldn't do anything. Many tutorials and references were written that described this method. A better way to get this behavior is to add return false; to the end of the event handler. By returning false, we can prevent the browser from following the link. As we will see below in *Higher-Order Scripts*, on page 224, this is one of the first steps to building higher-order scripts that maintain accessibility.

Avoiding Event Lockout

JavaScript interaction is based around providing handlers for device events. By relying exclusively on handlers for a specific input type, sites are rendered inaccessible to people who don't have the ability to use that device. The two general types of device are pointers and keyboards. As usual, however, we can assume only that the user has a keyboard equivalent device.

---

1. And in fact I wasn't going to until someone passed me a recently written JavaScript tutorial that actually recommended exactly this usage.

This doesn't mean we shouldn't support the mouse at all—after all, some users with mobility impairments may have more difficulties with keyboards than with pointers—what we really need to do is provide support for multiple devices.

Whenever you find yourself writing an event for a pointer event, you need to make sure the same functionality is available with a keyboard triggered event as well. The only exception to this would be where a function isn't essential for interacting with the site or the functionality is available without an event handler. The shopping cart in *Higher-Order Scripts*, on page 224, is an example of this. The drag-and-drop feature presented would require mouse events, but the provided link can be activated without an event handler.

Two JavaScript events need special consideration in terms of accessibility. The onchange event doesn't always behave as expected, specifically for <select> elements. In some browsers, each time a cursor key moves the selected position of the <select> element, it issues an onchange. This means that keyboard users can select only the first option in the list. Your choices for working around this are either to add a submit button and avoid onchange or to add handlers for key events to interrupt the onchange event.[2]

The onclick event is also misunderstood to be a pointer-only event. In modern browsers, pressing Return while an item is active results in an onclick, so this event should be considered available to keyboard users as well. If you still aren't comfortable with this, similar functionality can be developed by filtering keyCode with the onkeypress event. The filter is important to make sure you don't inadvertently capture other keyboard events (such as the ones the user might be sending to their assistive technology).

Progressive Enhancement for Graceful Degradation

In conversations about scripting and styling, you will run into the phrases *graceful degradation* and *progressive enhancement*. What we're really talking about here is making sure our pages operate in the best possible fashion for our users. These two ideas approach this goal from opposite directions and will directly influence how we view our usage of scripts.

---

2. One solution for this problem is described by Cameron Adams on the web page at http://www.themaninblue.com/writing/perspective/2004/10/19/.

The perspective of graceful degradation is that pages start out feature-rich. The developer then has to find ways to strike out parts of the style or functionality to allow the page to continue working. We might have to go back and add static links and page refreshes that take the place of scripts that we had previously written to perform a task. The flaw of this perspective is that it puts the blame on the user for not doing what the developer expects them to do.

Progressive enhancement takes the opposite perspective. In this case, we design pages starting with basic content and function. Styling and scripts are then added to the page as additional features and enhance the user experience for the users who are able to use them. This is a more user-centric point of view as well as one that makes accessible development easier to manage.[3]

Ultimately the difference between these two is largely philosophical—you can easily look at progressive enhancement as a great way of implementing graceful degradation and avoid getting into a debate about user-centric vs. developer-centric design. The important key is understanding how pages can be built to function and then customized with extra features. This has become extremely important as we watch the rise of the rich web application, which we'll look at next.

Act on It!

1. Search for href='#' and href='javascript:...' in your source. Eliminate with extreme prejudice.

2. Verify that if you are using device-specific event handlers, you aren't locking users out through your event choices.

3. Can you still use your site if JavaScript is turned off? If not, step back and make it work using the principles of progressive enhancement to bring in the scripted features.

---

3. That is why I recommend this kind of process in *Testing As a Design Decision*, on page 58.

34   Higher-Order Scripts

This is the approach of stratified design, the notion that a complex system should be structured as a sequence of levels that are described using a sequence of languages.
  ► Harold Abelson and Gerald J. Sussman, **The Structure and Interpretation of Computer Programs**

The latest concern for web accessibility professionals is the utilization of higher-order script techniques. I'm using the phrase *higher-order* to refer to JavaScript frameworks that are used to implement rich web interfaces including those use the Ajax approach.[4] From my perspective, most of the concern stems from that JavaScript has usually meant inaccessibility, so higher-order scripting can only compound the problem. That doesn't have to be the case, however, and there are a few accessibility positive results of higher-order scripting to consider.

We need to cut the hype, though—and there's a lot of it. People have credited higher-order techniques with everything from bringing applications to the Web (which it's about ten years too late to have done) to completely reinterpreting the design of the Web (insert version number here). The reality is that we're still just talking about a pile of tags and scripts. That's it. That's also where bringing accessibility to higher-order scripting is a win for everyone—it's already well on the way.

Higher-Order Accessibility

Most of the magic of higher-order scripting lies in manipulation of the page's Document Object Model (DOM). For this to work well, the HTML should be designed using clean semantics and standards-based markup. It's also better if the presentation is moved out into CSS rules that apply to the semantics and markup of the page design—is this sounding familiar yet? If we add the principle of progressive enhancement to what already needs to be done to let the scripting work, we're already well on our way to accessible higher-order scripting.

The first question I get about this is "How can my application provide these rich interfaces and not require JavaScript?" Essentially it can't—

---

4. Ajax has been used to refer to all types of higher-order scripting, but I think this does a disservice to the asynchronous model described in "Ajax: A New Approach to Web Applications" (http://www.adaptivepath.com/ideas/essays/archives/000385.php) by Jesse James Garrett, so I'll use "Ajax" only to refer to that particular practice.

the real goal is to provide the highest-quality interactions that you can *without* JavaScript and enhance that model with script handlers for the people who can use them.

The essential tool for achieving this is understanding the difference between <a href='#' onclick='[do something]'> and <a href='[URL]' onclick= '[do something and return false]'>. When scripts are available in the browser, these behave identically (except in the second version, where you don't have the # character magically appearing in the URL all the time—another bonus). When scripts are turned *off*, the user is directed to the URL assigned to href=. This means we now know the user doesn't have scripting, so we can react by doing things through basic page flipping. It may not be as exciting as an automatically updating application, but it's much more useful than being blocked from the application because of enhanced features. Now we have the best of both worlds—we can add features for users who can use them without shutting out parts of our audience. Using progressive enhancement in this way takes us a long way toward accessibility, but there are a few other issues we should consider.

Ajax: Across the State Line

The *A* in Ajax means *asynchronous*. This refers to the use of the XML-HttpRequest object to send and receive information without triggering a page refresh. This makes web applications appear to behave more like conventional desktop applications. It can also lead to some confusion for your users, however. Because the convention thus far has been for pages to refresh on actions, some users find that Ajax applications don't feel like they're doing anything. Additionally, screen readers generally don't refresh their view of the page when an update occurs, so these page transitions may go unnoticed for users with visual impairments.[5] Three interim solutions to this problem come to mind:

- *Use visual or aural feedback to indicate page updates*: This helps the users who are simply unused to Ajax pages, but it doesn't resolve the screen reader refresh problem; therefore, this might be a useful addition, but we'll need to go further.
- *Explain to the user that the page automatically refreshes its content and how they can initiate a reload or turn off JavaScript if they're*

---

5. And the history of screen reader support for the Web doesn't necessarily give hope that support will be coming rapidly.

> *using a screen reader*: Yeah, right. If you do this, I can explain to you why your screen reader–using audience thinks you're out of your mind. Remember that most of your users with disabilities fit the same profile as the general user populace. Many of your users are going to give up and leave if you start trying to explain JavaScript, Ajax, and stateful web applications to them. Remember that it's still *their* browser—and they're likely to be uncomfortable messing around with its settings.

- *Make a preference clearly available that allows users to select page refresh mode if they're using a screen reader or simply prefer to use the other version*: This isn't ideal—I really don't like the idea of asking the user to "turn on" accessibility, but I also don't see another clear path at this point in time.

Clearly, none of these solutions is *ideal*, but until screen readers adapt, we need to be ready to do what we can to assure an accessible experience for our users.

Multiple Inputs: It Doesn't Always Have to Be a Drag

Higher-order scripting has brought with it a wave of draggable interfaces. Without getting into a debate whether drag-and-drop interfaces are the best solution,[6] let's look at what we can do to make them accessible. If we've been progressively enhancing our sites, we already have a solution. Somewhere in the early phases, the interface will have had a standard link. If we retain these links, we can also open access to keyboard interfaces.

Consider the shopping cart examples in Figure 8.2, on page 141, and in Figure 8.3, on page 142. There is no reason we can't have the hybrid interface shown in Figure 12.1, on the next page. Better yet, since the first interface should have been enhanced into the second, we should effectively get it for free.

As another example, look at the interfaces in Figure 12.2, on page 228. These are designs for ranking authors by preference. In the first design, we simply have a collection of draggable elements. In the second, by adding "move up" and "move down" arrows, we do two things. We have enabled keyboard access by having links that can be activated, but we've also added indicators that signal that those items can be reordered.

---

6. If you have already read *Your Interface Has Some Explaining to Do*, on page 140, you've seen my opinion on the matter.

Figure 12.1: A HYBRID CART DESIGN OFFERS DRAG-AND-DROP OR BUT-
TON FUNCTIONALITY AND LETS THE USER DECIDE WHICH IS MORE USEFUL.

Overall, the second interface is better for all of your audience. Again, if you built a basic version and enhanced it with the draggable interface, having the links should simply be a matter of not getting rid of them.

When I've presented this interface, I've usually been asked whether reordering a list that way could be a little tedious. This is a valid point—there may be a better interface yet. That isn't the point, though. Although the link interface might be more inconvenient than the draggable interface, both are vastly better than not being able to interact with the list at all, which is what we subject some of our users to when we don't provide both solutions.

Letting Someone Else Help with the Heavy Lifting

Another nice characteristic of higher-order scripting is that the techniques are complex enough that we're beginning to see a number of APIs showing up that take care of the details. The presence of an API doesn't guarantee anything about accessibility, but when the API *is* designed for accessibility, it makes our lives as developers significantly easier.

Your Ranking		Your Ranking
Snicket		⬍ Snicket
Milne		⬍ Milne
Rowling		⬍ Rowling
Gaiman		⬍ Gaiman
Black		⬍ Black

Figure 12.2: DRAG-AND-DROP PREFERENCE RANKING. NOTE THAT THE SECOND EXAMPLE IS ACCESSIBLE BY KEYBOARD, AND IT SIGNALS THAT THE LIST CAN BE REORDERED.

The Yahoo! User Interface Library[7] has displayed a strong commitment to providing accessibility in its components. At this point, the Data-Table, Menu, and Grids components have documented accessibility features and provide significant pieces of useful functionality that would take considerable time to implement and test (and test for accessibility) on our own.

The rise of higher-order scripting has been controversial in accessibility circles, but I'm not sure it needs to be. The basic requirements for these scripts often overlap with accessibility requirements, and the presence of common libraries allows accessibility to be written once and shared by multiple developers. This has great potential to turn into a win across the board if we want. Further, because higher-order scripts are still located within the core browser, we can provide rich accessible applications without worrying about the availability and accessibility of plug-in technologies, which we'll look at next.

---

7. http://developer.yahoo.com/yui/

Act on It!

1. Think locally. Begin to transition toward the philosophy of progressive enhancement if you haven't already.

2. Can your interfaces be accessed without a pointer device? How about without a keyboard? What needs to be done to make this the case?

Isn't it queer: there are only two or three human stories and they go on repeating themselves as fiercely as if they had never happened before; like the larks in this country that have been singing the same five notes over for thousands of years.

▶ Willa Cather, ***O Pioneers!***

Chapter 13

Embedded Applications: Rinse and Repeat

In this chapter, we're going to look at the edge of the Web and discover that our ten principles for web accessibility from back in Chapter 1, *Introduction*, on page 3, can be used for other technologies as well.[1] Embedded applications are an important part of our web content, but most of the time, they don't feel very connected to web development at all. Most of the time, unless we're the one writing the application, we just add an <object> tag, and the application just sits there in our page layout in its own isolated box, providing data access, text chat, or some other functionality.

It's valuable for us to discuss the matter, however. First, the embedded parts often *are* critical pieces of our pages, so we need to understand *how* they can be made accessible. This includes understanding they have to be made accessible from the inside—if you receive a compiled component and it's inaccessible, there's nearly nothing you can do to fix it.

Even more important, embedded applications give us a different venue to look at accessibility. You'll find out in this chapter that all of the ideas and principles from HTML accessibility are applicable here too. We'll actually be spending most of our time looking at the differences in execution. We'll start out by looking at *The Many Faces of Flash* and then repeat the process in *Java: Is Your Brew Fair Trade?*

---

1. In fact, this is principle 10.

35   The Many Faces of Flash

It was the best of times, it was the worst of times.
▶ Charles Dickens, *A Tale of Two Cities*

Flash is a difficult topic for accessibility. On one hand, Flash has a bad reputation from old versions that didn't provide accessibility support and from the proliferation of annoying banner ads with blinking images and uncontrollable audio. On the other, tools like sIFR, described in *alt.text.odds-and-ends*, on page 170, use Flash to enhance the accessibility of web typography. The reality is that Flash is just a tool and can be used well or badly in terms of accessible development. Here, we'll be focusing on Flash CS3—the captioning features alone make this a must-have upgrade for accessible development. All of the basic principles of web accessibility also apply to Flash; it's mostly a matter of finding out where the accessibility information goes. Flash can be looked at in two ways, however. It can be seen as a web media player or as a platform for applications. We'll look at both cases and see what needs to be done. First, however, we need to look at a major caveat to accessible Flash development.

How Accessible Is Single Platform?

A major concern about Flash accessibility is that it is strictly platform restricted. Because Flash uses Microsoft Active Accessibility (MSAA), a bridging component that Windows provides to connect software applications with assistive technologies, accessibility features are available only to users of Microsoft Windows and Internet Explorer. This leaves us in a bad position—because we can't use the built-in accessibility functionality on all platforms that we might like to deploy to, we're left with two options:

- We could add audio overlays that act as a surrogate screen reader. This isn't ideal, but bypassing the need for a screen reader is one viable approach.

- If the functionality is essential to our site, we'll need an alternate form of the content anyway, so we could direct the user to that. This isn't nearly as nice of an approach, but it'll also work.

How this issue needs to be addressed will vary from project to project. For example, if all your Flash usage is as a media player and the controls are keyboard accessible, you may not have to worry about this too

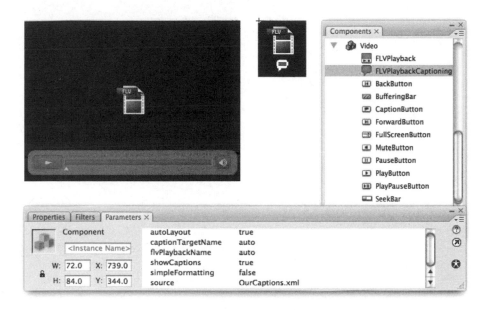

Figure 13.1: EMBEDDING DXFP CAPTIONS WITH THE FLVPLAYBACKCAP-
TIONING COMPONENT

much. On the other hand, if you have a complex application that isn't already self-voicing, you'll have some big decisions to make.

Flash: The Media Player

Because of its widespread availability, Flash is particularly useful for streaming media content. For a long time the problem has been jumping through component and ActionScript hoops to attach good captions to the media. Flash CS3 changes that with the introduction of the FLV-PlaybackCaptioning component. This new component combines with an FLVPlayback component to provide captioning.

The captions are added as an XML file by referencing the file in the source parameter to FLVPlaybackCaptioning, as shown in Figure 13.1. The captions need to be provided in DFXP format, which can be created with the MAGpie tool introduced in *On the Cutting-Room Floor*, on page 190. Flash takes over the heavy lifting at this point, so all you need to do is make sure to let the user control the playback and provide transcript alternatives.

Figure 13.2: ADDING ACCESSIBILITY PROPERTIES TO FLASH MOVIES
(LEFT) AND OBJECTS (RIGHT)

Flash: The Application Environment

When you're working with Flash applications, the job is a little more
complex. We'll need to add some information to describe our components and their order in the application. First up are text descriptions.
To add alternate text, we'll need to open the accessibility properties
viewer (Window → Other Panels → Accessibility), shown in Figure 13.2.
We have a few options here.

The Name and Description fields play the roles of alt= and longdesc=,
detailed in *To Put It Another Way*, on page 158, and in *More Than alt=
Can Say*, on page 163. The Auto Label option will attempt to automatically create text alternatives. Because there is no easy way to verify the
automatic choices, it is probably better to manually specify the alternatives. The Make Child Objects Accessible option should usually be
set unless the object acts as a container and provides alternative text
clearly describing the entire group of objects.

The Shortcut option is easily misunderstood. The content of this field does *not* create a shortcut key; it simply provides text to tell the user what the shortcut is. The actual shortcut key will need to be created separately.

If you've read *Tickling the Keys*, on page 137, you may be surprised to hear me tell you to set the Tab Index option for all available components. In Flash, there is no natural reading order to rely on as in HTML, so we'll have to organize the tab ordering ourselves.

Overall, there's nothing surprising here, just different ways of doing the same things we would with HTML. Flash *does* provide some automation of this process for some components, though. Labeling and keyboard access automation can be enabled by calling enableAccessibility() from ActionScript for the Button, Checkbox, Combo Box, Data Grid, List Box, Radio Button, Text Area, Text Input, and Tile List components. Remember that this functionality is not available by default—the ActionScript call is a necessary step.

A Note About Flex

The Flex framework for developing Flash applications has a similar issue with accessibility being turned off by default. The rationale is that it causes more bandwidth consumption by generating a larger file. If you're worried about bandwidth that much, accessible HTML will save you even more. There are three ways to turn on accessibility for Flex:

- Add ?accessible=true to the URL.

- Pass -accessible to the mxmlc compiler.

- Add <accessible>true</accessible>[2] to the server configuration.

Keep in mind that Flex supports accessibility for core components only under the same platform conditions as Flash. If you develop custom components, you'll need to generate your own MSAA information. Adobe recommends sticking with the included components for this reason.

Flash provides useful tools for web accessibility for distributing media and for deploying applications to environments where users with disabilities access the application with Windows and Internet Explorer. If you are deploying to broader environments, accessible Flash may still

---

2. If only accessibility were *this* easy!

Flash Satay: Quieting the Compliance Tools

One minor annoyance of working with Flash is the HTML used to place it on a page. For cross-browser support, the markup usually uses a combination of <object> and <embed>. Unfortunately, because <embed> isn't standards-compliant markup, your pages with Flash content end up failing validation. Drew McLellan, with some help from Jeffrey Zeldman, developed a clever solution to this problem called Flash Satay.

To load a streamed Flash movie using only <object> in a cross-browser way, we'll need to create a new Flash movie, loader.swf, with this script at frame 1 of the movie's root:

```
_root.loadMovie(_root.path, 0);
```

With this in place, we can load our *real* Flash content with the following:

```
<object type="application/x-shockwave-flash"
        data="loader.swf?path=YourMovie.swf"
        width="600" height="400">
  <param name="movie"
         value="loader.swf?path=YourMovie.swf" />
  <!-- AND you can stick a fallback alternative
       here for browsers that don't support Flash
  -->
</object>
```

And, by using <object>, we have a great location to place alternate content to our Flash file if the user doesn't have Flash installed. For a more detailed development and description of Flash Satay, see Drew McLellan's article "Flash Satay: Embedding Flash While Supporting Standards" (http://www.alistapart.com/articles/flashsatay).

require a fair amount of retooling for self-voicing and may not be as viable. By carefully evaluating your usage to determine whether Flash is the right tool for your content and by applying general accessibility principles, Flash doesn't necessarily have to be the accessibility "hands-off" zone that it once was.

Act on It!

1. Add captions to your Flash videos.
2. Add alternate text and keyboard access to your Flash applications. Better yet, work on making them self-voicing for multiplatform accessibility.
3. Spend a little bandwidth: make sure that your Flex components have built-in component accessibility enabled.

36 | Java: Is Your Brew Fair Trade?

Second verse, same as the first—a little bit louder and a little bit worse.
▶ Traditional

Java doesn't get the amount of buzz as a "web language" as it once did. However, along with Flash, Java is still one of the prominent ways to embed external applications in a web page. More important, Java gives us an opportunity to examine how what we've learned about accessibility applies to other venues. The tools and syntax for making Java applications accessible are different from the ones we use for HTML, but the principles and techniques are the same. All of the concepts covered earlier in the book about clear language, color, contrast, and media preparation apply to Java applications in the same way they did for web pages. We'll be taking a look at what the Java Accessibility API[3] gives us essentially for free, how to add basic accessibility features, and what tools are available to check the accessibility of Java applications.

Getting Something for Nothing (Well—Not for Much)

Because the accessibility API is supported by Swing components, some of our accessibility work is already done for us. Any component that has text attached to it will automatically provide that text to assistive technologies. For example, for these components:

```
JLabel  myLabel  = new JLabel("My Label");
JButton myButton = new JButton("Hello, Java!");
```

assistive technologies will be provided with the information to let the user know that there is a UI label with the text "My Label" and a button titled "Hello, Java!" Not all components have text attached to them, however, and we have ways to work with these as well. First, let's look at alternate text for images—in this case, the ImageIcon class. It is useful to know that, in addition to the plain constructors, there are alternative constructors that take a description parameter as well as a method setDescription() that we can use to provide alternative text:

```
// Why do this:
ImageIcon myImage = new ImageIcon("MyImage.jpg");

// When you can do this instead:
ImageIcon myImage = new ImageIcon("MyImage.jpg",
                                  "Description of My Image");
```

---

3. Found in the package javax.accessibility, accessibility API functionality is implemented into Swing.

```
// And if you need to change the description or if you
// prefer to not to use the constructor:
myImage.setDescription("Updated Description of My Image");
```

The description attribute becomes the alternative text exposed by the accessibility API. What about other components? We can address them through their accessibility context, obtained from the getAccessible-Context() method. The context has methods setAccessibleName() and set-AccessibleDescription that are used to set an associated text label and a functional description of the component:

```
// Get The Accessibility Context so we can set some attributes:
myButtonContext = myButton.getAccessibleContext();

// Explicitly set the name sent to assistive technologies:
myButtonContext.setAccessibleName("Hello, Java!");

// Describe the purpose of the button for the user:
myButtonContext.setAccessibleDescription("Play audio of a cat meowing.");
```

Often, you will find it better to describe the purpose of your components as a tooltip with setToolTipText(), but in cases like the example where sensory modalities come into play, setAccessibleDescription() may be a more appropriate choice.

Custom components can also be handled by the accessibility API, but you'll need to be a little careful in *how* you develop your components. JComponent does not support the accessibility API, so you'll want to inherit from JComponent.AccessibleJComponent instead. The accessibility API can't penetrate through inaccessible containers, however, so you'll also need to avoid using containers that don't implement the Accessible interface. Of course, you always have the option of extending a class and implementing Accessible on your own if that better suits your needs.

Helping Users Navigate

Beyond the functionality of the accessibility API, we can take a few more steps to make an application easier to navigate. In *Getting <form>al*, on page 130, we see the <label> used to tie an on-screen text label to the element to which it refers. JLabel has a setLabelFor() method that we can use to do the same:

```
myField = new JTextField(10);
myLabel = new JLabel("My JTextField:");
myLabel.setLabelFor(myField);
```

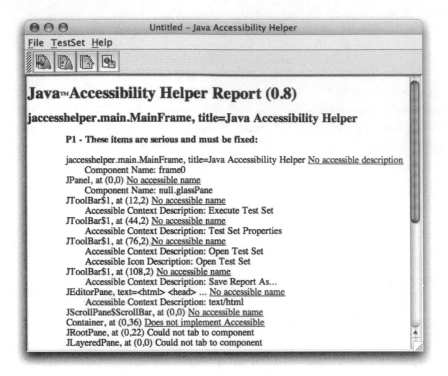

Figure 13.3: THE JAVA ACCESSIBILITY HELPER REPORTS ON ACCESSIBIL-ITY CONCERNS OF MULTIPLE SEVERITIES.

We also look at grouping related components with <fieldset>. In Java, JPanel should be used in a similar way to organize related items into a cohesive whole.

Testing for Accessibility in Java

Even though Java does all of these nice things for us in terms of accessibility, it doesn't eliminate the need to test. Although many of the methods covered in Chapter 5, *Testing for Accessibility*, on page 57, are still useful, none of these tools is. Fortunately, Sun has provided a few that'll keep our code in line:

- *Ferret* is provided with the Java Accessibility Utilities[4] as a way to

---

4. http://java.sun.com/products/jfc/jaccess-1.3/doc/

track the state of an on-screen component. Ferret tracks cursor focus and returns accessibility information about the object at the cursor. This allows manual checking that all components are exposing an appropriate accessible interface.

- *Monkey*, also part of the Java Accessibility Utilities, takes a different approach by tracking through the component tree and displaying comparative information about the actual component and its accessible representation. Monkey also allows you to see places where the Accessible interface isn't implemented, blocking access to child components.

- *Java Accessibility Helper*[5] works similarly to a web standards validator, sweeping through the application searching against a series of accessibility rules. The output, shown in Figure 13.3, on the preceding page, even looks quite a bit like a web evaluation, ranking the severity of observed problems and linking to further information.

As discussed in *Getting Your Hands Dirty*, on page 69, we always want to do plenty of manual testing, preferably involving testers with disabilities at some point in the process.

That covers the basics of getting started with Java accessibility. The important aspect to remember when approaching accessibility for *any* new platform is to leverage the principles you already know, find out what the local dialect is for applying those principles, and stop for a moment to put together the new toolbox necessary for working with the platform.

Act on It!

1. Add Java Accessibility API features to your applications in the places that there is no attached text or a need for greater description. Use the testing tools to check that the accessibility information makes sense.

2. Review the first three parts of this book. Think about how you would apply these ideas to accessible Java application development.

---

5. http://java.sun.com/developer/earlyAccess/jaccesshelper/

Part V

Understanding the Building Codes

Web Content Accessibility Guidelines 1.0

Up to this point, I have made only passing remarks about web accessibility guidelines. I think they are valuable tools but shouldn't dominate our thinking on the topic. In this part, we'll look more closely at the guidelines. We need to do this because many developers, managers, and clients are going to want to talk with us in terms of guidelines. When someone tells you "Guideline X says we need to do Y because of Z," you need to know whether that is true as well as how to respond. This chapter as well as Chapter 15, *Section 508*, on page 263, and Chapter 16, *Web Content Accessibility Guidelines 2.0*, on page 273, present walkthroughs of major guidelines. I'll break down what they're trying to tell us as well as point out where in the book we cover the concepts. If you have been reading the book in order, most of this should look familiar by now. If you've come here straightaway, the discussion will point you in the right direction.

In the beginning, web content was specialized communication between scientists, and HTML was a simple markup language with minimal design. Accessibility of content was easy—there were no images to create alternate text for and no tables to be abused for layout effects. This also meant that there were a lot of things that couldn't be said with web content.

As the web grew in scope and popularity, users wanted more functionality for including media, expressing complex information, and customizing look and feel. Because solutions weren't always provided quickly, developers found workarounds such as table-based layout to get the job done. In addition, competition between browser manufacturers gave rise to nonstandard features that harmed interoperability, and therefore accessibility suffered.

In 1997, W3C launched the Web Accessibility Initiative (WAI) with the goal of creating guidelines and tools to make the web accessible for people with disabilities. Two years later, the Web Content Accessibility Guidelines 1.0 (WCAG 1.0)[1] were made a W3C recommendation. WCAG 1.0 introduces a set of clear guidelines for the production of accessible web content, prioritized by importance and categorized as a series of checkpoints under each guideline. WCAG 1.0 is still the document most often referred to when discussing general principles of web accessibility.

14.1 Checkpoint Priorities

Each of the checkpoints in WCAG 1.0 is assigned a priority level. The priority level designates how critical the checkpoint is and signifies how comprehensively the guideline has been addressed. The level of conformance to WCAG 1.0 is determined by the priority levels of the checkpoints addressed. The priority levels are as follows:

- *Level 1 (must be satisfied)*: These are the checkpoints that *must* be done to meet a marginal level of accessibility. Providing alternate text equivalents and ensuring that content is readable with scripts and style sheets disabled are examples of level 1 priorities.

- *Level 2 (should be satisfied)*: Level 2 priorities are a mixed bag. Some of them are things that I would call essential. Others should be done as part of being a good host to your visitors or as good content development principles.

- *Level 3 (may be addressed)*: This is the priority where most web developers step down. Level 3 priorities are usually actions that qualify as going above and beyond for your users. Some, however, address problems that existed when WCAG 1.0 was written that have gone away. Others still have a feel of "We think this technology might happen soon, so let's try to address it." Of course, divining the future is a difficult art, and some of these technologies never came to pass.

---

1. http://www.w3.org/TR/WCAG10/

<u>**Claims to Conformance**</u>

It's good to be proud of a job well done, but I'm not a fan of conformance and validation banners on sites. They both strike me as being the same realm as the old "Best viewed in..." browser advertisement banners. If you want to make an accessibility statement somewhere in your "About This Site/Colophon" page, that's fine. In the interest of keeping your content neat and clean, however, lose the little banners—the users who need the accessibility functionality will notice that you've done a good job without them.

14.2 Conformance

We won't talk about conformance to WCAG 1.0 in terms of which checkpoints were satisfied for which guidelines directly. Instead, we'll look at three conformance levels based on the priority levels of the checkpoints. There are three levels of conformance:

- *A (all priority 1 checkpoints satisfied)*: OK, so you're accessible—marginally. You've just inched over the line where you can say you're accessible under WCAG 1.0, but many of your users with disabilities will still have a hard time with your pages. Is that really all you want to do? Sounds more like a C to me.

- *Double-A (all priority 1 and 2 checkpoints satisfied)*: This is the sweet spot for WCAG 1.0 compliance. At this level, you're doing the things that are most likely to improve the experience of users visiting your site.

- *Triple-A (all priority 1, 2, and 3 checkpoints satisfied)*: I would like to say that this is a good ideal, but as we'll see later in the chapter, some of the level 3 checkpoints relate to technologies that never quite took off or are otherwise not viable. I suggest that, rather than putting a lot of effort into attaining Triple-A compliance, your time be spent working beyond the guidelines to create usability and accessibility.

14.3 The Fourteen Guidelines of WCAG 1.0

In this section, we'll discuss the checkpoints one by one. I'll give a little bit of background on what they actually mean and point you to the places in this book that explain how to design content that satisfies the checkpoint where appropriate. The goal of this is not to start thinking about accessibility in terms of the guidelines but rather to give you the information that you need to understand what is being said by others who *are* guidelines focused.

1: Provide equivalent alternatives to auditory and visual content.

Providing multiple paths to access information is an essential theme to web accessibility. Look at *Multiple Access Paths*, on page 45, for more information.

- *1.1 [Priority 1] Provide a text equivalent for every non-text element (e.g., via "alt", "longdesc", or in element content). This includes: images, graphical representations of text (including symbols), image map regions, animations (e.g., animated GIFs), applets and programmatic objects, ascii art, frames, scripts, images used as list bullets, spacers, graphical buttons, sounds (played with or without user interaction), stand-alone audio files, audio tracks of video, and video.*

  This is the big one. At many points throughout this book, we return to the topic of creating alternative text representations. Particular focus on this topic is found in *To Put It Another Way*, on page 158; *More Than alt= Can Say*, on page 163; and *Words That Go [Creak] in the Night*, on page 181.

- *1.2 [Priority 1] Provide redundant text links for each active region of a server-side image map.*

  The short story is that there really isn't a good reason right now to be using server-side image maps at all. If you *do*, you'll need to have a list of links somewhere else in the page as an alternate.

- *1.3 [Priority 1] Until user agents can automatically read aloud the text equivalent of a visual track, provide an auditory description of the important information of the visual track of a multimedia presentation.*

"Until user agents…" hasn't happened yet. You'll still need auditory descriptions of the visual information. See *Describe It to Me*, on page 186.

- *1.4 [Priority 1] For any time-based multimedia presentation (e.g., a movie or animation), synchronize equivalent alternatives (e.g., captions or auditory descriptions of the visual track) with the presentation.*

Captions and auditory descriptions are our standard accessibility tool when dealing with video information. Chapter 10, *Video Killed the Something-Something*, on page 175, is dedicated to issues of accessible video.

- *1.5 [Priority 3] Until user agents render text equivalents for client-side image map links, provide redundant text links for each active region of a client-side image map.*

User agents seem to have gotten it right at this point. Adding alt= attributes to the <area> tag should do the trick. *To Put It Another Way*, on page 158, gives advice on writing appropriate alternative text. If you're concerned about users with older technologies that might still get client-side image maps wrong, you can add an alternate set of links as well.

2: Don't rely on color alone.

None of our web content should rely on *any* single sensory mode.

- *2.1 [Priority 1] Ensure that all information conveyed with color is also available without color, for example from context or markup.*

Whenever something is visually keyed, it should have an alternative representation that expresses the same intent. This includes alt= attributes for images and style sheet designs that don't obscure the difference between text and links.

- *2.2 [Priority 2 for images, 3 for text] Ensure that foreground and background color combinations provide sufficient contrast when viewed by someone having color deficits or when viewed on a black and white screen.*

The priority differentiation here makes sense only because, when style sheets are used appropriately, text color can be customized by the user. Really, both of these should be at least priority 2.

Testing contrast for accessibility is discussed in *Thinking in Terms of Black and White*, on page 153.

3: Use markup and style sheets and do so properly.

Many assistive technologies rely on the machine readability of your content. By using standard HTML and CSS, you allow these technologies to work better for their users.

- *3.1 [Priority 2] When an appropriate markup language exists, use markup rather than images to convey information.*

I'm not sold on this one. Some developers use this to recommend SVG markup over other image formats for accessible development. In reality, SVG isn't any better supported by assistive technologies, so you're still falling back to alternative text.

- *3.2 [Priority 2] Create documents that validate to published formal grammars.*

Using undocumented or browser-specific behaviors can make a page unreadable by assistive technologies. At all times, you will want to verify that your markup follows standard DTDs. Validation tools for HTML, CSS, and RSS are mentioned in *Building a Testing Toolbox*, on page 62.

- *3.3 [Priority 2] Use style sheets to control layout and presentation.*

We want to separate content and presentation to ensure that our pages are structured in a way that makes them understood for people who need assistive technologies to process the page for them or need to disable our style sheet. The basics of CSS style sheets are covered in *Styled to the Nines*, on page 95.

- *3.4 [Priority 2] Use relative rather than absolute units in markup language attribute values and style sheet property values.*

This one is a little obscure on first glance. The reason we want to use relative units such as ems or percentages is that absolute units such as pixels don't change if the font is scaled by the user. By using relative units, spacing on the page can change appropriately when the font scales.

- *3.5 [Priority 2] Use header elements to convey document structure and use them according to specification.*

Header tags (<h1>, <h2>, and so on) should be used only to mark the title of a section of content. By "according to specification," WAI means that heading numbers shouldn't be skipped (1 or 2 always follow 1, and 2 or 3 always follows 2). Whenever the next heading is a lower number (1 after 2, for example), it should mean that the section has concluded and the next is beginning.

- *3.6 [Priority 2] Mark up lists and list items properly.*

List items should be properly nested and *never* used to achieve a layout effect. The first is easily testable with HTML validation. The second is a direct result of separating presentation from content.

- *3.7 [Priority 2] Mark up quotations. Do not use quotation markup for formatting effects such as indentation.*

This is clearly WAI's response to the (in)famous use of <block-quote> as the universal indentation tool. Quotation tags such as <q>, <blockquote>, and <cite> should be used only to add semantic information about cited material.

4: Clarify natural-language usage.

The Web is international, so we need to provide information for assistive technologies to determine how a page should be processed.

- *4.1 [Priority 1] Clearly identify changes in the natural language of a document's text and any text equivalents (e.g., captions).*

To allow any screen reader that wants to implement multiple language support or spell out unknown foreign words, it is useful to signal that the language used in the document has changed.

- *4.2 [Priority 3] Specify the expansion of each abbreviation or acronym in a document where it first occurs.*

This is important for cognitively impaired users but also useful for *all* readers of your content. Abbreviation and acronym expansions also provide information that screen readers could use for proper output. Any new terminology, including abbreviations, that are unusual should be introduced in the text or placed into an easily searchable page glossary.

- *4.3 [Priority 3] Identify the primary natural language of a document.*

Again, this checkpoint is of greatest use to a screen reader that attempts to process multiple languages.

5: Create tables that transform gracefully.

Tables are a major accessibility problem for many web sites. Although this is largely a result of using tables for layout, complex tabular information requires extra information to be added for navigation. Chapter 7, *Round Tables*, on page 105 is an in-depth discussion of table accessibility.

- *5.1 [Priority 1] For data tables, identify row and column headers.*

    Tables need headings to express their content. *Setting the Table*, on page 106, describes adding descriptive information to tables.

- *5.2 [Priority 1] For data tables that have two or more logical levels of row or column headers, use markup to associate data cells and header cells.*

    For more complex tables, we can define relationship attributes for table cells that clarify the organization of the table. You can find information on these attributes in *Ah, <table>, I Hardly Knew Ye!*, on page 110.

- *5.3 [Priority 2] Do not use tables for layout unless the table makes sense when linearized. Otherwise, if the table does not make sense, provide an alternative equivalent (which may be a linearized version).*

    Let's just revise this to "Do not use tables for layout." Seriously. CSS is not new technology anymore and hasn't been for some time. If you decide to add a layout table anyway, at least check out *Layout and Other Bad Table Manners*, on page 117, to find out how to do it without completely trashing your site's accessibility.

- *5.4 [Priority 2] If a table is used for layout, do not use any structural markup for the purpose of visual formatting.*

    See checkpoint 5.3. If you *do* choose to create a layout table, you get to use <table>, <tr>, and <td>. That's *it*—none of the other table-related tags.

- *5.5 [Priority 3] Provide summaries for tables.*

    A brief description of the data contained in a table should be provided to the user. This is done either with surrounding text narrative or with the summary= attribute.

- *5.6 [Priority 3] Provide abbreviations for header labels.*

Because header labels may be repeated frequently by screen readers, it is useful to provide abbreviated versions of the header with the abbr= attribute.

6: Ensure that pages featuring new technologies transform gracefully.

This goes back to our one valid assumption: our users are capable of sending and receiving text information. If our images, style sheets, and scripts go away, the content still needs to be usable.

- *6.1 [Priority 1] Organize documents so they can be read without style sheets. For example, when an HTML document is rendered without associated style sheets, it must still be possible to read the document.*

As mentioned in *Getting Your Hands Dirty*, on page 69, accessibility testing should always include checking that the page makes sense and is usable with style sheets turned off.

- *6.2 [Priority 1] Ensure that equivalents for dynamic content are up dated when the dynamic content changes.*

Remember that multiple access paths are useful only if they represent the same information. If anything changes in one, the others need to be updated as well.

- *6.3 [Priority 1] Ensure that pages are usable when scripts, applets, or other programmatic objects are turned off or not supported. If this is not possible, provide equivalent information on an alternative accessible page.*

My recommendation is to do everything in your power to make this possible. Alternative pages are another way of Writing Everything Twice. Take a look at *Don't Get WET!*, on page 49, to see why you don't want to do this and *Unassuming Scripts*, on page 220, to learn how to make your scripts step out of the way.

- *6.4 [Priority 2] For scripts and applets, ensure that event handlers are input device-independent.*

True input device independence isn't possible unless you build pages that don't take input from users. Again, we look at the assumption that our users can send text to the browser.

This doesn't mean we can't use pointer-based events at all. In fact, we should allow pointer interaction for users with mobility impairments, among others. See *Linking It All Together*, on page 92, for more information on browser events and which ones pose accessibility problems.

- *6.5 [Priority 2] Ensure that dynamic content is accessible or provide an alternative presentation or page.*

Make sure that the "alternative presentation or page" provides the same experience as the original if you go that route. Alternative pages are particularly prone to the WET dilemma. It is far better to build a single page with multiple representations as needed.

7: Ensure user control of time-sensitive content changes.

Depending on the type of assistive technologies your users have, they may not be able to go through your page at the rate you would predict that they would. In general, unless there is a compelling reason to do so, we don't want to take away control of the browser from the user. Look at *It's Their Web—We're Just Building in It*, on page 126, for more.

- *7.1 [Priority 1] Until user agents allow users to control flickering, avoid causing the screen to flicker.*

- *7.2 [Priority 2] Until user agents allow users to control blinking, avoid causing content to blink (i.e., change presentation at a regular rate, such as turning on and off).*

User agents still don't allow users to control flickering and blinking, and I'm not entirely sure how they could as a general rule. See *It's Not Polite to Flash the Audience*, on page 177, for more on preventing flicker. As far as the <blink> tag, just pretend it never existed—it never officially did.

- *7.3 [Priority 2] Until user agents allow users to freeze moving content, avoid movement in pages.*

This one, like 7.1 and 7.2, have important consequences related to photosensitive epilepsy. In addition, however, audio elements that automatically play can cause problems with cross-talk for users of screen readers. It is better to load multimedia elements in a stopped state and let the user decide when they want to interact with it. *Never use audio or video content that cannot be stopped!*

- *7.4 [Priority 2] Until user agents provide the ability to stop the refresh, do not create periodically auto-refreshing pages.*

  Better yet, don't cause periodic refresh without the user specifically requesting it. Changing content while it's being read is disorienting and negatively impacts comprehension.

- *7.5 [Priority 2] Until user agents provide the ability to stop auto-redirect, do not use markup to redirect pages automatically. Instead, configure the server to perform redirects.*

  If you're redirecting the user, don't stop and give them a couple of seconds to read that you're redirecting them. Either transparently take them to the new location or give them a link and let them move on to the new location on their own.

8: Ensure direct accessibility of embedded user interfaces.

- *8.1 [Priority 1 if functionality is important and not presented elsewhere, otherwise Priority 2] Make programmatic elements such as scripts and applets directly accessible or compatible with assistive technologies.*

  Any embedded applications need to be made accessible for the page as a whole to be accessible. In Chapter 13, *Embedded Applications: Rinse and Repeat*, on page 231, we see that the same principles and techniques that we use for web accessibility generally apply to these technologies as well. When we use media formats that use plug-in software for display, there needs to be at least one implementation available that provides an accessible interface (and if the technology is very new, we *should* let your users know where to get that implementation).

9: Design for device independence.

Device independence simply means providing more than one channel through which our users can interact with our content. We always need to pay attention to two classes of input device: the keyboard and the pointer. Assistive technologies always provide some equivalent to keyboard input and a version of pointer input where possible.

- *9.1 [Priority 1] Provide client-side image maps instead of server-side image maps except where the regions cannot be defined with an available geometric shape.*

Server-side image maps don't provide links that can be used with a keyboard interface or screen reader. The "where the regions cannot be defined" bit is moot. Any shaped region that cannot be reasonably defined with <area shape="poly"> is probably too visually and navigationally complex for even users without disabilities.

- *9.2 [Priority 2] Ensure that any element that has its own interface can be operated in a device-independent manner.*

  This is really a consequence of checkpoint 8.1. See Chapter 13, *Embedded Applications: Rinse and Repeat*, on page 231, for more on this.

- *9.3 [Priority 2] For scripts, specify logical event handlers rather than device-dependent event handlers.*

  This is a matter of giving preference to event handlers that make no assumptions about input devices such as onfocus and onselect rather than those that do such as onclick and onkeypress.

- *9.4 [Priority 3] Create a logical tab order through links, form controls, and objects.*

- *9.5 [Priority 3] Provide keyboard shortcuts to important links (including those in client-side image maps), form controls, and groups of form controls.*

  These are references to the tabindex= and accesskey= attributes. As shown in *Tickling the Keys*, on page 137, I am not convinced that these are the best solutions. I certainly think that logical tab ordering is important but that it should be done as a consequence of content ordering. Access keys are a nice idea but pose too many potential problems for the end user.

10: Use interim solutions.

Many of the interim solutions given in WCAG 1.0 are still useful for other reasons, but sometimes the solution causes a different problem.

- *10.1 [Priority 2] Until user agents allow users to turn off spawned windows, do not cause pop-ups or other windows to appear and do not change the current window without informing the user.*

  Pop-up blockers are available now, but it still isn't a good idea to take control of the user's browser without their direct action.

- *10.2 [Priority 2] Until user agents support explicit associations between labels and form controls, for all form controls with implicitly associated labels, ensure that the label is properly positioned.*

Labels can be associated with form controls at this point, but there are still concerns about the positioning of the label relative to the control. See *Getting <form>al*, on page 130, for information on labeling form elements.

- *10.3 [Priority 3] Until user agents (including assistive technologies) render side-by-side text correctly, provide a linear text alternative (on the current page or some other) for all tables that lay out text in parallel, word-wrapped columns.*

Table layout: Just Say No.

- *10.4 [Priority 3] Until user agents handle empty controls correctly, include default, place-holding characters in edit boxes and text areas.*

The problem of empty controls has been addressed for a long time now. Default placeholders are problematic in their own right because they look to some assistive technologies such as fields that have already been filled in.

- *10.5 [Priority 3] Until user agents (including assistive technologies) render adjacent links distinctly, include non-link, printable characters (surrounded by spaces) between adjacent links.*

This is a debatable issue. Neighboring links *should* be discernible by the user, but that can be done in multiple ways. You can place characters between links as suggested, or if the context is clear, you may not need to do so. The thing you should avoid is sentences where each word is a different link—it isn't clear that there are multiple links.

11: Use W3C technologies.

With all due respect to W3C, this is an incredibly pretentious guideline. W3C has had a generally good track record for producing technologies with accessibility support, but they are certainly not the only provider out there. A more appropriate guideline is this: "Use accessible technologies from stable providers with a good accessibility reputation."

- *11.1 [Priority 2] Use W3C technologies when they are available and appropriate for a task and use the latest versions when supported.*

This is the same thing as checkpoint 11 along with an appeal to use the latest supported version. As long as the latest supported provides the same or better accessibility support, I would agree.

- *11.2 [Priority 2] Avoid deprecated features of W3C technologies.*

This one has merit. Many deprecated features were deprecated because they broke separation of content and presentation. See *Minding Your <p>'s and <q>'s*, on page 89, for a list of deprecated tags in HTML and how they should be handled.

- *11.3 [Priority 3] Provide information so that users may receive documents according to their preferences (e.g., language, content type, etc.)*

This comes back to multiple access paths. The checkpoint also brings up language preference. I think that translations are fantastic, but I don't consider them to be an issue of accessibility for users with disabilities.

- *11.4 [Priority 1] If, after best efforts, you cannot create an accessible page, provide a link to an alternative page that uses W3C technologies, is accessible, has equivalent information (or functionality), and is updated as often as the inaccessible (original) page.*

I'm sorry, but if your best efforts lead to an inaccessible page, you need to step back in your design process to figure out what went wrong. Punting by deliberately trying to bandage the problem is the wrong answer. See *Don't Get WET!*, on page 49.

12: Provide context and orientation information.

You should write content that is well-structured and semantic. This includes properly nesting content and making it clear how different parts of the content are related. In *Say It with Meaning*, on page 78, we cover issues of organizing our content in a semantic way.

- *12.1 [Priority 1] Title each frame to facilitate frame identification and navigation.*

- *12.2 [Priority 2] Describe the purpose of frames and how frames relate to each other if it is not obvious by frame titles alone.*

These two checkpoints specifically deal with organizing frames. I usually deal with it by not using them. If you need to use frames, make sure to give them titles and appropriate <noframes> alternatives. Just keep in mind that some alternative browsers don't handle them well at all.

- *12.3 [Priority 2] Divide large blocks of information into more manageable groups where natural and appropriate.*

This checkpoint is pretty much common sense. Long documents should use well-structured headings for logical sections with additional navigation, and you should add hierarchy to long lists of links or form options.

- *12.4 [Priority 2] Associate labels explicitly with their controls.*

That is, use the <label> tag, and tie it to form elements rather than just putting text next to them.

13: Provide clear navigation mechanisms.

Good content is irrelevant if our users can't make their way through it. In Chapter 8, *The Accessible Interface*, on page 125, we cover many issues of interface including navigation.

- *13.1 [Priority 2] Clearly identify the target of each link.*

This one of the most self-explanatory checkpoints in WCAG 1.0: don't use links with titles such as "Click here."

- *13.2 [Priority 2] Provide metadata to add semantic information to pages and sites.*

I agree that semantic information gives assistive technologies more to work with, but I don't know of an example where the <meta> and <link> tags mentioned in connection with this checkpoint have ever been used to successfully do this. I prefer to add semantics through tagging rather than with metadata.

- *13.3 [Priority 2] Provide information about the general layout of a site (e.g., a site map or table of contents).*

I'm not specifically against site maps and tables of contents, but they *do* raise a red flag for me. The first thing you should ask before adding site maps is, what is wrong with the standard navigation that makes one necessary?

- *13.4 [Priority 2] Use navigation mechanisms in a consistent manner.*

Does this *need* to be said? Has inconsistent navigation ever seemed like a good idea? The gist is that when you place navigation in the same place, it is easier to users to find or skip it.

- *13.5 [Priority 3] Provide navigation bars to highlight and give access to the navigation mechanism.*

I prefer "Make your navigation system clear and understandable." Often a navigation bar is the best solution, but it isn't the only way to go.

- *13.6 [Priority 3] Group related links, identify the group (for user agents), and until user agents do so, provide a way to bypass the group.*

The first two parts of this are a matter of organization. When many links appear in series, they should be sorted and placed in categories for easier navigation. User agents do not provide a convenient way to skip past groups of links, but it is simple to create a link to skip to a point just after the group.

- *13.7 [Priority 3] If search functions are provided, enable different types of searches for different skill levels and preferences.*

This isn't *really* a matter of accessibility—it's one of general usability. Your search systems should be easily usable by all of your users.

- *13.8 [Priority 3] Place distinguishing information at the beginning of headings, paragraphs, lists, etc.*

Some users navigate by skipping through headings. I don't know that I agree that it is our responsibility as content designers to help our users read information out of context. What we should do, however, is eliminate redundant prefix text in our headings. For example, don't create headings like "My Really Interesting Book's Title, Chapter 3: The Plot Thickens, Section N" for each section.

- *13.9 [Priority 3] Provide information about document collections (i.e., documents comprising multiple pages).*

This is another checkpoint that is about general usability more than accessibility. It isn't a checkpoint to worry about because the concept of bundled documents that use <link> to express relationships was never implemented in the way described by W3C.

- *13.10 [Priority 3] Provide a means to skip over multi-line ASCII art.*

I don't know why this is priority 3. Screen readers don't play well with ASCII art, and a link to skip it is easy to add. Call it priority 1.

14: Ensure that documents are clear and simple.

We need to communicate our content clearly, particularly for our users with cognitive disabilities. By creating easy-to-follow content, we add value for all of our users.

- *14.1 [Priority 1] Use the clearest and simplest language appropriate for a site's content.*

  Don't try to impress your audience with your vocabulary—try to impress them with your content. Staying clear and simple is the focus of *Keeping It Simple Is Smart*, on page 84.

- *14.2 [Priority 3] Supplement text with graphic or auditory presentations where they will facilitate comprehension of the page.*

  When communicating complex ideas, people who can use images may benefit from diagrams or charts that clarify the content. These shouldn't be used as an excuse for writing overly complex narratives, however.

- *14.3 [Priority 3] Create a style of presentation that is consistent across pages.*

  As always, consistency is an important usability factor. In terms of accessibility, it means navigation and understanding are made easier for the user.

That completes our walkthrough of WCAG 1.0. Many discussions are available online about these guidelines and their implementation. If you would like to see W3C's recommendations for satisfying the checkpoints, WAI has produced documents outlining general,[2] HTML,[3] and CSS[4] techniques. WCAG 1.0 is the current standard for accessible web development, so it is important to understand. You'll also find many local and national government standards on web accessibility to be based on or compatible with WCAG 1.0. In the United States, for example, you will find parallels between these guidelines and Section 508.

---

2. http://www.w3.org/TR/WCAG10-CORE-TECHS/
3. http://www.w3.org/TR/WCAG10-HTML-TECHS/
4. http://www.w3.org/TR/WCAG10-CSS-TECHS/

Section 508

The United States federal government has mandates that prevent it from purchasing inaccessible web content. These mandates were added to Section 508 of the Rehabilitation Act of 1973 in 1998. Section 508 is important both at the federal level and in many U.S. states that have based their own policies on Section 508. How do you know whether your work falls under section 508 mandates? Section 508 applies to the development, procurement, maintenance, and use of electronic and information technologies. Services and information provided by the federal government must be made accessible to federal employees and to the public at large. That's fairly comprehensive.

Section 508 does *not* apply directly to nonfederal web sites, though the Section 508 criteria could be used as a baseline for accommodation in an Americans with Disabilities Act suit. This is relatively unlikely, but it means that the mandates of Section 508 *could* be potentially applied to private businesses. If you are a nonfederal developer working under a federal contract, however, Section 508 applies to your work. The notion of operating under contract has been interpreted very widely, including direct contracts, grants, acceptance of federal loans, and more. It is safe to assume that if your project is in any way funded with money that originated at the federal level, you should be aware of Section 508.

As web developers, three sections of Section 508 apply to the work that we do under federal funding, though we are often told only about Section 1194.22. Let's walk through sections 1194.21, 22, and 24 to see how we can meet these mandates.

Undue Burden

The notion of *undue burden* gets brought up along with Section 508. Undue burden is the exception provided when the implementation of accessibility would be financially or technologically impossible to achieve. It is not usually viable to claim undue burden for web accessibility—usually physically engineered objects are more eligible to make this claim. Claiming undue burden is a risky line to walk and is the sort of risk that is not in your interest to take without expert advice. If you find an accessibility matter that seems to impose an undue burden, it is important to pass it up the chain to legal counsel or an accessibility coordinator. In short, *never* assume undue burden on your own.

15.1 Software Applications & Operating Systems (§1194.21)

You won't see §1194.21 brought up often in terms of web accessibility. Many people believe it to apply only to stand-alone desktop applications. This is beginning to change, however. If the content you produce is best described as a "web application," you should be keeping an eye on §1194.21. When Section 508 was written, there was a clear distinction between web and desktop applications, but this distinction has become unclear with the rise of rich Internet applications. Some of the mandates of this section are taken care of for us by the web browser, but we should always be aware of when this is or is not the case.

(a) When software is designed to run on a system that has a keyboard, product functions shall be executable from a keyboard where the function itself or the result of performing a function can be discerned textually.

Here we return to the one assumption of web accessibility: that our users can be expected to have the ability to send and receive text-based content.

(b) Applications shall not disrupt or disable activated features of other products that are identified as accessibility features, where those features are developed and documented according to industry standards. Applications also shall not disrupt or disable activated features of any operating system that are identified as accessibility features where the application programming interface for those accessibility features has

been documented by the manufacturer of the operating system and is available to the product developer.

In short, don't take control of the user's system. You should avoid automatically playing audio and video elements to prevent cross-talk with a screen reader, and as shown in *Tickling the Keys*, on page 137, access keys should be handled with caution if you use them so you don't inadvertently override important keyboard behaviors for the user.

(c) A well-defined on-screen indication of the current focus shall be provided that moves among interactive interface elements as the input focus changes. The focus shall be programmatically exposed so that assistive technology can track focus and focus changes.

This functionality is generally provided at the browser or system level.

(d) Sufficient information about a user interface element including the identity, operation and state of the element shall be available to assistive technology. When an image represents a program element, the information conveyed by the image must also be available in text.

We need to assign labels to form elements and create alternate text. The browser usually handles reporting the state of an element (such as checked or unchecked).

(e) When bitmap images are used to identify controls, status indicators, or other programmatic elements, the meaning assigned to those images shall be consistent throughout an application's performance.

Vector images aren't common yet, but this applies to them as well— never use a graphic element to mean more than one thing.

(f) Textual information shall be provided through operating system functions for displaying text. The minimum information that shall be made available is text content, text input caret location, and text attributes.

The browser, operating system, and installed assistive technology take care of presenting alternative text to the user so long as we have added it correctly.

(g) Applications shall not override user selected contrast and color selections and other individual display attributes.

With web applications, we don't have a way to know the users' display attributes, but when we create our presentation with style sheets and test that they degrade gracefully, we know that our users can use their own custom style sheets if they choose.

(h) When animation is displayed, the information shall be displayable in at least one non-animated presentation mode at the option of the user.

Animated elements should be accompanied with a transcript detailing the information presented in the animation.

(i) Color coding shall not be used as the only means of conveying information, indicating an action, prompting a response, or distinguishing a visual element.

See *Stoplights and Poison Apples*, on page 148, for information and examples on this topic.

(j) When a product permits a user to adjust color and contrast settings, a variety of color selections capable of producing a range of contrast levels shall be provided.

If you provide multiple color schemes that are user selectable, some of them should be tailored to the needs of users with color perception or contrast impairments.

(k) Software shall not use flashing or blinking text, objects, or other elements having a flash or blink frequency greater than 2 Hz and lower than 55 Hz.

We need to test all moving images against the flash threshold for photosensitivity. See *It's Not Polite to Flash the Audience*, on page 177, for more information.

(l) When electronic forms are used, the form shall allow people using assistive technology to access the information, field elements, and functionality required for completion and submission of the form, including all directions and cues.

This is a higher-level accessibility mandate. Forms must be provided in an accessible format. Specifically, scanned images of forms are not acceptable unless we separately provide their information in an accessible format. See *Getting <form>al*, on page 130, for more on accessible forms.

15.2 Web-Based Intranet and Internet Information & Applications (§1194.22)

This section is the most important for web accessibility. If you have already read Chapter 14, *Web Content Accessibility Guidelines 1.0*, on page 245, and are familiar with WCAG 1.0, most of these paragraphs will be familiar because they are equivalent to WCAG 1.0 checkpoints. I will give pointers to the appropriate checkpoints as we go through these.

(a) A text equivalent for every non-text element shall be provided (e.g., via "alt", "longdesc", or in element content).

As always, alternative text is key to web accessibility. This paragraph is parallel to WCAG 1.0 checkpoint 1.1. Alternative text is discussed in depth in *To Put It Another Way*, on page 158, and in *More Than alt= Can Say*, on page 163.

(b) Equivalent alternatives for any multimedia presentation shall be synchronized with the presentation.

Alternatives aren't equivalent if they do not occur in parallel to the default information. WCAG 1.0 checkpoint 1.4 is parallel to this paragraph, and *On the Cutting-Room Floor*, on page 190, discusses formats for synchronizing your alternatives.

(c) Web pages shall be designed so that all information conveyed with color is also available without color, for example from context or markup.

As a sensory modality, coding only with color is unacceptable for accessibility. WCAG 1.0 checkpoint 2.1 also makes this assertion, and an example of how to eliminate color coding is available in *Stoplights and Poison Apples*, on page 148.

(d) Documents shall be organized so they are readable without requiring an associated style sheet.

Documents should be written in natural reading order whenever possible, as described in *Say It with Meaning*, on page 78. This is equivalent to WCAG 1.0 checkpoint 6.1.

(e) Redundant text links shall be provided for each active region of a server-side image map.

I prefer "Server-side image maps shall not be used." See paragraph (f) as well as WCAG 1.0 checkpoint 1.2.

(f) Client-side image maps shall be provided instead of server-side image maps except where the regions cannot be defined with an available geometric shape.

As I stated in my discussion of WCAG 1.0 checkpoint 9.1, the sibling to this paragraph, the presence of <area shape="poly">, means that there is no viable reason to require the use of server-side image maps.

(g) Row and column headers shall be identified for data tables.

(h) Markup shall be used to associate data cells and header cells for data tables that have two or more logical levels of row or column headers.

Paragraphs (g) and (h) are equivalent to WCAG 1.0 checkpoint 5.1 and 5.2 as well as the subject of Chapter 7, *Round Tables*, on page 105.

(i) Frames shall be titled with text that facilitates frame identification and navigation.

I really prefer to avoid frames whenever I can because they are not well supported in many alternative browsers. WCAG 1.0 checkpoint 12.1 makes a similar appeal, but reasons for avoiding frames entirely are discussed in *Minding Your <p>'s and <q>'s*, on page 89.

(j) Pages shall be designed to avoid causing the screen to flicker with a frequency greater than 2 Hz and lower than 55 Hz.

Section 508 gives a more specific mandate for flicker control than WCAG checkpoints 7.1 and 7.2 by specifying a flicker frequency. In *It's Not Polite to Flash the Audience*, on page 177, we borrow the flash threshold definition from WCAG 2.0 because it provides a compatible definition and tools are available to measure it for us.

(k) A text-only page, with equivalent information or functionality, shall be provided to make a web site comply with the provisions of this part, when compliance cannot be accomplished in any other way. The content of the text-only page shall be updated whenever the primary page changes.

Like WCAG 1.0 checkpoint 11.4, Section 508 gives us a way out by Writing Everything Twice. In *Don't Get WET!*, on page 49, I recommend avoiding this at all costs. If your interface can't be made accessible, it may be that you're trying to build the wrong interface.

(l) When pages utilize scripting languages to display content, or to create interface elements, the information provided by the script shall be identified with functional text that can be read by assistive technology.

Our scripts need to fall away and allow the user to access information when they don't have scripting available or choose to turn it off. In *Unassuming Scripts*, on page 220, we look at how to write scripts that do this.

(m) When a web page requires that an applet, plug-in or other application be present on the client system to interpret page content, the page must provide a link to a plug-in or applet that complies with §1194.21(a) through (l).

This is the recursive clause. When we embed other types of documents and applications into our pages, their interfaces and content need to be accessible as well. Chapter 13, *Embedded Applications: Rinse and Repeat*, on page 231, as well as most of the rest of Part IV are focused on bringing accessibility to these external elements.

(n) When electronic forms are designed to be completed on-line, the form shall allow people using assistive technology to access the information, field elements, and functionality required for completion and submission of the form, including all directions and cues.

Implementing accessible forms is the focus of *Getting <form>al*, on page 130. Forms that are not intended to be filled out online need to be provided in an accessible format as well, rather than as scanned images. An important note here is that any related instructions must also be made accessible—but that isn't surprising

(o) A method shall be provided that permits users to skip repetitive navigation links.

This appears so many times in various documents about usability and accessibility that I am astounded that there is no explicit call to provide skip links from the beginning to the end of groups of links. It's easy to do, so just do it.

(p) When a timed response is required, the user shall be alerted and given sufficient time to indicate more time is required.

This is something that should have been part of WCAG 1.0 Guideline 7: "Ensure user control of time-sensitive content changes." Unless the nature of a page requires timed responses, they should be eliminated entirely. *It's Their Web—We're Just Building in It*, on page 126, discusses the issue of user control and timing effects.

15.3 Video & Multimedia Products (§1194.24)

This section, like §1194.21, isn't usually brought up in discussions of Section 508 and web accessibility. I suspect that this has a lot to do with people starting to read the first two paragraphs and assuming this is all about television. If your web presence is used to provide video and multimedia content, however, the last three paragraphs are important to your adherence to section 508.

(a) All analog television displays 13 inches and larger, and computer equipment that includes analog television receiver or display circuitry, shall be equipped with caption decoder circuitry which appropriately receives, decodes, and displays closed captions from broadcast, cable, videotape, and DVD signals. As soon as practicable, but not later than July 1, 2002, widescreen digital television (DTV) displays measuring at least 7.8 inches vertically, DTV sets with conventional displays measuring at least 13 inches vertically, and stand-alone DTV tuners, whether or not they are marketed with display screens, and computer equipment that includes DTV receiver or display circuitry, shall be equipped with caption decoder circuitry which appropriately receives, decodes, and displays closed captions from broadcast, cable, videotape, and DVD signals.

(b) Television tuners, including tuner cards for use in computers, shall be equipped with secondary audio program playback circuitry.

Clearly these first two paragraphs are not directly applicable to us as web developers, but I thought it better to give them here than leave you wondering where (a) and (b) went.

(c) All training and informational video and multimedia productions which support the agency's mission, regardless of format, that contain speech or other audio information necessary for the comprehension of the content, shall be open or closed captioned.

This is *very* broadly stated. The only video elements exempt from this paragraph are those of purely decorative function and those that contain no audio to be captioned. See *Words That Go [Creak] in the Night*, on page 181, for more on captioning audio content.

(d) All training and informational video and multimedia productions which support the agency's mission, regardless of format, that contain visual information necessary for the comprehension of the content, shall be audio described.

This is simply the auditory description version of §1194.24 (c). This book covers auditory description in *Describe It to Me*, on page 186.

(e) Display or presentation of alternate text presentation or audio descriptions shall be user-selectable unless permanent.

I am not particularly an advocate for either exclusively open or closed production of captions and auditory descriptions. Both have advantages and disadvantages for you and for your end users. Closed production refers to captions and auditory descriptions that can be turned on or off by the user, where open production is mastered onto the video in a permanent manner. Some of the formats discussed in *On the Cutting-Room Floor*, on page 190, allow closed production, and some do not. It is probably nicer to allow them to be turned on and off, but I am more concerned that the content is there than I am about how it is presented.

That completes our look at Section 508. If you have been following WCAG 1.0 guidelines, there shouldn't have been many surprises, and everything you need to know in order to meet these mandates is given at the referenced points in the book.

Web Content Accessibility Guidelines 2.0

WCAG 1.0 has been a useful guideline, and as we'll see in Chapter 17, *Meanwhile, in the Rest of the World...*, on page 291, it has been influential on the development of many other guidelines and regulations pertaining to web accessibility. WCAG 1.0 has aged, however, and doesn't always reflect the current state of web development. Additionally, WCAG 1.0 also takes an approach that is tightly wedded to HTML, and there are many document types other than HTML that we need to think about when we work in web development. Responding to these issues, the WAI, rather than issuing a revision to WCAG 1.0, chose to develop an entirely new set of guidelines that would take all of these things into account. The new set of guidelines, WCAG 2.0, is intended to be a more comprehensive general guideline for web accessibility.

The path to WCAG 2.0 has been a long one, however, and it has yet to be finalized. This chapter will look at WCAG 2.0 as it existed in the May 2007 Working Draft. It seems that some progress has been made toward finalization, but there is no set date for finalization, so it is still very likely that the guidelines will continue to change. An up-to-date copy of the guidelines can be found at the WAI's WCAG 2.0 site.[1] At this point, WCAG 2.0 isn't something that will concern you on a day-to-day basis, but you should have some basic familiarity with it. It's useful to stay informed about where the WAI wants to take web accessibility as well as to see some suggestions for issues not covered in WCAG 1.0.

---

1. http://www.w3.org/TR/WCAG20/

16.1 The Basics of WCAG 2.0

WCAG 2.0 is a significantly more complex set of guidelines than WCAG 1.0, and the related documents attest to this. In addition to the main guidelines document, extensive Techniques[2] and Understanding[3] documents describe the intent and meaning of the guidelines in depthly. To assist the casual user in finding their way through these large documents, a Quick Reference[4] allows you to narrow down appropriate techniques and recommendations based on the technologies you use and the level of conformance you want to attain.

Conformance has also changed a bit in WCAG 2.0. The three levels of conformance (A, Double-A/AA, and Triple-A/AAA) are similar to WCAG 1.0, but some useful clarifications have been made:

- Only known accessible technologies can be used to meet success criteria.

- Nonaccessible technologies cannot prevent accessible use of the page by preventing keyboard access, generating flicker, or otherwise interfering with content accessibility while turned on or off.

- Conformance claims are made for full web pages only (but see the upcoming exception).

- For determining conformance, alternative content is considered part of the page.

- If any page in a sequence, such as a wizard, is inaccessible, then the entire sequence of pages is to be considered inaccessible.

Most of these clarifications boil down to common sense. Clearly, if the accessible parts of your pages are available only by going through inaccessible content, the accessibility becomes pointless. There is one exception made for the rule about full-page compliance, however. If you have user-submitted content such as message boards or wikis, you have two options.

First, you can claim conformance based on your best knowledge of the site. If you do this, however, you need to make sure any inaccessible content is repaired or removed when it is discovered. The other option is to make a statement of partial compliance.

---

2. http://www.w3.org/TR/WCAG20-TECHS/
3. http://www.w3.org/TR/UNDERSTANDING-WCAG20/
4. http://www.w3.org/WAI/WCAG20/quickref/

This can be done only for content that isn't under the author's control and only when the user is made clearly aware of which content may be inaccessible. Saying something like "The parts we don't have control over" doesn't count—you'll need to be *specific* like "The comments for this article."

Compared to the relative simplicity of WCAG 1.0 and U.S. Section 508, even the basics of WCAG 2.0 may seem verbose or difficult to follow. You wouldn't be the first to feel this way—this issue is only one of the controversies regarding WCAG 2.0.

16.2 Concerns About WCAG 2.0

WCAG 2.0 has been controversial among accessibility experts and web developers alike. First and foremost, many developers have backed away from web accessibility because of difficulty in understanding or implementing WCAG 1.0. It is counterintuitive to believe that releasing a more complex set of guidelines will reverse this situation.

Another point of concern is that of *testability*. One of the core philosophies of WCAG 2.0 is that the success criteria be constructed in a way that is either machine testable or can be interpreted by human testers in a consistent manner. Although the idea of consistency is nice, the downside is that WCAG 2.0 has nearly no coverage for issues of cognitive disability because they are difficult to test.[5]

There has been some question whether the problems of WCAG 2.0 can be resolved at all. Some are hopeful that the WAI will remove the testability requirement and simplify the guidelines, while others, including a group of developers under the name WCAG Samurai[6] think the WCAG 2.0 guidelines are not likely to be fixed and that a better solution would be to issue proper errata for WCAG 1.0.[7] Regardless of the final fate of WCAG 2.0, it is clear that the wait will go on for some time yet, so any discussion of how WCAG 1.0 should be approached in the meantime should be valuable for all developers of accessible web sites.

---

5. Gian Sampson-Wild has written an in-depth discussion on the problems imposed by testability requirements at http://www.alistapart.com/articles/testability.

6. http://wcagsamurai.org/

7. Joe Clark's reasons for founding the WCAG Samurai are described in the article "To Hell with WCAG 2" (http://alistapart.com/articles/tohellwithwcag2).

16.3 The WCAG 2.0 Guidelines

WCAG 2.0 is organized according to the four principles of perceivability, operability, understandability, and robustness. Each of these principles is described by one or more guidelines that can be met by conformance to specified success criteria. The criteria are divided by level (A, AA, AAA), much like they were in WCAG 1.0, and all success criteria of a level must be met in all guidelines to claim the corresponding level of conformance. In other words, if you meet all of the criteria marked A, your site is A compliant, if you also meet all of the AA criteria, then you can claim AA compliance. With that, let's take a look at what the guidelines and criteria mean for us while we design as well as where in the book you can find more information about satisfying the requirements of the guidelines.

Principle 1: Perceivable—Information and user interface components must be perceivable by users.

I understand the desire to have the POUR acronym for the principles, but in this case, it obscures the intent. What we're really trying to do under the first principle is ensure that we're not relying on our users being able to use a particular sense to understand our content.

Guideline 1.1: Provide text alternatives for any non-text content so that it can be changed into other forms people need such as large print, braille, speech, symbols or simpler language

This guideline comes off as being far too ambitious. Clearly we want text alternative, but in practice, the translation to braille, symbols, or simplified language isn't something that's going to happen automatically. Users of magnification software and screen readers need access to alternative text, however.

Level A

- *1.1.1 Non-text Content: All non-text content has a text alternative that presents equivalent information, except for the situations listed below.*

    - *Controls-Input: If non-text content is a control or accepts user input, then it has a name that describes its purpose. (See also Guideline 4.1.)*

This is where <label> from *Getting <form>al*, on page 130, comes in.

- *Media, Test, Sensory: If non-text content is multimedia, live audio-only or live video-only content, a test or exercise that must be presented in non-text format, or primarily intended to create a specific sensory experience, then text alternatives at least identify the non-text content with a descriptive text label. (For multimedia, see also Guideline 1.2.)*

If the nature of the media makes it impossible to create a text alternative, we still don't want to leave the user completely out of the loop, so we should at least describe the media rather than leaving a blank space.

- *CAPTCHA: If the purpose of non-text content is to confirm that content is being accessed by a person rather than a computer, then text alternatives that identify and describe the purpose of the non-text content are provided and alternative forms in different modalities are provided to accommodate different disabilities.*

CAPTCHA is generally problematic. For more on this topic, see *alt.text.odds-and-ends*, on page 170.

- *Decoration, Formatting, Invisible: If non-text content is pure decoration, or used only for visual formatting, or if it is not presented to users, then it is implemented such that it can be ignored by assistive technology.*

This means setting alt=" for decorative images and using CSS to set noncontent images where possible.

Guideline 1.2: Provide synchronized alternatives for multimedia

Level A

- *1.2.1 Captions (Prerecorded): Captions are provided for prerecorded multimedia, except for multimedia alternatives to text that are clearly labeled as such.*

We look at creating good captions in *Words That Go [Creak] in the Night*, on page 181, and we need to provide these for all multimedia that has an audio track. Clearly, it doesn't make sense to create alternative text for the cases where the media is an alternative *to* text.

- *1.2.2 Audio Description or Full Text Alternative: Audio description of video, or a full text alternative for multimedia including any interaction, is provided for prerecorded multimedia.*

  WCAG 2.0 also notes that there's no need to audio describe media that has nothing to describe. See *Describe It to Me*, on page 186, if you don't know what to look for.

Level AA

- *1.2.3 Captions (Live): Captions are provided for live multimedia.*

  When you have the resources to do such, live material should be captioned as well.

- *1.2.4 Audio Description: Audio description of video is provided for prerecorded multimedia.*

  The level A equivalent to this criterion also provides the option of a full-text alternative. When possible, it's better to provide the audio description as well.

Level AAA

- *1.2.5 Sign Language: Sign language interpretation is provided for multimedia.*

  I have mixed feelings about this criterion. If you have the capacity to create sign language "bubbles," it's certainly a useful thing to add. On the other hand, I don't think provision of sign language interpretation should outweigh the need to provide captions, which serve a wider audience.

- *1.2.6 Audio Description (Extended): Extended audio description of video is provided for prerecorded multimedia.*

  Not all level AAA criteria are applicable in all situations. Sometimes it is necessary to pause video playback to fit audio description so this applies only to those cases.

- *1.2.7 Full Text Alternative: A full-text alternative for multimedia including any interaction is provided for all prerecorded multimedia, except for multimedia alternatives to text that are clearly labeled as such.*

Full-text alternatives, described in *Describe It to Me*, on page 186, are a nice addition to all sites. Because you often need to generate a script for captions and audio descriptions anyway, it's also not usually a lot of extra effort to provide.

Guideline 1.3 Create content that can be presented in different ways (for example spoken aloud, simpler layout, etc.) without losing information or structure

Level A

- *1.3.1 Info and Relationships: Information and relationships conveyed through presentation can be programmatically determined or are available in text, and notification of changes to these is available to user agents, including assistive technologies.*

This one isn't very clear—all we're doing here is expressing our content semantically. See *Say It with Meaning*, on page 78.

- *1.3.2 Meaningful Sequence: When the sequence in which content is presented affects its meaning, a correct reading sequence can be programmatically determined and sequential navigation of interactive components is consistent with that sequence.*

This is our warning to use natural reading order. Figure 7.3, on page 120, is an example of a page where the meaning is confused when read sequentially.

- *1.3.3 Size, Shape, Location: Instructions provided for understanding and operating content do not rely on shape, size, visual location, or orientation of components.*

This comes down to not assuming that our user can receive more than text. In a text-only presentation, none of these indicators makes any sense.

Guideline 1.4: Make it easier for people with disabilities to see and hear content including separating foreground from background.

Level A

- *1.4.1 Use of Color: Any information that is conveyed by color differences is also simultaneously visually evident without the color differences.*

Color keying is another sensory modality issue that we need to avoid. Figure 9.3, on page 152, shows an example of avoiding exclusive color keying.

- *1.4.2 Audio Turnoff: If any audio plays automatically for more than 3 seconds, either a mechanism is available to pause or stop the audio, or a mechanism is available to control audio volume which can be set independently of the system volume.*

Particularly for users of screen readers, we don't want to force uncontrolled audio. This is a specific case of keeping the user in control of their own system. See *It's Their Web—We're Just Building in It*, on page 126.

Level AA

- *1.4.3 Contrast (Minimum): Text (and images of text) have a contrast ratio of at least 5:1, except if the text is pure decoration. Larger-scale text or images of text can have a contrast ratio of 3:1.*

Poor contrast makes your content illegible. See *Thinking in Terms of Black and White*, on page 153, for examples of this as well as information on measuring contrast.

- *1.4.4 Resize text: Visually rendered text can be resized without assistive technology up to 200 percent and down to 50 percent without loss of content or functionality.*

This criterion seems a bit weak. With CSS, we can use relative sizing to keep our layout in place while the font resizes, but the percentages seem arbitrary. For example, if I design with 6-point type, 200 percent is still going to be too small for many users with visual impairments.

Level AAA

- *1.4.5 Contrast (Enhanced): Text (and images of text) have a contrast ratio of at least 7:1, except if the text is pure decoration. Larger-scale text or images of text can have a contrast ratio of 5:1.*

This is just the "more is better" equivalent to criterion 1.4.3.

- *1.4.6 Low or No Background Audio: Audio content that contains speech in the foreground does not contain background sounds, background sounds can be turned off, or background sounds are at least 20 decibels lower than the foreground speech content, with the exception of occasional sound effects.*

Some users may have trouble understanding foreground audio if there is too much background noise. WCAG 2.0 notes that the threshold for background noise is about 25 percent of foreground volume.

- *1.4.7 Resize and Wrap: Visually rendered text can be resized without assistive technology up to 200 percent and down to 50 percent without loss of content or functionality and in a way that does not require the user to scroll horizontally. (Level AAA)*

This criterion is a real problem. It combines the issues of 1.4.4 with the requirement to not require horizontal scrolling. Ultimately this is intractable—in the worst case, a narrowly sized browser window with a long word could force this to fail (try the WCAG 2.0 page in Firefox if you don't believe me).

Principle 2: Operable—User Interface components must be operable by users.

Operability is the mirror to perceivability—we can't assume that our user has a particular physical ability in order to use our content.

Guideline 2.1: Make all functionality available from a keyboard.

Level A

- *2.1.1 Keyboard: All functionality of the content is operable through a keyboard interface without requiring specific timings for individual keystrokes, except where the underlying function requires input that depends on the path of the user's movement and not just the endpoints.*

This addresses two issues. First, we can never assume the user has the ability to use a device other than a keyboard equivalent. This doesn't mean we can't support mouse input—in fact, some users will have easier access if we do. The other issue is that we should never take control away from the user if we don't have to by setting arbitrary timing constraints. The exception given is when the input doesn't have any reasonable keyboard equivalent.

For example, some tools in a drawing application don't have a sensible keyboard mapping. You should make sure this is the case, though. I have heard people incorrectly argue that the drag-and-drop examples shown in *Higher-Order Scripts*, on page 224, fall under this exception.

Level AAA

- *2.1.2 Keyboard (No Exception): All functionality of the content is operable through a keyboard interface without requiring specific timings for individual keystrokes.*

This criterion seems unreasonable—our job is to make our web content as accessible *as possible*. If the nature of an application requires nonkeyboard input, nothing can be done to make it more accessible. Apparently we have to settle with a maximum compliance of AA in that case.

Guideline 2.2: Provide users with disabilities enough time to read and use content

Level A

- *2.2.1 Timing: For each time limit that is set by the content , at least one of the following is true:*

  - *Turn off: the user is allowed to turn off the time limit before encountering it; or*

  - *Adjust: the user is allowed to adjust the time limit before encountering it over a wide range that is at least ten times the length of the default setting; or*

  - *Extend: the user is warned before time expires and given at least 20 seconds to extend the time limit with a simple action (for example, "hit any key"), and the user is allowed to extend the time limit at least ten times; or*

  - *Real-time Exception: the time limit is a required part of a real-time event (for example, an auction), and no alternative to the time limit is possible; or*

  - *Essential Exception: the time limit is part of an activity where timing is essential (for example, time-based testing) and time limits can not be extended further without invalidating the activity.*

Obviously, as discussed in *It's Their Web—We're Just Building in It*, on page 126, we want to avoid timeouts wherever possible. If we can't, we need to give the user the greatest degree of control possible, and the Adjust and Extend options both seem reasonable. If it is simply impossible to alter the time limit, as in the real-time exception, there's nothing we can do. I give a small caveat for the Essential exception, however. In the time-based testing example given, contact information should be given for the person who people with disabilities should discuss alternate test-taking arrangements with.

Level AA

- *2.2.2 Blinking: Content does not blink for more than three seconds, or a method is available to stop all blinking content in the Web page.*

Preferably, moving content should load in a stopped state and be left in control of the user. Blinking should always be treated as a potentially serious problem—see *It's Not Polite to Flash the Audience*, on page 177.

- *2.2.3 Pausing: Moving, blinking, scrolling, or auto-updating information can be paused by the user unless it is part of an activity where timing or movement is essential. Moving content that is pure decoration can be stopped by the user.*

As always, it is best to leave the user in control of the system wherever possible. When the timing or movement is essential, the user should be warned if there is *any* level of blinking that would raise a photosensitivity concern.

Level AAA

- *2.2.4 Timing: Timing is not an essential part of the event or activity presented by the content, except for non-interactive multimedia and real-time events.*

Like 2.1.2, this criterion seems to unreasonably disqualify those applications for which timing is essential from AAA status.

- *2.2.5 Interruptions: Interruptions, such as updated content, can be postponed or suppressed by the user, except interruptions involving an emergency.*

This criterion just seems strange. Certainly, we'd like to allow the user to control interruptions from the page. I would generally assume that the user would still be open to receiving emergency information, so sure—why not?

- *2.2.6 Re-authenticating: When an authenticated session expires, the user can continue the activity without loss of data after re-authenticating.*

I'm not convinced that this is really an *accessibility* issue so much as one of usability. It also seems unclear whether this implies that the current page should automatically save—which makes an unacceptable insistence that scripting be available. More likely, it means the user's current session should be stored—again, an issue of general usability rather than accessibility specifically.

Guideline 2.3: Do not create content that is known to cause seizures

Level A

- *2.3.1 Three Flashes or Below Threshold: Content does not contain anything that flashes more than three times in any one second period, or the flash is below the general flash and red flash thresholds.*

Flickering content threatens the health of your users. Not all flashing content is likely to be harmful, though. If the content tests well against the flash thresholds, described in *It's Not Polite to Flash the Audience*, on page 177, it should be safe to use.

Level AAA

- *2.3.2 Three Flashes: Content does not contain anything that flashes more than three times in any one second period.*

This is simply the restrictive form of 2.3.1 that bars *all* flashing content that might pose a threat.

Guideline 2.4: Provide ways to help users with disabilities navigate, find content and determine where they are.

Level A

- *2.4.1 Bypass Blocks: A mechanism is available to bypass blocks of content that are repeated on multiple Web pages.*

It's better for users who navigate by keyboard if they can use a skip link that points to a point just past a large block to simplify navigation.

- *2.4.2 Page Titled: Web pages have descriptive titles.*

In particular, the page title shouldn't be the same on each page. Instead of "MyCorp," use "MyCorp - Products - Spice Weasel."

- *2.4.3 Focus Order: If a Web page can be navigated sequentially, focusable components receive focus in an order that follows information and relationships conveyed through presentation.*

Simply put, build your pages in natural reading order, as set out in *Say It with Meaning*, on page 78.

- *2.4.4 Link Purpose (Context): The purpose of each link can be determined from the link text and its programmatically determined link context.*

Links should usually be presented in a context that makes it clear what will happen if the user clicks it. This is really another usability issue.

Level AA

- *2.4.5 Multiple Ways: More than one way is available to locate content within a set of Web pages where content is not the result of, or a step in, a process.*

I've never been convinced that multiple navigation methods are strictly necessary. They certainly don't hurt, but when they're needed, I often ask what's lacking the primary navigation method.

- *2.4.6 Labels Descriptive: Headings and labels are descriptive.*

This is a parallel to 2.4.2. Headings and labels are often used to rapidly navigate a page, so they should let the user know what they're going to see. Nondescriptive headings and labels often seem to mean something has gone wrong with the semantics of the document. You'll want to check to make sure the tags are being used for meaning.

Level AAA

- *2.4.7 Location: Information about the user's location within a set of Web pages is available.*

  Providing breadcrumb-style navigation is particularly useful for users who may have difficulty concentrating on content while maintaining a mental map of the site.

- *2.4.8 Link Purpose (Link Text): The purpose of each link can be identified from the link text.*

  Descriptive link text is useful, but usually a good link context should be sufficient. The primary argument for this is from users of technologies that let them navigate links without reading the surrounding context. I don't think that it is generally necessary to make the site specifically easier to use in this case.

- *2.4.9 Section Headings: Where content is organized into sections, the sections are indicated with headings.*

  Sectioned documents are generally also long documents. By providing headings, users are better able to navigate the section they need.

Principle 3: Understandable—Information and operation of user interface must be understandable by users.

This one is kind of a "well, yeah" moment. Web pages are meant to provide information and services to users. If we can't make it understandable, we've failed on a fundamental level. For this reason, a lot of the guidelines in this part fall more into general usability than they do into accessibility.

Guideline 3.1: Make text content readable and understandable.

Level A

- *3.1.1 Language of Page: The default human language of each Web page within the content can be programmatically determined.*

  As discussed in *Keeping It Simple Is Smart*, on page 84, lang= can be used with the <html> element to provide information about the native page language.

Level AA

- *3.1.2 Language of Parts: The human language of each passage or phrase in the content can be programmatically determined.*

  The lang= can also be used with other elements to describe language usage within a page. Keep in mind that this is not necessary for words that have been adopted into the page's primary language.

Level AAA

- *3.1.3 Unusual Words: A mechanism is available for identifying specific definitions of words or phrases used in an unusual or restricted way, including idioms and jargon.*

- *3.1.4 Abbreviations: A mechanism for finding the expanded form or meaning of abbreviations is available.*

  Whenever *any* unusual language usage needs to be understood to comprehend the page, it should be defined on first use. It is also useful to provide a glossary for reference, particularly if there is a significant amount of terminology to learn.

- *3.1.5 Reading Level: When text requires reading ability more advanced than the lower secondary education level, supplemental content or an alternate version is available that does not require reading ability more advanced than the lower secondary education level.*

  I disagree with this guideline for nongeneral use sites. For example, content created for medical practitioners will necessarily have language more advanced than the lower secondary level. This is perfectly appropriate as long as the language is at a basic level for the intended audience.

- *3.1.6 Pronunciation: A mechanism is available for identifying specific pronunciation of words where meaning is ambiguous without knowing the pronunciation.*

  Pronunciation guides for the user seem useful but not necessarily related directly to accessibility concerns. Pronunciation information provided for text-to-speech devices, on the other hand, would be a direct accessibility feature (though not a commonly used one at this point in time). See *Welcome to the Future*, on page 99.

Guideline 3.2: Make Web pages appear and operate in predictable ways:

Level A

- *3.2.1 On Focus: When any component receives focus, it does not initiate a change of context.*

- *3.2.2 On Input: Changing the setting of any user interface component does not automatically cause a change of context unless the user has been advised of the behavior before using the component.*

  Launching new windows or submitting forms should be something done with deliberate intent by the user—in other words, Don't Take Control from the User.

Level AA

- *3.2.3 Consistent Navigation: Navigational mechanisms that are repeated on multiple Web pages within a set of Web pages occur in the same relative order each time they are repeated, unless a change is initiated by the user.*

- *3.2.4 Consistent Identification: Components that have the same functionality within a set of Web pages are identified consistently.*

  Particularly for users who need to use accessibility features such as skip links, it's important that navigation and controls stay consistent rather than changing position or function.

Level AAA

- *3.2.5 Change on Request: Changes of context are initiated only by user request.*

  This eliminates the exception of 3.2.2 where you can take control as long as you tell the user you're going to do it.

Guideline 3.3: Help users avoid and correct mistakes.

Level A

- *3.3.1 Error Identification: If an input error is automatically detected, the item that is in error is identified and described to the user in text.*

  This criterion just clarifies that we can't rely on color, sound, or another sensory effect to convey the error.

Level AA

- *3.3.2 Error Suggestion: If an input error is detected and suggestions for correction are known, then the suggestions are provided to the user, unless it would jeopardize the security or purpose of the content.*

The user's mental effort can be reduced by providing clear instructions on how to correct errors in their input.

- *3.3.3 Error Prevention (Legal, Financial, Data): For forms that cause legal commitments or financial transactions to occur, that modify or delete user-controllable data in data storage systems, or that submit test responses, at least one of the following is true:*

  1. *Reversible: Transactions are reversible.*
  2. *Checked: Submitted data is checked for input errors before going on to the next step in the process.*
  3. *Confirmed: A mechanism is available for reviewing, confirming, and correcting information before finalizing the transaction.*

These are all great suggestions for interaction design. On the other hand, there's absolutely nothing about any of these that are specific issues of accessibility.

- *3.3.4 Labels or Instructions: Labels or instructions are provided when content requires user input.*

As described in *Getting <form>al*, on page 130, all form elements should be labeled. Additionally, nontrivial forms should be clearly explained to the user.

Level AAA

- *3.3.5 Help: Context-sensitive help is available.*

- *3.3.6 Error Prevention (All): For forms that require the user to submit information, at least one of the following is true*

  1. *Reversible: Transactions are reversible.*
  2. *Checked: Submitted data is checked for input errors before going on to the next step in the process.*
  3. *Confirmed: A mechanism is available for reviewing, confirming, and correcting information before finalizing the transaction.*

Again, both of these checkpoints fall into general usability.

Principle 4: Robust—Content must be robust enough that it can be interpreted reliably by a wide variety of user agents, including assistive technologies.

Robustness is a touchy issue. Although the two checkpoints for this principle are basically about standards-compliant design, the real problems of providing robust content show up when dealing with non-standards-compliant browser implementations.

Guideline 4.1: Maximize compatibility with current and future user agents, including assistive technologies.

Level A

- *4.1.1 Parsing: Content implemented using markup languages has elements with complete start and end tags, except as allowed by their specifications, and are nested according to their specifications.*

  Simply put: use the tools in *Building a Testing Toolbox*, on page 62, to validate your content and make sure it's standards compliant.

- *4.1.2 Name, Role, Value: For all user interface components, the name and role can be programmatically determined; states, properties, and values that can be set by the user can be programmatically determined and programmatically set; and notification of changes to these items is available to user agents, including assistive technologies.*

  The gist of this is that if you create your own custom controls, make sure their properties are available to assistive technologies.

This finishes our trip through WCAG 2.0. It's definitely a large topic, and some parts of it seem to need a little more time to evolve before they're completely ready for general use. It's good to know where these are going, however. As we'll see next, if WCAG 2.0 can reach the level of use that WCAG 1.0 did, it may become a reference document for many other guidelines and laws.

I want you to be concerned about your next-door neighbour.
Do you know your next-door neighbour?
► Mother Teresa of Calcutta

Chapter 17

Meanwhile, in the Rest of the World...

In this part of the book, we've looked at general guidelines from W3C as well as U.S. accessibility law—but the laws in other countries are equally compelling. Many countries and international bodies have been very active in developing standards and mandates. Before we finish up, let's take a brief look at the state of web accessibility on the international front.

We have a few really good reasons to do this. First, you may be from one of these countries, and I'd like to give you a few resources to get you moving. It's also possible that you're developing for companies internationally. Global development has become common, and the more you can expand your skill set to adapt to this reality, the better off you'll be in the long term.[1]

Finally, it's useful to look at standardization on the global front to better understand our local standards. Many localities base their standards closely on WCAG, while others have opted to develop their own. Some countries have mandates only on public web sites, while others, like the United States, have mandates on private industry as well. By looking at these differences, we gain insight about our local situation.

---

1. For more on the issue of adapting to globalization, I highly recommend taking a look at Chad Fowler's excellent book, *My Job Went to India* [Fow05].

17.1 Australia

Australia mandates accessibility for public-sector and private-sector web development as part of the Disability Discrimination Act (DDA) of 1992. The DDA makes it illegal to discriminate against someone who has a disability when providing goods, facilities, and services. Further, terms can't be added that change the conditions or manner of delivery for people with disabilities. This makes the DDA a particularly powerful piece of legislation.

The manner of provision clause has been particularly interesting on the legal front. There has been considerable controversy over PDF media in Australia. Currently, the stance of the Human Rights and Equal Opportunity Commission (HREOC) is that PDF is not sufficiently accessible, and alternative formats must be provided and preferred. Opponents counter that PDF has become more accessible in recent years and should be reconsidered because of its widespread usage.

Beyond controversies over document format, the accepted standard for web accessibility in Australia is WCAG 1.0. The common understanding, however, is that single-A compliance is absolutely minimal and ultimately undesirable, while double-A compliance is significantly more desirable.

A brief guide to the DDA. . .
. . . http://www.hreoc.gov.au/disability_rights/dda_guide/dda_guide.htm
The HREOC's "getting started" site to outline and introduce the Disability Discrimination Act. The guide is written in straightforward language and also provides links to frequently asked questions, other materials, and state and territorial guides.

Web Publishing Guide. . . . . http://webpublishing.agimo.gov.au/
The Australian Government Information Management Office guide is provided to help departments and agencies implement web site standards. This document gives information about all areas of web development including accessibility and equity issues.

17.2 Canada

Web accessibility in Canada is explicitly mandated for government sites by the Treasury Board. Like many nations, the standard follows closely from W3C. In the case of Canada, the rule of the day is WCAG1.0 *double-A level compliance* and a requirement of validation against

XHTML 1.0 Strict.[2] The story of clear and explicit accessibility ends with the government, however.

Web accessibility is not explicitly mandated for the private sector in Canada. That said, it is widely considered to be mandated by the Canadian Human Rights Act and informed by the Ontario Human Rights Code as well as by legal decisions in Australia and the United Kingdom. The prevailing current opinion seems to be that private-sector sites be designed to WCAG 1.0 double-A.

Common Look and Feel for the Internet 2.0. . .

. . . http://www.tbs-sct.gc.ca/clf2-nsi2/

The Treasury Board of Canada's Common Look and Feel is an overall guide on designing governmental web sites in accordance with standards. The second part of the guide includes guidance and examples for accessibility, usability, and interoperability.

Web Accessibility Law in Canada . . . http://www.zvulony.com/accessibility.html

Gil Zvulony and Jaime Weinman provide an extensive overview of accessibility laws and precedents in Canada and why the general view is that private-sector web accessibility is probably covered by the Canadian Human Rights Act.

17.3 The European Union

The European Union calls upon its members to improve the availability of accessible information technologies in Europe. The European Union, through its financial support and by formal resolutions, has supported WCAG 1.0 and the activities of the WAI.

European Union web accessibility has become part of the larger goal of *e-Inclusion*. The goal of the e-Inclusion initiative is to work for progress in accessibility-related areas such as aging, lifelong learning, social participation, increased well-being of economically disadvantaged areas, and inclusive government in web settings. Although enabling accessibility is still a stand-alone goal, the techniques of accessible web development prove useful in all of these other areas as well.

Many European Union states, including France, Germany, Ireland, Italy, Spain, Sweden, and the United Kingdom, have, in addition to supporting EU work, enacted national legislation mandating public-sector or private-sector web accessibility.

---

2. http://www.w3.org/TR/xhtml1/

e-Inclusion. . . . . http://ec.europa.eu/information_society/activities/einclusion/
The EU's e-Inclusion activity site includes information about policy and practice related to developing web content for all populations. Issues of accessibility for persons with disability and the aging population are core focuses of e-Inclusion.

EDeAN. . . . . http://www.e-accessibility.org/
The European Design for All e-Accessibility Network is a network of EU organizations that collaborate to communicate and provide resources on accessibility issues. In particular, EDeAN focuses on the Design for All goals of the EU's e-Inclusion plan.

17.4   Japan

Japan does not have a legal mandate for web accessibility in the private sector though there has been significant support from the industry for Japan Industrial Standard (JIS) X 8341-3. This standard has been referred to as the Web Content JIS and is titled "Guideline for older persons and persons with disabilities—information and communications equipment, software and services." Although JIS X 8341-3 is not a legal mandate, there has been some consensus that the standard falls in the realm of general best practice. Additionally, accessibility mandates from trade partners make accessible design an important issue.

JIS X 8341-3 is largely modified from WCAG 1.0 and some pieces of a 2004 draft of WCAG 2.0. In general, JIS 8341-3 differs from the two WAI guidelines by disregarding pieces of WCAG 1.0 that were perceived as dated and including particularly useful notions from an incomplete WCAG 2.0. Also notable are a number of specific guidelines that are more strict about the usage of font and text formatting to address specific issues of the Japanese language.

Web Content JIS Compliance. . .
. . . http://www.mitsue.co.jp/english/column/backnum/20040625a.html
Kazuhito Kidachi provides a high-level introduction to JIS X 8341-3 and rationale for the importance of accessibility in the Japanese market.

JIS Web Content Accessibility Guideline. . .
. . . http://www.comm.twcu.ac.jp/~nabe/data/JIS-WAI/
Takauki Watanabe's 2004 CSUN presentation describing JIS X 8341-3. This presentation is useful for understanding the background and decisions made in implementing accessibility in an Asian-language environment.

17.5 United Kingdom

As in the United States and Australia, accessibility is legally mandated for public-sector and private-sector web sites. Part III of the Disability Discrimination Act (DDA)[3] is the law of the land for the United Kingdom. The DDA uses a model of services provided and introduces mandates to do the following:

- Not refuse to provide any service to a person with a disability that is provided to the public.

- Not reduce the standard or manner of service to a person with a disability.

- Make all "reasonable adjustments" necessary to allow a person with a disability to make use of services impossible or unreasonably difficult to use.

These obligations make it clear that all services must be made to the best possible degree for all audiences and that few exceptions are to be considered. In terms of application, WCAG 1.0 is looked to as the base guideline for web accessibility, but in general, there seems to be a greater focus on practical outcomes for users with disabilities.

DDA Code of Practice . . . . http://www.drc-gb.org/PDF/CoP_Access.pdf
The U.K. Disability Rights Commission's Code of Practice is a comprehensive guide to the DDA. Although not tailored specifically to web development, focus on services makes this a useful guide to the language and intent of the DDA, which is focused on the idea of service provision rather than specifics to the means of provision.

Disability Rights Commission . . . . http://www.drc-gb.org/
The Disability Rights Commission provides a wide variety of resources on all issues related to disability in the United Kingdom. The library portion of the site is particularly useful, including web site accessibility resources such as PAS 78, a guide to good practice in commissioning accessible web sites.

17.6 United Nations

The United Nations have also been considering issues of accessibility as part of the Convention on the Rights of Persons with Disabilities.

---

3. Similar to but not the same as the Australian legislation with the same name.

The convention has been signed by more than 100 member nations and focuses on accessibility as a human rights issue. As web developers, Article 21 should be of great interest:

Article 21: Freedom of expression and opinion, and access to information

States Parties shall take all appropriate measures to ensure that persons with disabilities can exercise the right to freedom of expression and opinion, including the freedom to seek, receive and impart information and ideas on an equal basis with others and through all forms of communication of their choice, as defined in article 2 of the present Convention, including by:

(a) Providing information intended for the general public to persons with disabilities in accessible formats and technologies appropriate to different kinds of disabilities in a timely manner and without additional cost;

(b) Accepting and facilitating the use of sign languages, Braille, augmentative and alternative communication, and all other accessible means, modes and formats of communication of their choice by persons with disabilities in official interactions;

(c) Urging private entities that provide services to the general public, including through the Internet, to provide information and services in accessible and usable formats for persons with disabilities;

(d) Encouraging the mass media, including providers of information through the Internet, to make their services accessible to persons with disabilities;

(e) Recognizing and promoting the use of sign languages.

The UN has, to promote this convention, been working to build collaborative environments to understand and resolve issues of web accessibility. The first major result was the December 2006 publication of the Global Audit of Web Accessibility.

United Nations Enable . . . . http://www.un.org/esa/socdev/enable/
Enable is the central point for following progress of the UN in accessibility. Mandates, resolutions, and resources are regularly being added.

UN Global Audit of Web Accessibility...

...http://www.nomensa.com/resources/research/
united-nations-global-audit-of-accessibility.html

The report commissioned by the UN as the first audit of web accessibility on a global level. The report, while not deeply comprehensive, evaluates 100 sites in five key industries from 20 countries. The results were not terribly inspiring but give insight about the next steps to take.

17.7 More Information

We have seen only a small portion of what's happening on the global accessibility front. Accessibility guidelines and legislation are rapidly developing in many places. Not all countries are equal in terms of web accessibility for many of the same reasons that not all countries are equal in terms of web availability.

One thing that seems certain is that as widespread connectivity continues to advance, the question of accessibility will come up. As we've seen in this chapter, whether you're concerned with Section 508, the DDA, a variant of WCAG, or something else entirely, there will be some differences in how the question is answered. When you focus on the basic principles of accessibility that we've used throughout this book, however, you'll find that the answers to the questions will remain the same.

Policies Relating to Web Accessibility.......http://www.w3.org/WAI/Policy/
The WAI Education and Outreach provides information about legislation, documents, guidelines, and responsible parties for a variety of countries.

WebAIM World Laws...............http://www.webaim.org/articles/laws/world/
WebAIM provides information and links to many world accessibility laws.

An ideal world is left as an exercise to the reader.
  ► Paul Graham, ***On Lisp***

Chapter 18

Final Thoughts

Well then, we're almost at the end of our time together, so it's time for you to continue this path on your own. You have a solid set of principles that you can use to design accessible web sites. You know how to put them into action (and if you've been following the "Act on It!" sections, you already have a few times). You're familiar with the major web guidelines and how they relate to accessibility principles. In other words, you're ready to go. Before you do, however, I have a couple more thoughts to leave you with.

18.1 Keep Trying

I'll put it as gently as I can—no matter how long you work in accessibility, it's still going to go wrong for you on occasion. There's always going to be a situation you hadn't accounted for or a technology that doesn't behave the way you thought it would. That's just the way it is. It's not the end of the world. Users with disabilities understand that there are bugs too. I have yet to hear about a site that strives for accessibility getting sued over an honest mistake. Your goal should simply be to respond to the problem, apologize for the inconvenience, and understand what happened so you can prevent it from happening again.

18.2 Stay Informed

Although the technologies of the Web don't change as rapidly as they once did, our understandings of them do. You should always be on the look-out for new additions to your understanding of accessible web development. There are many great sites for keeping up with current accessibility issues.

Here are a few I recommend:

Juicy Studio . . . . http://juicystudio.com/
Gez Lemon says that his site is about best practices. This, more often than not, means accessibility. The articles are always well thought through, and the selection of tools on Juicy Studio makes it a must-add for your bookmark bar.

WebAIM . . . . http://www.webaim.org/
WebAIM hosts a wide collection of accessibility articles and resources as well as the WAVE evaluation tool.

A List Apart . . . . http://www.alistapart.com/
A List Apart is a must-read for *any* web developer who wants to keep up with content design. Accessibility is only one of many content focuses.

456 Berea St. http://www.456bereastreet.com/
Roger Johansson's articles and tutorials about high-quality accessibility and usability are informative and sure to keep you thinking.

Standards schmandards . . . . http://standards-schmandards.com/
Peter Krantz's site is a nice place to watch for information on techniques and tools (Peter wrote the Fangs and RAAKT tools) as well as articles that keep you thinking about the big picture of accessibility.

Accessify . . . . http://www.accessify.com/
Accessify provides tools, wizards, and tutorials to aid in accessible development as well as news about web accessibility.

The Web Standards Project . . . . http://www.webstandards.org/
WaSP is the place to go for information on standards-compliant web design. The accessibility task force has been following the development of WCAG 2.0 closely with many well-informed analyses.

Accessify Forum . . . . http://www.accessifyforum.com/
If you want to ask some questions, see what other developers are up to, or keep up with emerging issues in accessibility, this is a great place to be. If it's about accessibility, you'll often find someone here who has already been there.

18.3 Have Fun

Seriously. *Have Fun.* We have the pleasure of working in a dynamic media with fantastic creative opportunities. Many accessibility solutions, like other web development, started by simply asking "What if?" and playing around to see what happened. Play with the media. Create great things.

Just make sure to bring everyone you can along for the ride.

Start by doing what is necessary; then do what is possible; and suddenly you are doing the impossible.

—St. Francis of Assisi

Bibliography

[Fla06]   David Flanagan. *JavaScript: The Definitive Guide*. O'Reilly & Associates, Inc, Sebastopol, CA, fifth edition, 2006.

[Fow05]   Chad Fowler. *My Job Went To India: 52 Ways to Save Your Job*. The Pragmatic Programmers, LLC, Raleigh, NC, and Dallas, TX, 2005.

[HT00]   Andrew Hunt and David Thomas. *The Pragmatic Programmer: From Journeyman to Master*. Addison-Wesley, Reading, MA, 2000.

[Kei05]   Jeremy Keith. *DOM Scripting: Web Design with JavaScript and the Document Object Model*. friends of ED, Berkeley, CA, 2005.

[Ras00]   Jef Raskin. *The Humane Interface: New Directions for Designing Interactive Systems*. Addison-Wesley, Reading, MA, 2000.

[RD05]   Johanna Rothman and Esther Derby. *Behind Closed Doors: Secrets of Great Management*. The Pragmatic Programmers, LLC, Raleigh, NC, and Dallas, TX, 2005.

[Rob06]   Jennifer Niederst Robbins. *Web Design in a Nutshell*. In a Nutshell. O'Reilly & Associates, Inc, Sebastopol, CA, third edition, 2006.

[Rot07]   Johanna Rothman. *Manage It!: Your Guide to Modern, Pragmatic Project Management*. The Pragmatic Programmers, LLC, Raleigh, NC, and Dallas, TX, 2007.

Index

Web 2.0

Welcome to the Web, version 2.0. You need some help to tame the wild technologies out there. Start with *Prototype and script.aculo.us*, a book about two libraries that will make your JavaScript life much easier.

If you'd like to learn Ajax, then a great place to start is *Pragmatic Ajax*.

Prototype and script.aculo.us

Tired of getting swamped in the nitty-gritty of cross-browser, Web 2.0–grade JavaScript? Get back in the game with Prototype and script.aculo.us, two extremely popular JavaScript libraries that make it a walk in the park. Be it Ajax, drag and drop, autocompletion, advanced visual effects, or many other great features, all you need is write one or two lines of script that look so good they could almost pass for Ruby code!

Prototype and script.aculo.us: You never knew JavaScript could do this!
Christophe Porteneuve
(330 pages) ISBN: 1 934356-01-8. $34.95
http://pragmaticprogrammer.com/titles/cppsu

Pragmatic Ajax

Ajax redefines the user experience for web applications, providing compelling user interfaces. Now you can dig deeper into Ajax itself as this book shows you how to make Ajax magic. Explore both the fundamental technologies and the emerging frameworks that make it easy.

From Google Maps to Ajaxified Java, .NET, and Ruby on Rails applications, this Pragmatic guide strips away the mystery and shows you the easy way to make Ajax work for you.

Pragmatic Ajax: A Web 2.0 Primer
Justin Gehtland, Ben Galbraith, Dion Almaer
(296 pages) ISBN: 0-9766940-8-5. $29.95
http://pragmaticprogrammer.com/titles/ajax

Enterprise Ready

Your application is feature complete, but is it ready for the real world? See how to design and deploy production-ready software and *Release It!*.

Did you know Ruby could glue together all sorts of enterprise technologies? See how in *Enterprise Integration with Ruby*.

Release It!

Whether it's in Java, .NET, or Ruby on Rails, getting your application ready to ship is only half the battle. Did you design your system to survive a sudden rush of visitors from Digg or Slashdot? Or an influx of real-world customers from 100 different countries? Are you ready for a world filled with flakey networks, tangled databases, and impatient users?

If you're a developer and don't want to be on call at 3 a.m. for the rest of your life, this book will help.

Design and Deploy Production-Ready Software
Michael T. Nygard
(368 pages) ISBN: 0-9787392-1-3. $34.95
http://pragmaticprogrammer.com/titles/mnee

Enterprise Integration with Ruby

See how to use the power of Ruby to integrate all the applications in your environment. Learn how to
• use relational databases directly and via mapping layers such as ActiveRecord • harness the power of directory services • create, validate, and read XML documents for easy information interchange
• use both high- and low-level protocols to knit applications together

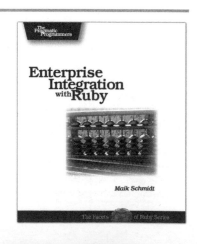

Enterprise Integration with Ruby
Maik Schmidt
(360 pages) ISBN: 0-9766940-6-9. $32.95
http://pragmaticprogrammer.com/titles/fr_eir

Pragmatic Projects

See what an agile project is supposed to feel like in the award-winning *Practices of an Agile Developer.*

Have you ever noticed that project retrospectives feel too little, too late? What you need to do is start having *Agile Retrospectives.*

Practices of an Agile Developer

Agility is all about using feedback to respond to change. Learn how to apply the principles of agility throughout the software development process
• establish and maintain an agile working environment • deliver what users really want • use personal agile techniques for better coding and debugging • use effective collaborative techniques for better teamwork • move to an agile approach

Practices of an Agile Developer: Working in the Real World
Venkat Subramaniam and Andy Hunt
(189 pages) ISBN: 0-9745140-8-X. $29.95
http://pragmaticprogrammer.com/titles/pad

Agile Retrospectives

Mine the experience of your software development team continually throughout the life of the project. Rather than waiting until the end of the project—as with a traditional retrospective, when it's too late to help—agile retrospectives help you adjust to change *today.*

The tools and recipes in this book will help you uncover and solve hidden (and not-so-hidden) problems with your technology, your methodology, and those difficult "people issues" on your team.

Agile Retrospectives: Making Good Teams Great
Esther Derby and Diana Larsen
(170 pages) ISBN: 0-9776166-4-9. $29.95
http://pragmaticprogrammer.com/titles/dlret

Ruby and Rails

Interested in learning Ruby, or in learning how to use a scripting language the right way? Start with *Everyday Scripting with Ruby: For Teams, Testers, and You.*

If you know Java, and are curious about Ruby on Rails, you don't have to start from scratch. Read *Rails for Java Developers*, and you can catch up to the industry leaders by learning this exciting new technology.

Everyday Scripting with Ruby

Don't waste that computer on your desk. Offload your daily drudgery to where it belongs, and free yourself to do what you should be doing: thinking. All you need is a scripting language (free!), this book (cheap!), and the dedication to work through the examples and exercises. Learn the basics of the Ruby scripting language and see how to create scripts in a steady, controlled way using test-driven design.

Everyday Scripting with Ruby: For Teams, Testers, and You
Brian Marick
(320 pages) ISBN: 0-9776166-1-4. $29.95
http://pragmaticprogrammer.com/titles/bmsft

Rails for Java Developers

Enterprise Java developers already have most of the skills needed to create Rails applications. They just need a guide that shows how their Java knowledge maps to the Rails world. That's what this book does. It covers: • the Ruby language • building MVC applications • unit and functional testing • security • project automation • configuration • web services This book is the fast track for Java programmers who are learning or evaluating Ruby on Rails.

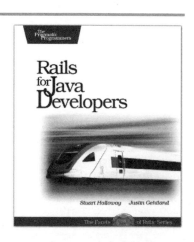

Rails for Java Developers
Stuart Halloway and Justin Gehtland
(300 pages) ISBN: 0-9776166-9-X. $34.95
http://pragmaticprogrammer.com/titles/fr_r4j

Erlang and More

New challenges call for new solutions. The coming multicore crunch makes parallel programming a necessity, not a luxury. Learn how to do it right with *Programming Erlang*.

And whatever language you use, you'll need a good text editor, too. On the Mac, we recommend TextMate.

Programming Erlang

Learn how to write truly concurrent programs—programs that run on dozens or even hundreds of local and remote processors. See how to write high-reliability applications—even in the face of network and hardware failure—using the Erlang programming language.

Programming Erlang: Software for a Concurrent World
Joe Armstrong
(536 pages) ISBN: 1-934356-00-X. $36.95
http://pragmaticprogrammer.com/titles/jaerlang

TextMate

If you're coding Ruby or Rails on a Mac, then you owe it to yourself to get the TextMate editor. And, once you're using TextMate, you owe it to yourself to pick up this book. It's packed with information that will help you automate all your editing tasks, saving you time to concentrate on the important stuff. Use snippets to insert boilerplate code and refactorings to move stuff around. Learn how to write your own extensions to customize it to the way you work.

TextMate: Power Editing for the Mac
James Edward Gray II
(200 pages) ISBN: 0-9787392-3-X. $29.95
http://pragmaticprogrammer.com/titles/textmate

The Pragmatic Bookshelf

The Pragmatic Bookshelf features books written by developers for developers. The titles continue the well-known Pragmatic Programmer style and continue to garner awards and rave reviews. As development gets more and more difficult, the Pragmatic Programmers will be there with more titles and products to help you stay on top of your game.

Visit Us Online

Design Accessible Web Sites' Home Page
http://pragmaticprogrammer.com/titles/jsaccess
Source code from this book, errata, and other resources. Come give us feedback, too!

Register for Updates
http://pragmaticprogrammer.com/updates
Be notified when updates and new books become available.

Join the Community
http://pragmaticprogrammer.com/community
Read our weblogs, join our online discussions, participate in our mailing list, interact with our wiki, and benefit from the experience of other Pragmatic Programmers.

New and Noteworthy
http://pragmaticprogrammer.com/news
Check out the latest pragmatic developments in the news.

Save on the PDF

Save on the PDF version of this book. Owning the paper version of this book entitles you to purchase the PDF version at a terrific discount. The PDF is great for carrying around on your laptop. It's hyperlinked, has color, and is fully searchable.

Buy it now at pragmaticprogrammer.com/coupon.

Contact Us

Phone Orders:	1-800-699-PROG (+1 919 847 3884)
Online Orders:	www.pragmaticprogrammer.com/catalog
Customer Service:	orders@pragmaticprogrammer.com
Non-English Versions:	translations@pragmaticprogrammer.com
Pragmatic Teaching:	academic@pragmaticprogrammer.com
Author Proposals:	proposals@pragmaticprogrammer.com